# Topics in Afro-American Studies

*Edited by*
*Henry J. Richards*

BLACK ACADEMY PRESS, INC.
Buffalo, New York

*Published by*
Black Academy Press, Inc.
Box 366, Ellicott Station
Buffalo, New York 14205

Printed in the United States of America
Artcraft-Burow, Buffalo, N. Y.
25

| Chapter | | Page |
|---|---|---|

# INTRODUCTION: BLACK STUDIES, THE LIBERAL ARTS AND ACADEMIC STANDARDS

*by*

HENRY J. RICHARDS

Lately, there has been a great deal of talk by educators about a new liberal education and I find the concept of a new liberal education interesting and significant for two good reasons. In the first place, it is clear that the potential validity of the traditional liberal education is generally recognized. In the second place, this attention to a new liberal education is evidence that something has been happening to transform the old concept of a liberal education in such a way as to actualize its validity. I speak of the actualization of the validity of the liberal education because this is what, of necessity, will be achieved as attempts to bring the traditional liberal arts closer to achieving their stated goals become more successful. In this introduction I intend to focus attention on the role of black students and black studies in the transformation of the traditional liberal arts curriculum.

If we were to consider carefully the objectives of a liberal education as stated in university and college catalogs and the means used to attain them, a conflict between means and ends becomes quite evident. It is affirmed, for example, that the colleges of liberal arts attempt to develop in their students those qualities which will make them effective participants in their world.* But the curricula themselves militate against the attainment of this goal. These programs reflect the hypocrisy and the narrowness of vision of their designers who have excluded from them vast and legitimate academic areas. It is common knowledge, I believe

---

\* The objectives of a liberal education discussed in this paper are those outlined in several college and university catalogs.

that the neglect of these areas is not accidental but rather represents conscious negation of their validity. On the basis of what I have just stated, it should be clear that there exists a remarkable contradiction between the stated goals of the traditional liberal arts curriculum and the goals that it is equipped to achieve. As black students began to appear on university and college campuses in appreciable numbers the majority of white educators, white students and white observers were quick to express their fears that the presence of large numbers of "educationally and culturally disadvantaged" Blacks in the university environment would result in the lowering of academic standards. Contrary to that notion, however, one may argue convincingly that at all white institutions where black students have been admitted in significant numbers the latter contributed to elevating academic standards. In order to amplify the preceding statement, it is necessary to define in very general terms what education is. Education may be defined as something that students acquire in a special environment (primary school, secondary school, college or university); it involves (1) the interaction between young people (students) and older people (teachers or professors) (2) an emphasis on learning and (3) participation by teachers and students in the search for truth. Genuine academic standards, therefore, should be measured according to the following criteria: (1) the extent to which there is interaction between students and teachers in the academic environment (2) the degree to which there is emphasis on learning and (3) the extent to which teachers and students participate in a genuine search for truth. The demands for the establishment of black studies curricula by black students represented a constructive challenge to the educational establishments of the institutions of higher learning to develop curricula that would truly function for the attainment of goals associated with the liberal arts; in other words they represented a cry for the elevation of academic standards. It should be pointed out here that in all efforts at developing black studies programs there has been a healthy interaction between students and faculty members; there has been a great emphasis on learning about all aspects of the world black experience; and all of these recent attempts by black students and scholars to explore the world black experience testify to a genuine participation in the search for truth not in the traditional uni-dimensional and limited form associated with white scholarship but rather in a multi-dimensional form.

In the colleges and universities where the challenge by black students was met by serious efforts to develop sound black studies programs, the way for the liberal arts to attain all they are capable of attaining was opened. In fact, the development of black studies programs has set the stage for the development of ethnic studies curricula which will ultimately serve to make students more effective participants in their world which, after all, is a multi-ethnic world. Black studies programs have had a significant impact, therefore, on the liberal arts that truly attempt to prepare students to be world citizens. Thanks to black studies, the new liberal arts curricula are attempting to realize goals which heretofore were treated as worthy but unattainable ideals. And, let us not forget the contribution of black students and black studies to the elevation of academic standards.

It is also stated that the student in whom the objectives of the college of liberal arts have been measurably realized will acquire competence in the skills needed for extending his understanding and appreciation throughout the range of human experience. Again, however, the very restrictiveness of the traditional liberal arts curriculum tended to militate against the attainment of this goal. The narrowness about which we speak stems from the almost total commitment of the liberal arts to exploring the achievements and ideals of Western Civilization. Demands for the inclusion of black studies in the liberal arts curriculum represent, therefore, a serious questioning of the validity of this drive to acquaint students exclusively with the Western tradition. What is clear here is that the proponents of black studies programs were, in effect, taking the position that an education that is unqualifiedly fixed and rigid cannot be responsive to the needed changes in the intellectual, social and political conditions of a society. The total commitment to the propagation of Western ideas and ideals in the twentieth century when news media and rapid modes of transportation contribute to awareness of other civilizations and other cultures is indeed anachronistic. The demands of black students on university and college campuses for recognition of the legitimacy of black studies through their inclusion in liberal arts curricula forced all involved, be they black or non-black, to take a second look at American society and to recognize the process of symbiosis at work in it. It should be evident, I believe, even to the most casual observer that contact between the Mexican-American, Puerto-Rican American, Afro-American and Indian-American cultures and the dominant white culture has given rise to a composite culture with heterogeneous characteristics. However, conflicts between the oppressed and the oppressor have tended to obscure the integrity of

America's multi-ethnic and multi-cultural composition. I would affirm here that black studies, by their inclusion in the liberal arts, have contributed to creating a genuine awareness of the multi-ethnic nature of the American society. In this I see some movement toward recognition of the validity of non-European cultures. The kind of awareness that will eventually be developed as a result of this new focus will inevitably culminate in the development of a pluralistic perception of reality whereby minority cultural and racial differences will be accepted and respected even by the dominant cultural group and will not be dismissed as deviant and lacking in value. It is my belief that proper emphasis given to the true nature of American society and indeed of the world will lead to an understanding and appreciation of cultural pluralism. This, in turn, will contribute more than any other factor to the resolution of problems which have their basis in attitudes that have been nurtured by the Western dualistic vision of reality.

This leads us to another of the goals of the liberal education according to which the liberal arts student is expected to develop the ability to reason effectively by applying critical analysis and constructive solutions to problems as they arise. In the traditional liberal arts education the objective stated above seems to be regarded more as an ideal rather than as an attainable goal. It is a well known fact that the liberal arts curriculum has not, in fact, addressed itself to the solution of problems. This may be due perhaps to the tendency toward elitism that has been part of the liberal arts from their earliest beginnings. Black students with the opportunity to study in colleges and universities in increasing numbers represent a group of Americans who have real problems and who have chosen to direct a great deal of effort toward resolving them. This attitude, in turn, contributes to the achievement of one of the objectives of the liberal education, the development of the ability to creatively resolve real problems thereby making significant contributions to society. Black studies programs with their problem-solving orientation, once included in the liberal arts curriculum, serve to revitalize the liberal arts so that a major objective of the liberal education is treated not as an unattainable ideal but as a worthwhile and attainable goal.

The liberal arts student, it is expected, will be free to pursue truth by reading, listening, observing and acting. But the narrowness of the traditional liberal arts curriculum, exemplified by the rigid compartmentalization of knowledge into disciplines, curtails free academic growth thereby frustrating the achievement of one of the stated objectives of liberal education. This strict compartmentalization of knowledge also militates against the development in the student of the very important skill of grasping the analogies between the various disciplines. Black studies curricula, as a whole however, are attempting to break away from this narrow system by espousing a broader and more realistic interdisciplinary approach to education. This, in effect, is evidence of the recognition of the interrelatedness of the many aspects of the human experience which can most effectively be presented and studied through a fully interdisciplinary approach to education.

The student who receives a liberal education, it is assumed, will gain through his study an understanding of his total environment. He will develop a knowledge of the values which society has formulated in dealing with its problems. He will also develop an appreciation of the values which man has discovered through his own creative expressions and interpretations in such forms of art as literature, drama, music, painting and sculpture. Over the years, however, there has been the wholesale exclusion of the creative interpretations of the black experience from the traditional liberal arts curriculum. This denial of the validity of the black experience by educators in the liberal arts inevitably imposed limitations on the attainment of the goals outlined above. Black college students openly identified the contradiction in an educational system which affirms the importance of certain objectives yet develops a curriculum that militates against their attainment. It was to this contradiction, which went unchallenged for generations, that the demands for the black studies called attention. I believe that positive response to the call for black studies cannot but have a significant influence on the liberal arts education for they have infused into it a real commitment to the attainment of stated goals which no longer stand as unattainable ideals. The role of black studies in the development of this trend can hardly be overemphasized.

While some segments of the university populations have been haggling, for some time, over the question of effective student participation in the educational processes, the black students and black faculty have, from the very inception of the black studies concept, recognized the importance of full cooperation of both students and faculty in the educational venture. In fact, efforts have been made to close the traditional gap between students and faculty so that both groups may develop a relationship in which all involved in the programs will be  viewed in the dual role of student and teacher. Freedom, therefore, espoused in theory in the traditional liberal arts is, in fact, one of the hallmarks of the new liberal education to which black studies have so significantly contributed.

The recent widespread use of the words "relevance" and "survival" may be traced back to expressions by the first proponents of the inclusion of black studies in university curricula. Black students and black faculty who have been working for the development of black studies have spoken constantly, and with good reason, of the importance of black studies for the survival of black people. For it is inconceivable to have educated men who have control of significant bodies of knowledge, who think clearly, who are articulate, who are prepared to solve problems and make a contribution to their world, yet who have not developed the ability to survive nor the awareness of the need for concern over the question of survival. On this question, black studies have again effectively challenged the traditional concept of the liberal education. Blacks involved in the development of black studies have introduced to the liberal arts a feature that has perhaps been taken for granted too long—the need for concern about survival. It is, I contend, no accident that on the heels of the call by black people for greater concern over their survival has come a sudden concern about real threats to national survival that have heretofore been ignored.

If we agree that the goals of the liberal arts as outlined in college and university catalogs are worthwhile then we must accept as worthwhile those factors which further the attainment of these objectives. In my brief examination of the role of black studies in the liberal arts I have tried to emphasize the fact that liberal arts curricula, in general, have tended by their rigidity and narrowness of focus to work against the achievement of the acknowledged goals of a liberal education. I have also attempted to show how the inclusion of black studies in liberal arts curricula serves to revitalize them and open the way for real progress toward attainment of the goals of the liberal education. The inclusion of black studies in the liberal arts have brought us closer to providing students the opportunity to receive a relevant education, one which will enable them to understand clearly the nature of their society and equip them to develop effective solutions to problems. Students who have had the benefit of this type of educational experience will undoubtedly make significant contributions to their society. Awareness of the interrelatedness of the total human experience which is fostered in black studies through the interdisciplinary approach enables students to develop the ability to see relationships and alternatives that rarely become evident to those who are the products of the traditional liberal arts curriculum characterized by the rigid compartmentalization of knowledge into narrow disciplines. Black studies as part of the liberal arts curriculum play a significant role in developing in students an awareness of and respect for all cultural entities of the world as opposed to the almost exclusive concern with the ideas and ideals of Western Civilization which has characterized the traditional liberal arts curriculum.

The selection process used in collecting the pieces that follow was colored by two important factors. In the first place there was an attempt to include statements on the black experience by scholars from various disciplines. Secondly, in selecting the pieces, I was moved by a desire to include statements which focus on the experience of black people in a variety of cultural settings. It is my hope, therefore, that the papers which constitute the body of this anthology will, by their thematic variety, call attention to the vastness of the field of black studies and to the global nature of the black experience. And lest it be forgotten, let me affirm once more that black students in their demands for the inclusion of black studies in American college and university curricula have contributed in a very significant manner to the elevation of academic standards at these institutions. I must also add that the tremendous impact of black studies will be felt for generations to come not only in the educational structure of the United States but also in educational systems throughout the world.

# 2

# WHAT DIRECTION BLACK STUDIES?

*by*

DONALD HENDERSON

## INTRODUCTION

Over the past several years a great many colleges and universities have undertaken a variety of efforts in response to the demands of black students and faculty members for improving the status of blacks on their campuses. A bewildering variety of structures, processes and practices have been established in the wake of these demands. They all tend to fall under the general rubric of black studies and include such diverse undertakings as (1) recruitment programs for blacks and other minorities; (2) remedial, compensatory and tutorial programs; (3) the inclusion into the standard curriculum of courses designed more or less to deal with aspects of the black experience; (4) separate programs of courses dealing with the black experience for black students; (5) the establishment of Centers, Institutes, etc. that deal in some fashion with blacks; (6) and other activities such as recruitment and assistance of black graduate students. The situation is further confused by the fact that it is not unusual to find that all of these activities are being carried out simultaneously and independently at the same institution. Unless there is a structure clearly labeled as black studies, any or all of these activities may be perceived as the University's black studies program. For example, at one university, with which I am familiar, when black students requested a black studies program they were told by a representative of the Administration that the school had such a program and that it had been operative for two years. The administrator was making reference to a special recruitment and tutorial program for persons from minority groups while the students were requesting a substantive curricular effort. Further

confusion often arises from the feeling that whatever effort is being
carried out for black students it should address itself to all of their
problems. While it is elementary, it seems necessary for many
institutions to distinguish between recruitment and supportive
programs for black students and programs of substantive academic
effort aimed at teaching (and research) about the black experience.
This alone, however, will not clear up the major sources of
confusion. In the main it would seem that the most difficult
problems to solve center around questions of the nature, content
and structure of substantive efforts in the area of Black Studies.
In the state of Illinois, in the fall of 1969, for example, sixty-four
institutions offered a total of 548 courses that were labeled as
black studies offerings. About half of these institutions indicated
that they were in the process of expanding their offerings in this
area. There seemed to be, with the exception of standard courses
in Negro History and Race and Minority Relations, almost as
many different course titles as there were courses. The courses
were offered by traditional departments, such as history and
sociology and by newly devised structures, such as departments of
Black Studies and Afro-American Centers and Institutes. It is
worth noting that most frequently these courses were offered by
social science departments.

In short, in the area of black studies there is, at present, an
enormous lack of coherence and coordination at all levels. The
activities and structures that characterize black studies across the
nation undoubtedly have resulted from the headlong rush of universities to offer something black. In this light it is worth questioning the sincerity of the institutions that implement such programs. There is reason to believe that most academicians do not
believe that these programs have any real academic or intellectual
validity. In the main, they are perceived as strategically useful
ways of "cooling out militant black students". In most cases black
studies programs, however they are construed, have their reasons
for existence firmly based in political considerations and were only
rarely introduced as academic undertakings in the host institutions.

There are a great many objections to black studies efforts.
These objections range from academic considerations on the one
hand to political considerations on the other. In the main, several
arguments seem to predominate. (1) Black Studies programs are
viewed of as chauvinistic attempts on the part of blacks to
advocate black superiority and to glorify the history of blacks in

the United States. (2) Black Studies programs are held to be efforts directed at circumventing the conventional and more difficult performance standards of higher education in order to enable ill-prepared and equally inept students to acquire the credentials of higher education. (3) Black Studies programs are the core efforts in the training of militant revolutionary agents to do battle with the white university community on a local level and the wider white community on a wider level. It is also argued that these efforts are directed toward developing separate educational structures for blacks and as such reflect "racism" in reverse. Perhaps, the most frequently used objection (which occurs usually with one or several of those noted above) is that black studies "by its very nature" lacks intellectual and academic validity—in short there is nothing worthwhile in the undertaking of such efforts. These arguments are used to deprecate black studies programs that are extant and to deny their legitimacy as a part of the offerings of universities. Most importantly they are the instrumentalities for withholding the resources that are necessary for their planning, implementation, growth and stability. The lack of resources, of course, dooms these efforts to failure from the outset.

On the other side of the issue those who argue for the development of black studies programs are by no means unified in their notions about what they should be, how they should be structured, where they should be housed, what the content should be, etc. For example, some people argue that black studies should be geared toward developing and fostering racial awareness and racial pride among blacks. Others contend that such a program should not only foster racial pride but should also "teach black people how to be black" as an antidote to their present educational experiences that are designed to teach them to be white. Another school of thought contends that these efforts must actively undertake the political education and unification of the black community thus enhancing its position in the society. Another argument holds that the "true black studies program" must be community based and community controlled and aimed at the resolution of the myriad problems of the black community. These and a number of other arguments contribute to the confusion that characterizes the attempts to develop black studies programs around the country. Obviously, closure on these issues will take time and many of the problems can only be worked out as attempts are made to establish and cultivate viable programs of this type.

Nevertheless some thought must be given to notions that promise to structure, order and give coherence to black studies all over the country. Like any other limited undertaking black studies cannot be all things to all men—nor should it be.

Looking at the arguments of the dissenters and the aims of the supporters it is possible to see some legitimacy in them. It is conceivable that a move toward separation or a development of race pride for example may result from the operation of a black studies program. It is also conceivable that such programs can serve as an "antidote" to some present educational ills that devastate black youngsters. These occurrences in all probability will be spin-offs from black studies programs and as such should not be conceived of, either individually or collectively, as the sum and substance of these efforts. My objection to all of these notions derives from a hidden implication in each of them that suggests that a black studies program cannot be an academically and/or intellectually legitimate undertaking for every college or university. The implication referred to above is related to one of the cardinal tenets of racism as I understand it—namely—there is nothing in the world black experience that is worthy of serious and extended intellectual activity or capable of contributing anything of value to our understanding of the universe or man's place in it. On the part of the detractors it smacks sharply of racism and on the part of the supporters, at very least, myopia and at worse an indirect subscription to the tenets of racism. Both are objectionable and cannot form the basis for a valid effort in the study of the world black experience.

At the same time one must not apologize for these spin-offs, if they in fact occur, nor can one attempt to design these programs to keep these things from happening. Sociology, for example, as far as I can tell was not designed in this fashion. It can be argued, as some do, that some of the notions of this discipline have contributed on the one hand to a number of "undesirable" social developments, particularly in the area of race relations, and on the other to some widespread challenges to traditional values. Black studies, like any legitimate intellectual endeavor, must be left free to become whatever its dedicated scholars are capable of making it. Anything less than that will prove intellectually dishonest and will ultimately work to the disadvantage of both black and non-black peoples.

Considering the widespread confusion that obtains with respect to black studies it is worth asking—what of the future of such programs? An honest answer suggests that their future as an integral component of university activities does not look promising. Two outstanding impediments loom as formidable roadblocks. One of these is centered in faculty hostility while the other concerns problems of financial support.

In many cases black studies programs, as noted above, were undertaken as a "temporary expedient" to preserve peace and order on campus. As such, rarely was there an attempt made to provide them with sound academic bases or full faculty sanction. A good many "courses," for example, were to be designed and taught by students. Moreover, the course content very often covered the whole academic landscape. Activities like these may be, in part, a function of the fact the field is new and the footing is uncertain; at the same time, however, it is possible that such activities were permitted to enable their results to discredit black studies efforts. It is worth noting that in a great many places, university faculties are requesting a thorough evaluation of black studies programs with the results often being a dissolution of the efforts. That is to say that the very circumstances that led to and surround the establishment of black studies programs are now being utilized to bring about their demise.

Black studies programs are also either facing or will be shortly faced by the growing shortage of funds that is afflicting universities all over the country. This is particularly critical for these programs because in most cases they have been established with little if any real financial support and little serious commitment to their permanency. This lack of commitment and of a firm base of support seems to portend a serious cut-back if not dissolution of many programs as universities begin to tighten their financial belts. Obviously strategies must be devised (1) to broaden the support base for these programs and to enable their survival and necessary growth; and, (2) to ensure their entree into the academic system of the university as full-fledged programs with their own particular body of knowledge and requisite skills and technologies. The next three sections of this paper attempt to address the latter of these two issues. Strategies that enable the accomplishment of this objective will go a long way toward establishing the bases for realization of a satisfactory resolution of the problem of funding.

A PROPOSAL

As suggested above, there are presently a variety of notions as to what constitutes a bona-fide black studies effort. Accepting the risk of adding yet another I would like to submit my notions of what constitutes a legitimate black studies effort. I hasten to add that my principal interest here is in the intellectual and academic aspects of such an effort. It is not an attempt to suggest that the discipline, black studies has no social, personal or other action-oriented significances, for indeed it must. I must also confess a little discomfort with the need for calling what I wish to propose black studies because my proposal not only encompasses the universe of black studies but necessarily involves the study of whites albeit within a non-white framework. For want of a more appropriate rubric, however, I will use the designation black studies.

Let me begin by saying that black studies is as worthy and legitimate an intellectual and academic undertaking as any en-deavor presently being carried out in the university. It is such in its own right and need not be propped, buttressed, or sold by any means other than its own historical and contemporary im-portance. It should not be viewed as a compensatory or remedial program for so-called high-risk disadvantaged students, although such students may certainly be enrolled. Their enrollment, how-ever, should be unrelated to their "disadvantaged" status. Black studies should not be a program in rhetoric designed, as many seem presently to be, to teach black folks (or even Negroes) how to be black. In my opinion black people do not have to be taught to be what they already are and it is an affront for some blacks to presume that they can tell other blacks how they should define themselves or behave, value and aspire. This is what whites have been attempting to do to blacks for better than 300 years. The liberation of blacks from the ideological and attitudinal clutches of whites must not be at the cost of re-enslavement with misguided blacks pulling the strings. I do believe that black studies pro-grams can contribute immeasurably to the true liberation of blacks.

Black studies programs should not be community action pro-grams, although they can and should service black communities. In this regard, however, these programs should assess the nature of their resources and capabilities and on the basis of this assess-ment determine the types of services they can provide the com-munity and then deliver on such services one hundred percent. Heads of these programs must realize from the outset that the programs cannot care for all the needs of the community. They must not make the mistake of promising to resolve all community ills as administrators of most urban colleges and universities have done in the past. Above all, the university-based black studies effort should be an educative effort and as such its primary obligation must be the educational fulfillment of its student and faculty membership. The important question is how this can best be done within the confines of the university system.

It seems that several types of efforts must be established in order to fulfill the promise of black studies. For the moment I wish to deal with the nature of these efforts on university campuses. Careful thought suggests that three major types of programs can be established to fulfill both the academic promise and the service capability of these undertakings, namely: (1) the Black Studies Department; (2) the School or College of Ethnic Studies and (3) the Black Studies Research Center. A brief formulation of each of these structures follows.

## DEPARTMENT OF AFRICAN AND AFRO-AMERICAN STUDIES

The primary goal of this department should be to provide the student with an encompassing knowledge of the history, culture, life-styles and futures of Africans and/or Afro-Americans. Such a department, unlike present substantive departments, would have to be truly interdisciplinary. Its membership would of necessity represent most of the established departments of the social sciences and the humanities. It is conceivable that geologists, biologists, geneticists and others from the natural sciences might be responsible for certain aspects of this department's program. The department would offer a broad concentration in African and Afro-American studies which would include, for example, surveys of art, literature, history, philosophy, religion, biology, economics, etc. as these areas contribute to an understanding of the world black experience. A student would be able to specialize, for example, in African Studies or Afro-American Studies with emphasis on the black experience in anglo-saxon cultures, or Afro-American Studies with emphasis on the black experience in latin cultures. The student thus majoring would concentrate his efforts, beyond certain required core courses, in the area of his specialty. For example, he would become familiar with the specific history, art, economics, philosophy, religion, etc. of Afro-Americans of South America. He would of necessity study the linkages of that region to Africa and to North America and those unique features of the people themselves. In short, the student would become reasonably knowledgeable about the experiences of black people in a certain large geographical area and their relations to all other blacks in the world.

The department would most logically belong in the College of Liberal Arts and its students would of course be liberal arts majors. Upon graduation these young people would be able to acquire the types of positions that are usually available to liberal arts graduates. For those students wishing to continue their studies in one or more of these areas, graduate programs would be offered. The graduate programs would enable students to acquire an expert knowledge in one of the areas of study outlined above. For instance, a student may wish to specialize in Brazilian culture. He would of necessity then have to learn a good deal about Yoruba culture of Africa as many of the blacks in Brazil are descendants of this tribe. The lifeways of Brazilian blacks would be thoroughly examined through study of their religion, philosophy, art, music, family life, child-rearing practices, medicine, etc. The historical and contemporary similarities and dissimilarities between them and African Yoruba would be considered. The student would also be required to place the Brazilians into proper perspective vis-a-vis other blacks in the New World. This of necessity would require some knowledge about other New World peoples. At the same time, in order to place his work in world perspective he must learn, at least superficially, about the culture and lifeways, etc. of non-black people both in and out of the new world. His knowledge of cultural variety would be truly eclectic.

Ideally a good deal of time should be spent among the people being studied. The graduate student studying Brazilian blacks should be required to study in Brazil. It would be tremendously beneficial to this student if his "field work" in Brazil included, say, at least a year or two working and living as a Brazilian. He could, for example, teach in a Brazilian school and observe the scene as a Brazilian rather than anthropologize or do some other form of social sciencing during his "field work". His principal objective would be to understand Brazilian life from the point-of-view of the Brazilian. This might require the assumption of a perspective that at times would be decidedly non-objective.

As noted above, the structure of a department such as this must depart from what has been the norm for departments for most of the history of American universities. The Department of African and Afro-American Studies must be truly interdisciplinary and its members must be meta-disciplinarians. They must be academically and intellectually able to range across a variety of traditional areas with facility and sophistication. Obviously the selection of personnel will be a principal factor in the operation of such a department. The traditional and often arbitrary boundaries that divide sociology from history or philosophy from economics will not only be undesirable but dysfunctional in carrying out the mission of this department.

It seems reasonably clear that such a structure would be a desirable addition to the university complex. Not only would it provide exciting new areas for student and faculty attention but it would fill a void that has traditionally existed in the curricular structure of the American university. That void, of course, is a result of the almost total lack of attention to the world black experience or, what is worse, the abominable portrayals of that experience that resulted in the presentation of distorted versions of the history of both blacks and non-blacks. It would, of necessity, if only in the service courses it offered, begin to set the historical record straight for both blacks and whites.

## SCHOOL OF ETHNIC STUDIES

In thinking of the full scope of black studies in a university setting it is necessary to consider how such an effort can be construed in a fashion substantially broader than a department. I can see the need and desirability of establishing a School or a College of Ethnic Studies. I suggest ethnic studies because it is a more inclusive notion than black studies and because I can also see the value of the serious study of other ethnic groups. In any case, such a structure would enable a student to pursue a degree in one of the traditional disciplines and at the same time concentrate his study on one or more ethnic groups. In this school, for example, a student would be able to major in sociology while concentrating substantively on some aspect of the experience of the black world. That is, the student would learn the concepts, theories and methods of a particular discipline with the lifeways, beliefs and institutions of the black world serving as the substance through which the concepts and theories are exemplified. If, for example, the student were an economics major the communal economics of the African world or ghetto economics of Afro-America could be the substance that would "put the meat on the theoretical or conceptual bones". I must hasten to suggest that this kind of academic undertaking is not equivalent to taking an established discipline like sociology and "coloring it black". What I am suggesting is a bona-fide attempt at developing an appropriate understanding within the discipline of the experiences of the non-white (perhaps it is more appropriate to say non-American) world. Such, I believe, is the thinking that underlies the call for the establishment of black psychology for example.

I find it difficult to understand the almost total lack of offerings in African philosophy among departments of philosophy in American universities. In my various inquiries about the lack of such offerings I invariably got an incredulous stare followed by "African philosophy! — What's that? Why there's no such thing!" It should be reasonably clear to any free-thinking intelligent person that such an entity must exist or must have existed at one time. Indeed, a sensitive examination of African thought reveals the presence of a very sophisticated and elegant body of philosophical notions. These notions are in a great many ways quite different from those that we in the Western world have been used to granting the status of philosophical concepts. The denial of the existence of African philosophy by Western scholars is the result of their very provincial notion of philosophy. The standard against which their judgments are made is the extent to which African thinking parallels Western thought systems. We also seem to feel that our own thought systems are universal in time and space. Our explanations of the operation of the universe, for example, are arrogantly presumed to have exclusive validity. Therefore, when we are confronted by notions found in African thought that suggest the existence of some basic free-flowing power in the world that can be controlled and utilized by man through the selective use of the spoken word[1] we dismiss such notions as the primitive musings of savages. Such notions are not seen as elements in a complex thought-scheme for ordering the universe and explaining man's place in it. They are seen as primitive attempts to control the natural world through magic instead of science. These attempts at magic (which we understand to be wish-fulfilling rather than practical) are proof that such people have not yet evolved a systematic and logical way of thinking[2] and therefore could not have developed a system of philosophical thought in the grand sense of our philosophy. Hence—there is no such thing as African philosophy—it is at best "black magic".

I suggest that it is necessary to transcend such narrow notions. Although African notions of how the universe operates and the place of man in it may be entirely unfamiliar and alien to American philosophers they are nevertheless parts of a grand scheme that orders and structures the world in a fashion that is effective for those who subscribe to it. It has nothing to do with western philosophy nor does it need to be evaluated by western notions in order to assume the status of philosophy—it needs only to be seen as a philosophical system in its own right. The effort I am describing here would approach that study in just this way. A philosophy major would learn philosophy through concentrating on the understanding of African philosophical thought as a distinctively different system with its own history and dynamics.

It is obvious, however, that there is need for comparative work in such an undertaking. Our philosophy major would of necessity have to learn a good deal about non-African philosophy—but only because it will increase his knowledge of philosophy and as such is pedagogically sound; it should have no ideological, political or emotional motivating impetus. The work to be undertaken must be based on the meaningful education of the student who requires as full an educational experience as possible. This of necessity includes the examination of experiences of the non-black world.

The school of ethnic studies must obviously engage in graduate studies. It should be possible for a student to acquire any of the standard advanced degrees currently available. One should be able to acquire a master's or Ph.D. in one of the standard disciplines while concentrating his attention principally on the substance of the black world. Obviously one could also become involved in an elaboration of the undergraduate experience through increased involvement in research and teaching at this level. There is a desparate need for authentic and sensitive research in the many aspects of the black experience. Graduate students and their senior colleagues (professors) would be required to undertake such research.

## RESEARCH IN CONNECTION WITH BLACK STUDIES

It seems important to complement the Department of African and Afro-American Studies and the School of Ethnic Studies with research capability. In addition there is much that can be contributed through applied research to the resolution of some of the problems that presently beset the black community. This two-fold mission characterizes the purpose of the Center for Research in the World Black Experience. The Center would provide for both basic and applied research activities.

As noted earlier there is great need for serious effort to reconstruct the world black experience in an accurate way. Much of the work of contemporary African writers is seriously challenging

the formulations put forth by Western students. Continued and
expanded research influenced by African formulations promises to
be of immense value in realizing the accurate reconstruction of
the African historical experience. Reformulation of traditional
explanations of African life and thought stands as a major area
for research effort. Jack Mendelsohn suggests that such areas are
"the great unexplored subject (s) for research in Africa today."[3]
Indeed, Mendelsohn's own understandings themselves require this
kind of attention. A specific example derives from his discussion
of the direction of African thought in which he suggests,

> The Africans have left aside all attempts to discover physical laws
> and to domesticate matter; instead they have tried to discover the
> spirit of each being and object in order to enable man to move
> about the world according to its inner rhythm. This concept of the
> relations between man and the world surrounding him has resulted
> in a mode of existence which is so devoid of any dynamic principle
> that it is very near to mere equilibrium, though it has allowed the
> preservation of the black race and civilization in spite of its technical
> weakness.[4]

Mendelsohn's conclusions that Africans left aside the search
for physical laws, and that their efforts resulted in a mode of
existence near to equilibrium do not seem quite accurate. African
thought and African life suggest that they were fully aware of the
operation of physical laws and were also concerned with what
Mendelsohn has called the "inner rythms of the world". I suspect
that what is difficult for us (of the West) to understand is that
some of the African concepts are elegant to the point that they
encompass in their operation both the spiritual (man) and the
physical (not-man). The concept of "Nommo" so well described by
Janheinz Jahn[5] and Chief Fela Sowande[6] seems to involve notions
of physical energy (in the sense that physics defines it as the
capacity for doing work or overcoming resistance) and the nature
of man's spiritual ascendancy. In short, it seems to express the
relationship between man and the forces of the universe in both
theoretical and practical terms. At the same time it is possible
that Mendelsohn's characterization of African cultural life as "mere
equilibrium" is a misunderstanding that results from imposing
western standards on African belief systems. It is obvious from
Janheinz Jahn's discussion of the African notion of Kuntu[7] and
Fela Sowande's rendition of IFA,[8] that the African notion of life,
is anything but static. The dynamic quality of African life is expressed spiritually whereas we of the West perceive dynamism as
a function of changes in the material features of the world. The
continued creation of both spiritual and physical life (the birth

and naming of babies) and its counterpart in the spirit world (the creation of gods) expresses the dynamic quality of African life.

Now, I cite my disagreements with Jack Mendelsohn to point out the need for extensive research that is based on the forms of African understanding and at the same time capable of translation into western terms. In effect my disagreements are hypotheses that can be tested through research structures such as that described above.

I must hasten to add that there is need for extensive research into the experience of black folks in the New World. It would be important to determine the degree to which New World blacks (Afro-Americans) still retain remnants of their African past in their conceptions of the universe and man's place in it. Conceptions of morality, beauty, goodness among other things also seem to be open to this kind of research effort. No doubt such remnants have been extensively influenced by European forms but it is possible that they have retained their essential African quality. I am prepared to suggest, according to my best judgments, that E. Franklin Frazier was wrong in concluding that the African social and cultural heritage of American blacks was utterly devastated and replaced by European forms.[9] I submit that there is still a lot of African in most black Americans despite an incredible campaign of de-Africanization by both blacks and whites. One can hypothesize that such remnants can be observed in religious worship, food preparation, speech, walking and lounging behavior, social taboos, sexual taboos, family forms and functioning, child rearing and a variety of non-verbal cultural forms, such as listening behavior and the use of space, among other things.[10] It is likely that these "Africanisms" with various modifications were passed on from generation to generation at an imperceptible level of cultural transmission. That is to say, over time, elders who passed them on to youngsters became unconscious of the fact they were passing on "Africanisms." They probably saw their teaching as simply functional within the context of the life of blacks in an extremely hostile environment. It is critically important to begin to confront some of these issues in a serious and systematic way. There are, of course, innumerable other questions that beg answering. The Center for Research in the Black Experience can provide a resource through which a good many of the issues can be investigated.

The Center must also have its applied side. That is, its research should not be restricted solely to the scholarly undertakings of the "pure researcher." There are myriad problems that have immediate relevance to the way black folks live or fail to live their lives right now. The Center should have the capacity to meaningfully and successfully define and resolve certain of these problems. Moreover, the focus of the efforts of the Center should be directed toward problems that are articulated by lay people of the black community. That is to say, that the interests pursued should be for the most part a function of the expressed concerns of the people of the community. It is conceivable that the Center could investigate problems as diverse as whether foods such as milk and pork are in fact harmful to blacks and whether items sold in super-markets in black neighborhoods are more expensive than the same items sold in white neighborhoods. This component of the Center should provide a meaningful service to the black community.

The Center should over time develop a capacity for educational efforts in its own right. From the outset, however, it should involve the staff and students of the department of African and Afro-American Studies and the School of Ethnic Studies in its operation. It could provide a base and resources from which the students of these structures can carry out their research activities. The applied researchers should be full-time paid professionals, preferably individuals who have served a scholarly apprenticeship in the Center on their way to acquiring their professional competence. I suggest this because I believe it takes a good deal more than "being black" to teach in and service the black community. It requires competence and in most cases that competence will be unrelated to color.

It should be noted that what has been suggested here as an academic vehicle for African and Afro-American Studies and the research Center can be seen as appropriate for carrying out scholarly teaching and research on any ethnic group. Moreover, it is important for university and college personnel to realize this and respond appropriately. It is the absence of the legitimation of ethnicity in America (because of the "melting pot" nonsense) that lurks behind the complex responses of whites to the efforts of blacks to achieve a more equitable position in the society. Indeed, the absence of socially legitimate mechanisms for preserving ethnicity, and the insistence that all ethnic distinctiveness be left in the melting pot may prove to be an important element in racism. Ethnic research and study must become a more important area for scholarly concern.

## SOME GAINS TO BE ACCRUED FROM BLACK STUDIES

It is obvious that black studies will spin-off a variety of beneficial results apart from those noted above. I would like to discuss briefly several of these possible outcomes—obvious benefits that will accrue to blacks. Important among these will be an increased psychological and emotional liberation of black people. It is necessary at this point in the growth of black awareness for blacks to begin to establish evaluative standards against which, for example, the self-worth of blacks can be appropriately measured. Most of the existing standards are appropriate for white people but when applied to blacks can only yield self-denigrating assessments. I suspect that what results from the application of "white standards" to black behavior patterns and characteristics is what social scientists have identified as indicators of the self-hate that blacks supposedly have. Seen in another way, however, what blacks have been forced to do is to accommodate to the operation of cultural standards of, for example, beauty, content of which could only result in assessments that found them non-beautiful. These standards of beauty have been articulated around the physical characteristics of whites, thus the lack of such physical attributes by blacks leads to a negative valuation of the physical attributes of blacks by both blacks and whites. In response to this many blacks attempted to take on the attributes of whites by using skin lighteners, hair straighteners, etc. It was in effect an attempt to "live up" to the content of the white standard of beauty, in this case. It is obvious that any standard of beauty appropriate for blacks would have to be strongly influenced by the quality of their own racial attributes.

A good example of this kind of accommodation and the painful results it yields is illustrated in the following. All cultures have norms that apply to individual physical appearance. These norms identify certain physical qualities as desirable and others as undesirable e.g. beautiful and ugly. In an effort to fulfill the requirements of this norm the technical element of the culture produces instrumentalities (artifacts and techniques) for making oneself beautiful, or non-ugly. Now consider the need for grooming the hair (norm) and the comb (instrumentality) and the process of combing (technique) as a normative complex. Consider also that an operational definition of the verb "to comb" presupposes the presence of reasonably straight and flowing hair. Apply the normative complex to the grooming of kinky hair and the yield is an experience that can result in a negative evaluation of kinky hair. Blacks have over time accommodated in a number of ways to this normative bundle with what I consider negative yield. In Africa, specifically in Yorubaland, the same imperative for grooming the hair exists and the appropriate instrument is an *oya*. The requisite process is let's say *oyaing*. Now both this instrument and this technique is as appropriate to kinky hair as the comb is to straight hair. The absence of the *oya* in America and the corrollary possibility of *oyaing* the kinky hair of blacks led to a definition among blacks of kinky hair as *"bad hair"* and straight hair as *"good hair"*. Hair is still often classified in this fashion. The opposite would have been the case—the kinkier the hair the "gooder" the hair and straighter the hair the "badder" the hair—if the standards for judging hair quality had been appropriate to the attributes of black folks. It is for reasons such as these that these standards must be re-articulated in a fashion appropriate to blacks.

Black studies will also contribute to the development of a body of knowledge about blacks and their history that has been for the most part denied, ignored or deprecated. Along with this denial and deprecation went a denial and deprecation of blacks by whites and self-deprecation by blacks. Study of the black experience will yield a proper perspective of the world black experience in historical and contemporary affairs of the world. With this more accurate perspective will come a new sense of the importance of the non-white experience. Although this will be of especial significance for blacks, it will be greatly important for whites also. Whites need the knowledge of the black experience to temper their unearned sense of superiority. Moreover, such a contribution will place both the black and white experience in proper historical perspective and contribute to the correction of a good many historical untruths.

In another way the black studies efforts will force the conventional disciplines out of their present provincial mold. The theories of the present social science disciplines are narrowly cast and based on the experience of the western world. They tend to reflect the provincialism of European scholars who ethnocentrically order and interpret phenomena of the world from the disadvantage of their western-most evolutionary perch. It is not surprising that looking at the black experience "through the glass whitely", as it were, they concluded that Africans were primitive and savage. They were afflicted by an enormous case of cultural myopia and self-inflicted at that. Cultural myopia, the scientific method notwithstanding, has continued to afflict the western social scientists, both black and white. It is necessary for these myopic disciplines and their practitioners to discover the experience of the non-white world. This experience, to be truly understood, must be confronted in its own right and not through the screen of western evaluation. When this happens the theoretical formulations of these disciplines will be shown to be incapable in their present form of handling the data that derive from the black experience. It will also be necessary to re-cast these theories so as to make them applicable to the majority of the world experiences (the non-white elements of the world). Then and only then will these disciplines be prepared to become disciplines whose theories and bodies of knowledge are truly reflective of the entire world.

Finally, black studies, as I have outlined it here, will truly constitute what Matthew Holden has referred to as "education for black power". In Dr. Holden's formulation both black students and black professors need this type education. He suggests—

> Moreover, the new mission will be to avoid the speciousness of developing students into mere verbalists, sophists, and rhetoricians. If there is a single obvious difficulty with current students . . . it is their addiction to a language of social action, without an honest and sustained attention to the facts underlying that reality or the logic involved in any proposal to change that reality. If mature black intellectuals have failed in any significant way, it is that they have become intimidated by student militancy . . .[11]

Holden goes on to suggest a strategy for education for the wielding of black power—

> The business of the black intellectual, in forwarding the development of other black intellectuals (his students) is to tell the truth (or as much as he can discover) and to aid in imaginative searches for ways to make the truthful situation most productive. This is what we must mean—and must insist upon—in "the regimen of fact and logic."

> This is a vital part of our understanding of the liberal education— the education appropriate to a man who will be a man of power. To be a man of power means that one must acquire a strategic position such that one can survive, grow, and develop—even in adverse circumstances

> . . . the objective in black education, is, therefore to provide those forms of training which will most greatly enhance black men's capacities to penetrate the strategic points of influence and decision.[12]

I believe Dr. Holden's position to be entirely consistent with the notions of black studies as put forth here. I remind you again that these efforts hold potentially salutary outcomes not only for the university and our society but for the world. It is imperative that these activities be understood and undertaken by universities, colleges and other educational structures of our society.

## NOTES

1. C. F. Janheinz Jahn's discussion of Nommo in his book *MUNTU*, Grove Press, 1962, Chapter 5 "Nommo: The Magic Power of the Word" pp. 121-155.

2. This calls to mind Levy-Bruell's characterization of the Nuer as "prelogical".

3. Mendelsohn, Jack, *God, Allah and Ju Ju,* Beacon Press: Boston 1965, p. 84.

4. *Ibid,* p. 85.

5. Jahn, *op. cit.*

6. Sowande, Fela, *IFA,* Sowande: Institute of African Studies, University of Ibadan, Nigeria. (Chief Sowande, in his discussions of traditional Yoruba religious beliefs, describes a battle between factions of Irunmoles (angel-like beings). He reports these factions as being "armed to the teeth with *words* of terrible and awesome destructive power".)

7. Jahn, *op. cit.,* See Chapter 6 "KUNTU: Immutability of Style."

8. Sowande, *op. cit.*

9. Frazier, E. Franklin, *The Negro Church in America,* Schocken Books, Inc. New York, 1963.

10. Edward T. Hall, among others, has written extensively about these areas. c.f. *The Hidden Dimension,* Doubleday and Company, Inc. Garden City, 1966.

11. Holden, Matthew "Education for Black Power" Wayne State University mimeo. 1967, p. 13.

12. *Ibid,* p. 14.

# 3

# THE "RELEVANCE" OF ACADEMIC PSYCHOLOGY TO THE BLACK EXPERIENCE

*by*
Ross A. Evans

The present controversy over the desirability, necessity, or indeed, the legitimacy of Black Studies in the University has, if nothing else, succeeded in shaking traditionally complacent higher educators out of their dogmatic slumber. For as Charles Hamilton (1969) has aptly noted ". . . the Black Studies thrust has helped to expose . . . the blatant weaknesses and inadequacies of much of higher education." The question of the need for separate Black Studies curricula (or departments) shall not be considered here. A case for the legitimacy of a concerted effort to make higher education relevant to the problems of the black community (and vice versa) has been eloquently presented by others (e.g., McWorter, 1969). My purpose, on the contrary, is to employ the Black Studies *concept* as a framework for reevaluating the contribution of academic psychology to the black experience and the black struggle.

With this as an introduction, I have set for myself the task of identifying the inadequacies and deficiencies in academic psychology which the Black Studies movement has helped me to recognize. First, it is my opinion that American psychology, as a product of a racist society, has been unwilling to seriously confront and expose the racist elements which are buried in many of its fundamental assumptions, implicit as well as explicit. If one considers that one of the objectives of training in psychology is to enable the student to transcend his culture, then one has little choice but to view psychology's success in this area with extreme skepticism. Those of us who are products of the psychology taught in colleges and universities could hardly disagree with

Robert MacLeod's (1965) appraisal "that the conventional undergraduate curriculum in psychology is about as culture-bound as
any curriculum could be." And let's face it, American culture is
largely a culture of racism. Therefore, in my opinion, it would be
naive and gratuitous to suppose that American psychology has
managed to escape the pernicious and encumbering effects of
racism which have permeated every other facet of American life.

The major deficiencies in academic psychology, as they relate
to the black experience, may be subsumed under what might be
termed the inferiority assumption—an assumption which has led
to a general inferiority orientation of psychologists toward black
people. Modern American psychology, from its inception around
the turn of the century, tended largely to ignore the real problems
confronting the black American, and chose rather to concentrate
its efforts on pursuing "scientific" explanations of an inferiority
which was *assumed*. My purpose here is not to indict the psychologist of that day for making that assumption, but rather to consider
the continuing effects of that assumption on the course of scholarly
inquiry into questions relevant to the black condition.

The selective application of the inferiority assumption has been
so thoroughly and subtly incorporated into the academic style
of American psychology that it hardly appears to exist at all.
For example, take the question of intelligence testing. First, let us
observe that the two most commonly used individual intelligence
scales for children were initially constructed, pretested and stan-
dardized with a native born white reference population.* Non-
white and foreign born children were excluded from the item
selection and standardization samples on the assumption that
their inclusion would render the standardization norms unduly
low, and non-predictive for children from the majority culture.
But it is with revealing irony that one further observes that these
very tests are currently being used to consign minority children to
classes for the mentally retarded, or to the lowest educational tracks
in the public schools. Moreover, data from these instruments provide sanction for the increasingly numerous statements (issued
so casually by many professionals, including psychologists), which
instruct the lay public that fifty per cent of the school children in
this or that black community are mentally retarded. But what is

*The scales to which I refer are the Stanford-Binet Intelligence Test and
the Wechsler Intelligence Scale for children. It should be noted that the
Wechsler Scale was constructed in 1955 and has not since been revised. The
Stanford-Binet, which has undergone two major revisions—the latest published in 1960—has not to date corrected this deficiency.

even more disturbing than these assertions themselves is the professional reaction to them. The historically conditioned professional response has typically been the initiation of frantic activities directed toward discovering the causes of the assumed inferiority, in lieu of critical reevaluation of the measuring instruments themselves.

Perhaps the points I have been trying to make will be given perspective by considering two examples—taken from the history of American psychometry—in which the absence of the inferiority assumption is notable. During World War I, the United States Armed Forces undertook a massive psychological testing program in an effort to identify those individuals who were intellectually unsuitable for military conscription. The results of that testing program, inadequate as it was, revealed several dramatic differences as a function of race, socioeconomic status and geographic location: whites tended to score higher than blacks; Northern whites scored higher than Southern whites; Northern blacks performed better than Southern blacks; the scores of men from higher socio-economic brackets were higher than those of counterparts from lower socio-economic brackets; and so forth. These results have been well publicized, and are not of major importance here. What is of interest is the fact that fifty per cent of the *white* draftees failed to achieve a test mental age score of thirteen (13) years—an achievement level which was being proposed as a cut-off point for feeble-mindedness. This finding, suggesting that one-half of draft age white American males were feebleminded, understandably created tremendous controversy and disquietude. However, as Sarason and Doris (1969) point out ". . . despite the alarms, a saner view set in and both psychologists and the public at large soon realized that any definition of feeblemindedness that classifies 50 per cent of the population as feeble-minded must be suspect to say the least." One wonders when a saner view will set in with respect to the incidence of mental retardation among children from low income *black* communities.

The second example from the field of psychometry, in which the inferiority assumption is conspicuously absent, concerns the question of sex differences in intelligence. Consider the following excerpts from Anne Anastasi's (1961) *Psychological Testing* regarding the construction of the 1937 revision of the Stanford-Binet test:

> In the final selection of items, consideration was not only given to age differentiation and internal consistency, but also to the reduction and balancing sex differences in percentage passing of either sex,

on the *assumption* that such items might reflect purely fortuitous and irrelevant differences in the experiences of the two sexes (Italics my own) . . . . p. 194

She later states the following:

> For proper interpretation of test scores, the test user should be aware of such item selection procedures. A statement that boys and girls do not differ significantly in Stanford-Binet IQ, for example, provides no information whatever regarding sex differences in intelligence. Since sex differences were deliberately eliminated in the process of selecting items for the test, their absence from the final score merely indicates that this aspect of test construction was successfully executed. p. 195

In essence, what the above excerpts indicate is that the test constructors assumed *a priori* that there should be no sex differences in intelligence; therefore, they developed an instrument which precluded them. On the contrary, these same test constructors assumed *a priori* that there should be racial differences in intelligence (favoring whites). Thus, it should not be surprising, in my opinion, that this result has generally obtained.

It is true that some effort has been made toward the development of so-called "culture fair" tests; but the general consensus has been that these instruments have little practical utility since they do not correlate highly with the indicators of success (typically school achievement) within the majority culture. However, I believe that the question must be raised as to whether a "culture fair" test logically should be expected to predict success in a culture which is decidedly *unfair*. The relatively high correlation between the more culture-bound tests and such measurers as school achievement, in fact, may be simply a statistical artifact reflecting the ubiquitous effects of cultural and racial biases in American society. The ramifications of this likely state of affairs are far-reaching. On the one hand, psychologists are able to justify their continued use of admittedly biased measurement devices on the basis of empirical predictive validity; on the other hand, educators are able to rationalize their failure to teach black children on the basis of the learners' inferior intellectual potential. Thus, two related aspects of a biased system achieve equilibrium through the process of reciprocal reinforcement. The Black Studies thrust, I believe, can help expose the fuzzines and illogic of this kind of thinking, to the benefit of all concerned.

Another manifestation of the inferiority assumption in American psychology appears in its pathology orientation toward the collective adjustment problems and adjustment processes of black people. That is to say, American psychologists, in their effort to interpret behavioral and personality differences between whites and blacks, have attempted to apply psychological constructs based on *within* group deviations from white middle class standards to differences occurring *between* the two groups. Thus, for example, "hypersensitive" behavior on the part of the black people as a group becomes theoretically equivalent to ostensibly similar behavior occurring in a white psychiatric patient. The most glaring fallacy here is that one logically cannot apply clinical models based on individual deviations from a cultural norm to groups of individuals with different cultural experiences and standards; moreover, one should not even attempt to extrapolate from such models without at first taking into account the situational validity of the constructs involved. To be more concrete, if one is to infer that "hypersensitivity" without realistic provocation is indicative of a pathological condition, then one must establish the absence of such provocation in the situation under consideration. In the present example, this would raise the question as to whether "hypersensitivity" on the part of black people is, in fact, unrealistic, or whether it is actually a logical adaptive reaction to the circumstances of their everyday existence. This issue, I believe, has not been given adequate consideration in pathology-oriented research and theory pertaining to the social adjustment of black people.

The pathology orientation to the situational adjustment problems of black people has also led to a concentration on instances of social and/or personal maladjustment of blacks, while only philosophical attention has been paid to the adverse social and environmental factors which produce them. At the same time, the pathology orientation tends to ignore the positive aspects of adjustment on the part of black people, who constantly face conditions of intense and sustained adversity. The more meaningful question is not why so many black people become maladjusted, but rather why so many of them do not. I believe that important lessons on techniques for overcoming adversity could be learned from the examination of case studies of black people who have managed to neutralize the debilitating and degrading effects of racism and oppression. Why must only negative illustrations be represented in the psychological literature? And then again, when negative illustrations are presented, why must they be analyzed and interpreted within a pathology rather than a social adaptation framework? It is important to remember that all behavior is lawful and purposeful, even though some of it is regrettable and/or unsuccessful. Failure, however, should not be equated with pathology. Perhaps an analogy will help clarify my point.

Consider a situation in which three boys are walking through a cow pasture, when suddenly they observe a dangerous bull charging in their direction. All three boys react instantly by racing across the pasture toward a fence beyond which lies safety. Now as it happens, two of the boys are tall with long legs, while the third lad is built somewhat closer to the ground. Upon reaching the fence, all three boys attempt to leap over; however only the two taller youths are successful. The short boy does not make it simply because his legs are not long enough. Therefore, he scrambles around avoiding the bull until he decides to try crawling under the fence. This works, and the boys continue on their way.

An attempt to analyze the behavior of the short youth using the pathology model might proceed as follows: First of all, the short boy's initial effort to leap over the fence perhaps reflects an unrealistic level of aspiration resulting from low self esteem and feelings of self worthlessness. The fact that he imitated the behavior of the taller boys could reveal an internalization of tall boy standards, indicating a subconscious wish to be tall accompanied by a rejection of all short people, including himself; and so forth. On the other hand, a more parsimonious explanation may simply be that the short boy initially attempted a logical approach to the solution of a problem, which did not work. Whether or not he actually did model his behavior after that of the tall boys is irrelevant here, since imitation of successful behavior is certainly a logical strategy. The fact is that the approach did not solve the problem, and he had to try something different.

The above analogy, I believe, bears directly upon the historical attempts of blacks to overcome the social and economic barriers to full American citizenship. And it also characterizes the typical reaction of psychologists and other social scientists to those attempts. Historically, American social scientists have reacted to the problems of black people in a compartmentalized fashion. The problem of gaining entry into the social and economic mainstream of American life has confronted virtually every minority immigrant group (in varying degrees) since the nation's founding. Yet, the similarity between the adaptive reactions to these encumbrances utilized by the immigrant groups and those attempted by blacks has not been adequately appreciated.

Immigrant minority group members attempted to modify their physical appearance and social demeanor (e.g., adopting American haircuts, abandoning Old World customs, anglicizing surnames, etc.) in an effort to become more acceptable to Anglo-Americans; this effort was widely regarded as positive adaptive behavior designed to facilitate their assimilation into the American mainstream.* Similarly, black Americans attempted to modify their physical and behavioral characteristics, (e.g., straightening their hair, lightening their skin, talking "proper," etc.), perhaps also to make themselves more like the real Americans; however, in this case, the behavior was considered pathological, reflecting self rejection, self hatred and the rest. (This is not to suggest that the phenomenon of self hatred does not exist for some individual black people. However, I do not believe that wholesale imputation of this tendency to black people as a group, or even a substantial percentage of them, is justifiable.) The major point here, however, should not be obscured. The fact is that for the blacks, the early attempts at acquiring "white folks" characteristics and mannerisms simply didn't work to their advantage. But is this any reason to consider these attempts to be reflective of underlying group pathology? I think not.

Fortunately, today's black American—like the boy attempting to escape the bull—has decided on an alternative strategy, a strategy which has given rise to the Black Studies movement. In turn, the Black Studies movement has begun to dispel the myth that the Afro-American has presented a *unique* and incredibly overwhelming problem to the American system. More realistically, the incredibly overwhelming problem has been presented *by the American system* to the Afro-African.

The final manifestation of the inferiority assumption to be considered here concerns the cultural deviance approach to intervention-oriented research with black children from low income

---

*Let me point out that it is not my contention that immigrant groups were ever fully assimilated into the American socio-cultural fabric, as suggested by the "melting pot" myth. However, the degree of assimilation they did achieve is substantially greater than that attained by black Americans. But the major point here is that both immigrants and blacks did make concerted efforts to decrease the dissimilarity between themselves and the more established Anglo-American. For an insightful exposition of the question regarding the assimilation of immigrants and Blacks, the reader is referred to Colin Greer's *Cobweb Attitudes: Essays on Educational and Cultural Mythology*. New York: Teachers College Press, 1970.

families:* This approach—which bears similarity to the pathology orientation discussed above—evaluates child-rearing circumstances of low income homes in terms of the degree of their deviation from the characteristics of the middle class milieu, which is taken as an unequivocal standard of excellence in most if not all respects. It is not my contention that the conditions of slum life are equally conducive to intellectual stimulation and development as those of middle class environments; there is too much evidence to the contrary. Rather, my point is that behavioral researchers have been overly zealous in identifying a multiplicity of child-rearing and parent-child interactional *differences* between middle income whites and low income blacks which are automatically assumed to represent deficiencies in the upbringing of black children. I should like to emphasize that what I am referring to are not those obviously handicapping factors associated with slum living, such as overcrowded living conditions, hunger, the absence of the mother in the home due to her need to work, etc.; rather, the issue here pertains to those relatively subtle value-related life style variables, about whose effects on intellectual and personality development we know so little. Nevertheless, based on only scanty (and confounded) correlational evidence, researchers and practitioners have begun to propose interventional programs designed to restructure the life style and parent-child interactional patterns of large masses of low income black families. Moreover, as L. Alan Sroufe (1970) observes, ". . . these proposals have generated no more debate than surrounds a decision to alter the lighting in an experimental rat colony."

Perhaps the most disturbing aspect of this displacement of emphasis from early childhood education to the restructuring of family interactional patterns is that it seems clearly to be an example of buck passing; and the buck that is being passed is the same one which secondary school educators foisted upon the elementary schools, which, in turn, passed it on to preschool compensatory educational programs. Thus it appears that through this process of educational reductionism, we are gradually working ourselves back toward the point of conception. The immediate result of this tendency, in essence, has been the replacement of the concept of genetic inferiority with the concept of environmental inferiority (Sroufe, 1970). The justification may be different, but

*A stimulating discussion of this problem has been presented by L. Alan Sroufe in his article: "A Methodological and Philosophical Critique of Intervention-Oriented Research." *Developmental Psychology,* 1970, 2, 140-145.

the implications are the same; black people, on the whole, constitute an inferior breed. But ironically, while geneticists readily admit that they are nowhere close to being able to deal scientifically with the question of genetic inferiority, psychologists appear to be somewhat less modest. Compensatory educational programs continue to be evaluated; and with every negative finding reported, the concept of irreversible environmental inferiority is reinforced. As psychologists, we must ask ourselves why we continue to employ inadequate instruments to measure expected outcomes of socially important research without sharing with the public our awareness of these limitations. And as psychologists, we should state loudly and clearly that even if an interventional program does produce important behavioral changes, the state of the art of behavioral research is such that we are not even sure that we could detect them—especially on a short term basis. I am not suggesting that we should call a moratorium on important evaluative educational and social research until we have more adequate measurement instruments and research methodologies. What I am suggesting is that we stop leading the lay public to believe that we are presently equipped to do a job that we ourselves know we are not in a position to perform.

By way of summary, I would like to reiterate that the major purpose of this paper was to employ the Black Studies concept as a framework for reevaluating the relevance of academic psychology to the black experience. The Black Studies thrust, which grew out of a more general black awareness movement, arose from the expressed need of black people for a more positive evaluation of themselves. The major thesis presented was that the relevance of traditional academic psychology to the legitimate problems of black people has been impeded by the presence of institutionalized racist elements imbedded in many of its fundamental assumptions.

Based on this foundation, contemporary American psychology has generally adopted an inferiority orientation toward black people, which (among other things) has resulted in the misapplication of psychological principles and constructs to the collective problems of black Americans. More critically, yesterday's black student of psychology (especially black graduate students trained in white universities) readily accepted—or failed to challenge—the arbitrary assumptions of their disciplines; as well, many of the misguided interpretations and conclusions, regarding the black condition, which emanated from them were allowed to pass without serious opposition. Many of us subordinated the legitimacy of our own black experience in deference to the "objectivity" of the scientist.

The Black Studies movement, I believe, is a much needed impetus whose impact could go far toward identifying and eliminating the racial and cultural biases which exist within the field of psychology. But perhaps even more important, its momentum has already begun to provide a new perspective for evaluating what psychology is and what it should be.

## REFERENCES

Anastasi, Anne *Psychological Testing*. New York: The Macmillan Company, 1961.

Hamilton, Charles V. The Challenge of Black Studies. *Social Policy*, 1970, 1, 14-16.

MacLeod, Robert B. The Teaching of Psychology and the Psychology We Teach. *American Psychologist*, 1965, 20, 344-352.

McWorter, Gerald A. Deck the Racist Halls: The Case of Black Studies. In Armstead, L., Robinson, Craig, Foster, C., and Ogilvie, Donald H. (Eds.) *Black Studies in the University*. New Haven: Yale University Press, 1969, pp. 55-74.

Sarason, Seymour B. and Doris, John *Psychological Problems in Mental Deficiency*. New York: Harper and Row, 1969.

Sroufe, L. Alan A Methodological and Philosophical Critique of Intervention-Oriented Research. *Developmental Psychology*, 1970, 2, 140-145.

# 4

## THE AFRO-AMERICAN AND AFRICA

*by*

FELIX OKOYE

*"Colonization is no solution, but an evasion."*

In 1962 a North Carolina black minister argued that the African exiles in America were slow to abandon their "love and admiration for our native land" and their feelings of kinship with the inhabitants of the world's second largest continent.[1] This point of view had been articulated, as early as 1947, by the late Dr. DuBois.[2] Ten years later the distinguished scholar's opinion on the subject was still unchanged.[3] I did not find the pieces of evidence, which were put forth in substantiation of this viewpoint, altogether convincing. It was contended, for instance, that this attachment to the motherland could be seen in the fact that the transplanted blacks continued to label their organizations "African" right up to the Reconstruction period. What is fundamentally wrong with this assertion is that it creates a wrong impression in the reader's mind. It makes him feel that American Negroes willingly chose to remain unassimilated, that they were immensely proud of their "Africanness." This was not the case. They founded their African institutions only after the dominant whites had indicated, in no uncertain terms, that they could not endure any suggestion of equality between the two races, that the assimilationist ideal—as enshrined in the motto "E pluribus unum" —was nothing more than tall talk as far as black people were concerned.

Take the formation of independent black churches for instance. The Free African Society, the first of such institutions, was organized by Richard Allen and Absolom Jones; but not before both men had been tossed out of St. George, a predominantly Caucasian

church in Philadelphia.[4] Basic disagreements over policy soon led
to the revocation of Allen's membership from the Society. He
subsequently established his own church: Bethel African Methodist
Episcopal Church. Other black leaders hastened to emulate Allen's
example. They, too, set up African societies in several cities in the
states of Delaware, Maryland, New Jersey and Pennsylvania. In
1816 the various black churches were brought under the same
organizational framework. The new ecclesiastical institution was
called the African Methodist Episcopal Church and its first bishop
was Richard Allen.[5]

The white Methodists of New York had no intention of being
outdone by their counterparts in Philadelphia. They, too, thought
it was intolerable to worship God on a basis of equality with
Phoebus's children. They, therefore, introduced segregation into
the John Street Methodist Episcopal Church. The blacks, however, refused to be subjected to this blatant indignity. They
parted company with the Caucasian hypocrites and established
their own church—the African Methodist Episcopal Zion Church
—in 1796.[6]

The spirit of independence also manifested itself among the
black Baptists. And in each instance, identification with the
ancestral homeland was made only after they had been denied
social acceptance by their white compatriots. This, at least, was
true of the members of the Abyssinian Baptist Church of New York
City (1808) and the first African Baptist Church of Philadelphia
(1809).[7] We cannot help feeling that such an overt admission of
their kinship with Africans would never have been made had they
been integrated into the American social fabric. We would even
boldly suggest that the motive force behind this open acknowledgement of their ancestral background was not love for the African
way of life but sheer necessity. The black immigrants to Columbia
founded "African" churches, lodges, improvement and benevolent
societies because the hegemonic race vehemently opposed their assimilation into the political, economic and social life of America.
Having been generally rejected, there was no alternative except
to establish institutions which would make it possible for them to
achieve solidarity, status, self-esteem, respectability, dignity and
happiness.

The hostile attitude of the dominant whites towards the aspirations of black folk made it imperative for the latter to seek identification not with the world's second largest continent but with one another. For they were, as I have pointed out elsewhere, the little
Africa in America. If this fact is borne in mind it readily becomes

apparent that when they tagged on the African label to their organizations they were not in fact confessing their love and admiration for their brothers and sisters across the Atlantic. They were simply stressing the one thing about them which the white supremacists seemed determined not to forget, the one thing which kept them apart from other Americans, the primary reason for the blighting prejudice which encumbered their lives. The free blacks were surely dramatizing their conviction that their unique status in American society—neither free men nor slaves—had its origin in the white man's active contempt for the African complexion. They were so right. On August 20, 1817, Robert G. Harper practically confirmed their point of view in a letter to the Secretary of the American Colonization Society. This white supremacist from Baltimore admitted that the black color, in the United States, had become invested with special meaning and significance, had become a badge of inferiority, because of the social heritage of slavery.

> You may manumit the slave, but you cannot make him a white man; he still remains a Negro or a mulatto. The mark and the recollection of his origin and former state still adhere to him; the feelings produced by that condition in his own mind, and in the minds of the whites, still exist; he is associated, by his color and by these recollections and feelings, with the class of slaves; and a barrier is thus raised between him and the whites, that is, between him and the free class, which he can never hope to transcend.[8]

The man from Baltimore, of course, merely echoed sentiments which had been voiced, at an earlier date, by Thomas Jefferson, Robert Finley and Henry Clay, and a formidable list of Caucasians —Abraham Lincoln, Theodore G. Bilbo, George Lincoln Rockwell to name a few—would subsequently operate from the same assumptions in their efforts to make the United States a "Whiteman's Country."

Attention has been drawn to the pronouncements of these white racialists because they were crucially important in determining the attitudes of Afro-Americans towards Africa. A minority of the blacks took seriously the white supremacist contention that the children of the sun could never improve their lot in Columbia, that full manhood would forever be beyond their reach, that the two races could never live on a footing of equality. Members of this minority group have generally displayed a "disposition to exchange America for Africa."[9] In 1788, for instance, some black folk in Rhode Island wanted to return to their ancestral homeland but were prevented from so doing by a fraudulent agent.[10] Paul Cuffee, a free Negro, was the owner and skipper of a ship which was manned by an all-black crew. He visited Sierra Leone,

on the West African coast, at least twice because of the "deep
interest which he felt for the welfare of his brethren of the African
race."[11] In 1815 Captain Cuffee carried 38 persons of the "dispersed
race of Africa" from Boston to Sierra Leone. The enterprise cost
him about $4,000.[12] The American Colonization Society was
founded in December, 1816. Between 1820 and 1838 it sent 2122
free blacks to Liberia.[13] In 1859 Dr. Martin Robison Delany and
Robert Campbell journeyed through the western part of modern
Nigeria in search of a new home for American and Canadian
Negroes. On December 27, 1859, they obtained permission to set-
tle intelligent, educated and skilled Afro-Americans on any portion
of the unoccupied lands of Abeokuta, an Egba city-state. The treaty
was never implemented. The pilgrimage to Motherland, however,
was not a total failure. As a result of the trip, Mr. Campbell decided to adopt Abeokuta as his future home. He subsequently
returned to Nigeria and stayed in Lagos for a few years.[14] In
his *Official Report of the Niger Valley Exploring Party* Dr. Delany
recommended that Afro-Americans should always insist that Africa
is the patrimony of the African race and that only black people
have the right to shape the destiny of their continent.

> Our policy must be—and I hazard nothing in promulging it: nay,
> without this design and feeling, there would be a great deficiency
> of self-respect, pride of race, and love of country, and we might
> never expect to challenge the respect of nations—*Africa for the
> African race, and black men to rule them.* By black men I mean,
> men of African descent who claim an identity with the race.[15]

Africa for the African! The Harvard-trained physician seems to
have been one of the first to use this rallying cry of proponents of
a Pax Africana. His definition of the black man is full of interest
for he rigorously excluded all those who no longer possessed racial
pride, who were ashamed of their physical characteristics, who
desperately wanted to become identified with Caucasians. Being
black was not enough for this man who was so much concerned
with the elevation of the members of his race. One also had to
think and act black.

Nineteenth century Americans found Delany's extreme racial
consciousness quite disconcerting. This was particularly true of
Caucasians who had left no stone unturned in the effort to make
their black victims apologetic about their color. It was equally
true of Afro-American leaders who were concerned with stressing the fundamental humanity of all peoples. Frederick Douglass, for instance, was piqued by the African explorer's racial
consciousness. "I thank God for making me a man simply," said
he, "but Delany always thanks Him for making him a *black*

*man.*"16 For us, however, the physician's racial pride was consistent with the role he played, with the task he set himself. He sought the regeneration of the oppressed blacks. It was therefore only to be expected that he should seize every opportunity to aver "his faith in his race, and his deep identity with them."17 This racial consciousness manifested itself in the names of his progeny. These were Toussaint L'Ouverture, Charles Lennox Remond, Alexander Dumas, Saint Cyprian, Faustin Soulouque, Rameses Placido and Ethiopia Halle Amelia.18 It is hardly necessary to point out that a strict application of Delany's definition, today, would result in the rejection of the claims of many educated Africans—who unthinkingly style themselves "black Englishmen" or "black Frenchmen"—to membership in the sable race.19

On April 12, 1861, southern guns opened fire on Fort Sumter to perpetuate human inequality and forestall the realization of Black Power. The American Civil War made irrelevant the African Canaan project of Delany. He became an ardent supporter of the Unionist cause. On February 27, 1865, he received a commission as a major in the 104th Regiment, United States Colored Troops. He thus became the first black major in the history of the Republic. After the war, he worked in the Freedmen's Bureau as a Sub-Assistant Commissioner.20

The defeat of the Confederacy spelt the doom of slavery in the United States. The slaves were emancipated and between 1866 and 1875 serious efforts were made to assimilate those who, formerly, had been described as things, as excrescences on the body politic. Political power was also conferred upon those who had never enjoyed rights. The blacks were recognized as American citizens by the Fourteenth Amendment to the Constitution. The Fifteenth Amendment, which was ratified in 1870, gave the suffrage to Afro-Americans. The Force Act of 1870 placed all cases arising out of the fourteenth and fifteenth amendments under the jurisdiction of federal courts. By this enactment the Radical Republicans made it possible for black Americans to obtain justice from the courts. The Ku Klux Klan Act of 1871 sought to bring to a halt white violence against black folk. In 1875 a Federal Civil Rights Act was passed. And some Negroes, according to Dr. Woodward, "successfully tested their rights in railroads, steamboats, hotels, theaters, and other public accommodations."21 During the Reconstruction period Afro-Americans served as jurors and judges. They appeared in council chamber and legislative hall, at the state and national levels, and they voted in large numbers.

By 1875, therefore, the blacks seemed to be well on the road to achieving equality with the whites, to securing their Civil Rights, to acquiring political muscle. All this, however, was changed by the Compromise of 1877 which resolved the disputed Presidential election of 1876. By this Compromise the Afro-Americans were abandoned as the wards of the federal government and white southerners were given the right to determine, without outside interference, the Negro's "place" in society. In 1883 the Supreme Court dramatized the federal government's unwillingness to protect the blacks when it declared the Civil Rights Act of 1875 unconstitutional. This decision was clearly a "capitulation to racism." It was interpreted as such by the southern whites and they were not slow to disfranchise, ostracise and segregate the children of the sun. In *Plessy* versus *Ferguson*, which was decided in 1896, the United States' Supreme Court practically endorsed segregation as an acceptable way of life. It made respectable the "separate but equal" myth.

The blacks naturally resented these regressive developments. That much is clear from the writings and speeches of Henry McNeal Turner, Bishop of the African Methodist Episcopal Church. He was, as aptly pointed out by George Shepperson, a "major exponent" of the "Back-to-Africa" movement.[22] His book, *The Blackman's Burden*, was very critical of the Supreme Court decision of October 15, 1883.

> That revolting decision alone . . . sustains all the unjust discriminations, proscriptions, and robberies perpetrated by public carriers upon millions of the nation's most loyal defenders. It fathers all the Jim Crow cars into which colored people are huddled and compelled to pay as much as the whites who are given the finest accommodations. It has made the ballot of the black man a parody, his citizenship a nullity and his freedom a burlesque.[23]

He retained all through his adult life an unwavering contempt for the American flag. He repeatedly called it "a dirty rag." It had become sullied by the countless crimes committed in defense of White Supremacy. It aptly symbolized the racist soul of the nation: stripes for peoples of African descent and stars for Caucasians.[24] Because of Turner's intense dislike of oppression and hypocrisy, he always experienced feelings of disgust whenever the United States was described as the "sweet land of liberty."

On November 28, 1893, Turner addressed a meeting of the National Council of Colored Men. The Bishop from Georgia made it abundantly clear that he did not share the optimism of the overwhelming majority of black Americans—the faith that things would get better. He was convinced that the dominant whites had no intention of recognizing the manhood of the oppressed group. He claimed that Afro-Americans would forever remain "a dwarfed people" because of the color prejudices of the ruling race. Nor was education the answer to the problem of the inferior social status of the black man. Turner rightly noted that "book-learning" was of little value to a person who lacked motivation, rights, identity, true manliness, ambition, self-respect, self-confidence and opportunity.

> . . . and no amount of book-learning, divested of manhood respect and manhood promptings, will ever make us a great people; for underlying all school culture must exist the consciousness that I am somebody, that I am a man, that I am as much as anybody else, that I have rights, that I am the creature of law and order, that I am entitled to respect, that every avenue to distinction is mine. For where this consciousness does not form the substratum of any people, inferioration, retrogression and ultimate degradation will be the result.

The blacks, according to Turner, no longer possessed dignity or pride because they were denied the opportunities for improvement. Inadequate remuneration for their labors accounted for their lack of motivation. Only menial jobs—Pullman car porters and scullions for example—were open to Afro-American college graduates while the most ignorant white wretches could and sometimes did become congressmen and even governors of states. The inferior social status of the black man was attributable to the fact that the members of the hegemonic race, especially the poor white trash, seemed constantly on the lookout for ways to degrade and humiliate him.

Bishop Turner finally came to grips with the task of prescribing a remedy for the seemingly hopeless position of Afro-Americans. He disapproved of the blacks waging a war against their white oppressors on grounds that "physical resistance is literal madness," that only "an idiot would give it a moment's thought." A headlong confrontation was deemed sheer folly partly because of the overwhelming superiority of the Caucasians in numbers and resources and partly because such a course of action would give the white racialists a most convenient pretext for the realization of their fondest desire—the total extermination of black Americans. Turner dramatized the validity of the last point by reading a letter he received just before he left his home in order to attend the meeting in Ohio.

> You Negroes had better not provoke a conflict with the white people at your convention in Cincinnati, for if you do the whites, north and south, will join together and exterminate the last one of you from the face of the land. Take warning now, for I know the sentiment of the North, and the South justly hates you.

The writer of the letter was a resident of Philadelphia, the city of brotherly love! Salvation, in the view of the Georgian, was to be found in "a partial African emigration." What this amounted to was that only self-reliant Afro-Americans would be allowed to participate in African colonization. The money for the project was to come from the national coffers. Turner contended that the American Republic owed its black citizens the sum of forty billion dollars "for daily work performed." He, therefore, insisted that the federal government be asked to disgorge the relatively modest sum of $500,000,000 for the commencement of the nation-building enterprize.[25]

Turner's speech was, indeed, a priceless testimony of the love, loyalty, and patriotism of black people for "a nation that cares nothing for them." It was also a highly moving brief for the Back-to-Africa movement. Its origins and objectives were set forth in a most persuasive manner. Its origins lay deep in the inherent racism of American society, in the inhumanity of Caucasians, in the black man's despair that his appeals for justice were not heeded, in his dream of "being somebody," of "making it" like everybody else, in his search for dignity, self-respect and self-determination. The black Americans who espoused the cause of African colonization wanted to establish a nation of their own. They sought to escape from the crippling dominance of the white man. Their concern was fundamentally similar to that of Lena Younger, the mother of the tragic hero in Lorraine Hansberry's *A Raisin in the Sun*. "In my time," she said, "we was worried about not being lynched and getting to the North if we could and how to stay alive and still have a pinch of dignity too."[26] As a matter of fact it was the utter disregard of "the due process" requirement by white lynch mobs which compelled H. M. Turner to summon the 1893 Convention. He hoped that the delegates would evolve a plan which would make it possible for Afro-Americans to stay alive and still have a pinch of dignity too. We do not know whether such a plan materialized at the Cincinnati meeting. We do know, however, that the Bishop of the African Methodist Episcopal Church subsequently became the Chancellor of the Colored National Emigration and Commercial Association.[27] On March 1, 1896, Henry M. Turner personally supervised the departure of 321 Liberian emigrants—in the steamship "Laurada"—from Savannah, Georgia. The group consisted of 170 males and 151 females. The majority of these were drawn from "the better class" of Afro-American farmers from the Southern states. And many of them "had owned land or were otherwise well-circumstanced."[28] The latter fact definitely bears out Dr. DuBois's contention that the back-to-Africa movement "commended itself not simply to the inexperienced and to demagogues, but to the prouder and more independent type of Negro"— to those, that is, who could no longer endure the humiliating experience of "begging for justice and recognition" from men who had no intentions of being just or of recognizing the humanity of black folk.[29] This was true of Bishop Turner, of some of the sixty blacks who accompanied Alfred Charles Sam to the Gold Coast colony (Ghana) in 1914 and of thousands who joined Marcus Garvey's "Africa for the Africans" movement.[30] Dr. W. E. B. DuBois subsequently provided the strongest piece of evidence in substantiation of his viewpoint when he renounced his allegiance to the United States and accepted a Ghanaian citizenship. This immensely talented crusader for human dignity and human decency fittingly died in Accra on the eve of the gargantuan Civil Rights March on Washington in August, 1963. The call of Africa has been strong upon the proud and more independent Afro-Americans.

There is ample—nay preponderant—evidence that most black inhabitants of Columbia have always had a decided aversion for Africa, have always opposed all African colonization schemes, have been ashamed of their ancestral background. One could easily establish the validity of this contention by taking notice of the views, on the subject, of the few black voices which strove to make Negro Americans interested in the world's second largest continent. Rev. Alexander Crummell was such a voice. He wanted his black compatriots to participate in the evangelization of Africa. He hoped that the African exiles in the New World, especially those in the United States, the West Indies and Brazil—would play the leading role in the regeneration of our continent. As a matter of fact he anxiously looked forward to the day when Africa would be repossessed "in trade, commerce and moral power" by her "scattered children, in distant lands." The above-mentioned data were culled from a fifty-four page pamphlet which Crummell had been encouraged to write by Mr. Campbell and Dr. Delany upon their return from the Niger Valley expedition. For our purposes, however, what is significant is the reverend gentleman's assertion that many Afro-Americans had developed a "prejudice against everything African" from hearing exaggerated accounts of their relationship to our continent. He also remarked that the majority of black leaders were of the opinion that it was unfair "to disturb their residence in the land of their birth by a continued call to go to Africa." Crummell, on the very specific

issue of emigration or colonization, claimed that Frederick Douglass and Martin R. Delany represented the two polarities in the
thought of Negro leaders.[31] In 1893 Henry McNeal Turner in-
formed the National Council of Colored Men that his advocacy
of African emigration had conferred upon him the unenviable
honor of being the most abused man in the United States.[32] That
Bishop Turner was not a victim of paranoia was demonstrated in
1915 when R. R. Wright, Jr., editor of the *Christian Recorder*,
eulogized the Georgian. He said, among other things, that Turner
"was ridiculed from one end of the country to the other" because of his espousal of the cause of repatriation.[33] In 1895, the
Honorable J. H. Smyth, a former minister to Liberia, declared,
before the Congress on Africa, that

> (Negroes) are averse to the discussion of Africa, when their
> relationship with that ancient and mysterious land and its races is
> made the subject of discourse or reflection. The remoteness of Africa
> from America may be a reason for such feeling; the current opinion
> in the minds of the Caucasians, whence the American Negroes'
> opinions are derived, that the African is by nature an inferior man,
> may be a reason. The illiteracy, poverty, and degradation of the
> Negro, pure and simple, as known in Christian lands, may be a
> reason in connection with the partially true and partially false
> impression that the Negroes, or Africans, are pagan and heathen
> as a whole, and as a sequence hopelessly degraded beings. These
> may be some of the reasons that make the subject of Africa dis-
> cordant and unmusical to our ears. It is amid such embarrassments
> that the lecturer, the orator, the missionary must present Africa to
> the Negro in Christian America.[34]

Forty five years later Africa, to most black Americans, was still
something to be feared and resented.[35]

Today, the situation is different. There is now an increasing
tendency on the part of Afro-Americans to identify with our
continent. The black students now insist that they should be made
familiar with their African heritage. Some of them proudly wear
African clothes. The "natural look" has become quite fashionable.
It would be wrong, however, to conclude that the old image of
Africans—Carter Woodson's "terrible Africans"—no longer exists
in the minds of these "book-learners."[36] This, at least, has been
my experience at Tougaloo College, Mississippi. The few African
students at this predominantly black institution bitterly complain
that it is very difficult to establish meaningful relationships with
Negro Americans. The reason they give is that many black citizens
of Columbia fondly believe that the "Tarzan image" is a true one.
It is proper to remind our long-lost brothers and sisters that the
Tarzan movies were not produced in Africa. The "Tarzan image" of
Africa is simply another insidious effort, on the part of the domi-

nant race, to prove the "inferiority" of the black man. The racialists in Hollywood would be well-advised to pay heed to Ron
Karenga's telling comment on this subject. "As far as I know," the
black militant said, "only Tarzan swings from trees like monkeys
and he is a white man."

The most significant fact which emerged from the examination
of these writings was Smyth's assertion that Afro-Americans depended upon their white compatriots for their views about the
world's second largest continent. For it helps us understand why a
majority of Negro Americans tended to portray Africa negatively,
why they did not want to be associated with it, why they have
remained strongly attached to a nation which offered them nothing but stripes and scorn. This dependence upon Caucasians was
most unfortunate. It gave their oppressors the chance to brain-
wash them into believing that only in the United States could
they fully develop their potentialities. John C. Calhoun of South
Carolina indulged himself in the "Big Lie" when he tried, without success, to put an end to the anti-slavery petitions to Congress.

> Never before has the black race of Central Africa, from the
> dawn of history to the present day attained a condition so civilized
> and so improved, not only physically, but morally and intellectually.
> It came among us in a low, degraded and savage condition, and in
> the course of a few generations it has grown up under the fostering
> care of our institutions, as reviled as they have been, to its present
> comparative civilized condition.[37]

The brash senator opposed the Abolitionist movement on grounds
that the "peculiar institution" was a positive good to the African
"savage"!

This elaborate and unrelenting indoctrination of the blacks
was, perhaps, the most tragic aspect of American slavery. For many
of them, in time, came to believe the white man's lies. Phyllis (or
Phillis) Wheatley is a case in point. She was unquestionably the
most articulate African exile in colonial America. That she preferred life servitude in the New World to independence in Africa
was painfully made clear in several of her poems. Take for instance these lines which she addressed to the students of Harvard
University.

> 'Twas not long since I left my native shore
> The land of errors, and Egyptian gloom:
> Father of mercy, 'twas thy gracious hand
> Brought me in safety from those dark abodes.

Or the lines "To the Right Honorable William, Earl of Dartmouth,
His Majesty's Principal Secretary of State for North America."

Should you, my lord, while you pursue my song,
Wonder from whence my love of *Freedom* sprung
Whence flow these wishes for the common good,
By feeling hearts alone best understood.
I, young in life, by seeming cruel fate
Was snatch'd from *Afric's* fancy'd happy seat:
What pangs excruciating must molest,
What sorrows labour in my parent's breast?
Steel'd was the soul and by no misery mov'd
That from a father seiz'd his babe belov'd
Such, such my case. And can I then but pray
Others may never feel tyrannic sway?[38]

Africa as a land of errors, ignorance, and unhappiness! American slavery as benign, as an act of Providence, as a means of making the children of the sun acquainted with God! These falsehoods were taught her at the Boston home of the Wheatleys. This was the type of education Phillis received in "Christian" America. The smug attitude of this christianized African towards the cruel fate of millions of her race is strikingly different from that of John Atkins, an eighteenth century British surgeon who was familiar with West Africa and the overseas slave trade.

> To remove Negroes . . . from their Homes and Friends . . . to a strange Country, People, and Language, must be highly offending against the Laws of natural Justice and Humanity; and especially when this change is to hard Labour, corporal Punishment, and for Masters they wish at the D—L.[39]

Formal education had alienated Phyllis from Africa and Africans, had made this slave girl slavery's best apologist. This was surely too high a price to pay for "being brought from Africa to America." For—as Delany remarked one hundred and eighteen years ago— "we had rather be a Heathen *freeman,* than a Christian *slave.*"[40]

We are indebted to William Lloyd Garrison, the Abolitionist, for our finest example of the role played by American institutions of learning in setting the hearts of westernized Africans against their ancestral homeland. His newspaper, the *Liberator,* was founded in 1831. It provided the free blacks, especially the Northern ones, with the opportunity to make known their opposition to the designs of the American Colonization Society and its auxiliaries throughout the United States. Their views were happily and conveniently preserved for mankind in the second part of Garrison's *Thoughts on African Colonization.*

The free blacks left no doubts whatsoever that they regarded America as their "true and appropriate home," as their "native soil," as their "native land," as their "country." They explicitly stated that they did not want to be returned to Africa, that they had "no common interest" with the peoples of that "vast and extensive" continent, that their "language, habits, manners, morals and religion" were totally different from those of Africans. Their image of the world's second largest continent was overwhelmingly negative. Africa, to them, was "a howling wilderness," a "much neglected and benighted land," a "pestilential country." It was a land of "burning sun, arid plains and barbarous customs," a "land of sickness, affliction and death," a land "enshrouded in pagan gloom," a continent which was ruled by "barbarian despots." It was described as an "unknown land," a "strange land," a "foreign country." Its peoples were termed "ignorant." Its climate was deemed "uncongenial" and "fraught with disease and death."[41]

The most illuminating piece of information which emerged from the numerous resolutions passed by these opponents of the American Colonization Society was the statement that the second largest continent was unknown to them "except by geography."[42] Africa as a howling wilderness, as a land of benighted and ignorant people, as a land of disease and death, as a continent ruled by barbarian despots! This was the spurious geography which the Afro-Americans were taught by the dominant whites. It requires little imagination to realize that the effort was clearly to make the blacks ashamed of their African antecedents, to make them more easily reconciled to the harshness of their lot in Columbia, to make them feel grateful to those who kept them in a state of absolute subjection. How well the myth-makers succeeded may be seen in the cruel contrasts of "a colored Baltimorean."

> Why should we exchange a temperate and salubrious climate, adapted to our constitutions as Americans, for one, to us, fraught with disease and death? Why should we leave a land in which the arts and sciences are flourishing, and which is beginning to yield to our research, for one, where the irradiating beams of the sun of science have yet to be announced by the bright star of hope? Why should we leave a land illuminated with the blaze of gospel light, for one enshrouded in pagan gloom? Why should we, who are in tolerable circumstances in America, who enjoy many of the comforts of life, and are evidently on the advanced march of mind, cast away these certain, real, and growing advantages, for those which are precarious and chimerical? Why should we abandon our firesides, and everything associated with the dear name of *home*—undergo the fatigues of a perilous voyage, and expose ourselves, our wives, and our little ones, to the deleterious influences of an uncongenial sun, for the enjoyment of a liberty divested of its usual accompaniments, surrounded with circumstances which diminish its intrinsic value, and render it indeed "a dear earned morsel?"[43]

The success of the white racialists is evident in Peter Williams' brazen contempt for the land of his ancestors.

> We are to be improved by being sent far from civilized society.
> This is a novel mode of improvement. What is there in the burning
> sun, the arid plains, and the barbarous customs of Africa, that is
> so peculiarly favorable to our improvement?[44]

It is also discernible in the Negro American's passionate identification with the United States and in his efforts to repudiate his kinship with Africans. In 1831, for instance, the free blacks of Wilmington, Delaware, disclaimed "all connection with Africa" and refused to be repatriated on grounds that they possessed "no common interest" with the inhabitants of the second largest continent.[45] Two years later, James Forten, a highly prosperous sailmaker in Philadelphia, echoed the same sentiments: "My greatgrandfather was brought to this country a slave from Africa. My grandfather obtained his own freedom. My father never wore the yoke. He rendered valuable service to his country in the war of our Revolution; and I, though then a boy, was a drummer in that war. I was taken prisoner and was made to suffer not a little on board the Jersey prison-ship. I have since lived and labored in a useful employment, have acquired property, and have paid taxes in this city. Here I have dwelt until I am nearly sixty years of age, and have brought up and educated a family . . . . Yet some ingenious gentlemen have recently discovered that I am still an African; that a continent, three thousand miles, or more, from the place where I was born, is my native country. And I am advised to go home. Well, it may be so. Perhaps if I should only be set on the shore of that distant land, I should recognize all I might see there, and run at once to the old hut where my forefathers lived a hundred years ago."[46]

The intensity of the prejudice against our continent, early in the nineteenth century, may finally be demonstrated by calling attention to the attitude of most black leaders towards the members of the race who sought to escape the blighting effects of white racism. Every encouragement was given to those who were bound for Canada, Haiti or Mexico. The African emigrants, on the other hand, did not receive such encouragement. Instead they were vehemently denounced as traitors to their brethren, as persons who were too ignorant to realize that they had been duped into selling "their birthright for a mess of pottage."[47]

Theoretically speaking, the birthright of the free blacks was American citizenship and its concomitant rights and privileges. Most of them had been born in the United States and naturally regarded themselves as Americans. Many of them would have agreed with the black gentleman from Philadelphia who argued—

in the *Liberator* for January 22, 1832—that it was "a contradiction to say that a man is an alien to the country in which he was born."[48] But the dominant whites did not seem very much concerned with the question of logical consistency. They treated and regarded the free Negroes not as compatriots but as aliens. The black Americans were usually referred to as Africans. Lydia Maria Child, a friend of the oppressed blacks, admitted this when she wrote *An Appeal in favor of that Class of Americans called Africans*.[49] A fleeting glance at the life histories of two black Americans would buttress our contention. Andrew Bryan was born a slave in South Carolina in 1737. He was later taken to Savannah, Georgia, where he subsequently purchased his freedom for fifty pounds. He organized three African Baptist Churches which became, with the passing of years, "the beacon light" in the religious life of the blacks of Georgia. When he died in 1812 the all-white Savannah Baptist Association paid its respects to him as a "son of Africa."[50] Paul Cuffee was born in Massachusetts in 1759. On his death in September, 1817, he was eulogized as a "generous African" by white Americans.[51] Mr. Forten did not adhere strictly to the truth when he claimed that the members of the American Colonization Society had just discovered that he was still the son of Black Mother. Our pieces of evidence seem to indicate that the white racialists have always defined their black countrymen as Africans. In practice, therefore, the birthright of Columbia's sable children was not American citizenship but Jim Crow. It does not require too much intelligence to realize that a birthright of insult and persecution is hardly worth a mess of pottage!

Marcus Garvey once remarked that only a few white men were honest enough to write the truth about the black American.[52] The reason for this phenomenon is not far to seek. Human beings dislike embarrassment and the real story of what the black man has suffered and endured in this much vaunted land of liberty would always bring a blush of shame upon the cheeks of all the decent members of the hegemonic race. C. Vann Woodward is one of the few Caucasians who have attempted to explode the racialist myths which have cluttered the minds of Americans for so long. His book, *The Strange Career of Jim Crow*, is, in many ways, an excellent work. But his description of the plight of the free blacks during the Ante-Bellum period, leaves much to be desired.

> Denied full rights and privileges of citizens, deprived of equality in the courts, and restricted in their freedom of assembly and freedom of movement, the so-called free Negro shared many of the deprivations of the slave. In addition, measures of ostracism were leveled at members of this class to emphasize their status.[53]

The description is technically accurate but it does not evoke the proper responses in us. We ought to shudder at the inhumanity of Caucasians, to gasp in horror at the incredible degrading of black people. But we do not because Dr. Woodward had acted as a mental hygienist. He had—by a choice use of words—glossed over some discomforting details. A more apt description of the condition of black people, in the years before the Civil War, was given by David Walker, an Afro-American whose work was first published in September, 1829. His incomplete list of the crimes of white men against black folk is a priceless historical gem.

> First, no trifling portion of them will beat us nearly to death, if they find us on our knees praying to God—They hinder us from going to hear the word of God—They keep us sunk in ignorance, and will not let us learn to read the word of God, nor write—If they find us with a book of any description in our hand, they will beat us nearly to death—They are so afraid we will learn to read, and enlighten our dark and benighted minds—They will not suffer us to meet together to worship the God who made us—They brand us with hot iron—They cram bolts of fire down our throats—They cut us as they do horses, bulls, or hogs—They crop our ears and sometimes cut off bits of our tongues—They chain and hand-cuff us, and while in that miserable and wretched condition, beat us with cow-hides and clubs—They keep us half naked and starve us sometimes nearly to death under their infernal whips or lashes . . . . They put on us fifty-sixes and chains, and make us work in that cruel situation, and in sickness, under lashes to support them and their families.—They keep us three or four hundred feet under ground working in their mines, night and day to dig up gold and silver to enrich them and their children— They keep us in the most death-like ignorance by keeping us from all source of information, and call us, who are free men and next to the Angels of God, their property!!!!! They make us fight and murder each other, many of us being ignorant, not knowing any better—they take us, (being ignorant,) and put us as drivers one over the other, and make us afflict each other as bad as they themselves afflict us—And to crown the whole of this catalogue of cruelties, they tell us that we the (blacks) are an inferior race of beings! Incapable of self government!! —We would be injurious to society and ourselves, if tyrants should loose their unjust hold on us!!! That if we were free we would not work, but would live on plunder or theft!!!! That we are the meanest and laziest set of beings in the world!!!! That they are obliged to keep us in bondage to do us good !!!!!—That we are satisfied to rest in slavery to them and their children!!!!!—That we ought not to be set free in America, but ought to be sent away to Africa!!!!! That if we were set free in America, we would involve the country in a civil war, which assertion is altogether at variance with our feeling or design, for we ask them for nothing but the rights of man, viz. for them to set us free, and treat us like men,

and there will be no danger, for we will love and respect them, and protect our country—But cannot conscientiously do these things until they treat us like men.[54]

A few pages later the black insurrectionist continued his listing of the white man's crimes. He drew attention to the cruelties of Caucasians who were engaged in the overseas slave trade: their indiscriminate packing of humans, like sardines, in the holds of ships; their indifference to human suffering and their low regard for human life during the Middle Passage.[55]

The catalogue of crimes was quoted for two reasons. It helped sustain Walker's thesis that white Americans, of the ante-bellum period, were unsurpassed by any other people in cruelty and barbarism.[56] Of far more importance is the fact that it made it possible for us to understand why the free blacks who espoused the cause of African colonization were labelled traitors to their race.

Walker was well aware that the United States was viewed, by many foreigners, as "the most enlightened, humane, charitable and merciful" country in the world. This favorable image, he explained, was partly because such persons had no familiarity with the nation's most important social problem and partly because they were victims of the white American's "liberal" sympathy for the oppressed in far-away places. The black activist easily exposed the hypocrisy of his white compatriots:

> I saw a paragraph, a few years since, in a South Carolina paper, which, speaking of the barbarity of the Turks, it said: "The Turks are the most barbarous people in the world—they treat the Greeks more like *brutes* than human beings." And in the same paper was an advertisement, which said: "Eight well-built Virginia and Maryland *Negro fellows* and four *wenches* will positively be *sold* this day, *to the highest bidder!*" And what astonished me still more was, to see in this same *humane* paper!! the cuts of three men, with clubs and budgets on their backs, and an advertisement offering a considerable sum of money for their apprehension and delivery. I declare, it is really so amusing to hear the Southerners and Westerners of this country talk about barbarity, that it is positively enough to make a man smile.[57]

The black American has long been treated like an animal. As a slave, he was placed in the same category as horses, dogs and cattle. He was defined by the formulators of the Constitution as "three-fifths" of a man. By the Dred Scott decision of March 6, 1857, the Supreme Court lackeys of the slave power used his historic origins to deny his membership in the human family.

Nor did freedom bring about any significant improvement in his lot. Insults and ridicule remained his daily diet. He was the victim of unjust laws. In most of the slave states, every Afro-American who could not prove that he was a free man was to be sold as a slave. The magistrates of South Carolina were authorized to inflict twenty lashes on any free black who manifested a desire for mental culture. In Georgia, a free Negro who presumed to serve as a pedagogue to the members of his race was whipped thirty-nine times. The same punishment was meted out to his pupils. Any white man who attempted to enlighten the minds of free blacks was liable to a fine of five hundred dollars. In Virginia, the Justice of the Peace was empowered to administer twenty stripes on the backs of Afro-American children who were rash enough to go to school. In Louisiana, the penalty for teaching the Word to a free black was, for the first offence, five hundred dollars and death for the second! In Maryland any free Afro-American who dared defend himself against the physical assault of a Caucasian was to forfeit his ears whenever they were asked for by a Justice of the Peace. In Kentucky, the same "offence" brought upon the unfortunate child of the sun thirty lashes. Eight Negroes, in some states, could not assemble together for any purpose without incurring the judicial displeasure of the fear-ridden tyrants. In the nation's capital, any free black who held a dance in his house, without permission from the white Mayor, was to be fined about ten dollars. If he was still on the streets of Washington, D.C., after ten o'clock at night, he was to sleep in jail if he did not have a pass from a Justice of the Peace or "some respectable citizen." The following day he was fined ten dollars!

The bitter cup of oppression was also tasted in the free states. The Solons of Ohio ensured that the blacks would be barred from earning a livelihood when they enacted a law which placed upon any white man who gave an hour's employment to any member of the despised race the responsibility of supporting him for the rest of his life.[58] It was pointed out, in an earlier chapter, that Gustave de Beaumont—during his 1831-1832 trip to the United States— was shocked by his discovery that the free states of the north were in no mood to confer equality or liberty upon the blacks. The latter were segregated in theaters, railroad cars and buses. They were refused admission into museums and other public places of culture. They were denied service in restaurants. Every effort was made to keep them a deprived people—politically, economically and socially. Protests against such cruel and unjust treatment were of little avail in effecting an improvement in the social morality of white Americans. They merely provided the Caucasian monsters with the opportunity to bury their human victims in an avalanche of ridicule.

Attention has been drawn to these historical facts not simply because of their shock value but also because they help explain why the "back to Africa" idea was appealing to some of the black sons and daughters of Columbia. Life in America meant, for black people, caste-segregation. It meant being constantly assaulted by Caucasians. White racism inflicted incalculable damage upon Afro-Americans. That much was apparent to me after I had perused the journal of Charlotte Forten, a free black woman in pre-Civil War America. This highly sensitive grand-daughter of the Philadelphia sail-maker left in her *Journal* a vivid description of the crippling effects of color prejudice. She became imbued with a "constant, galling sense of cruel injustice and wrong." Apartheid made her feel "sick at heart." She could never forget her black color. The wrongs perpetrated against her race became the "all-absorbing subject." Caste-segregation made it immensely difficult for her "to love and trust" anyone whose skin was white. She regarded every Caucasian with a great deal of distrust and suspicion. She was convinced that all white Americans were her enemies.[59] Apartheid, in short, had developed in the black woman an intense racial consciousness.

Miss Forten's testimony received weighty corroboration from the pen of W. E. B. DuBois.

> Practically, this group imprisonment within a group has various effects upon the prisoner. He becomes provincial and centered upon the problems of his particular group. He tends to neglect the wider aspects of national life and human existence. On the one hand he is unselfish so far as his inner group is concerned. He thinks of himself not as an individual but as a group man, a "race" man. His loyalty to this group idea tends to be almost unending and balks at almost no sacrifice. On the other hand, his attitude toward the environing race congeals into a matter of unreasoning resentment and even hatred, deep disbelief in them and refusal to conceive honesty and rational thought on their part . . . .[60]

Much of the venom directed against the Afro-Americans who favored African colonization stemmed from this intense identification with one's racial group. The Liberian project was essentially the brain-child of Caucasians and was, therefore, suspect in the eyes of the majority of those at the receiving end of Apartheid. Most blacks believed, with Frederick Douglass, that repatriation was not a viable solution to the American race question. They felt it was an ingenious evasion of the burning question of freedom and citizenship for black Americans. They insisted that the United States—not Africa—was their home. This being so, it was inevitable that they should denounce the Liberian emigrants as traitors to their brethren. For they could not help feeling that

African colonization was a dangerous diversification of energies
and talents which were desperately needed in the fight for social
justice in America.

## NOTES

1. C. A. Chick, Sr., "The American Negroes' Changing Attitude Toward
   Africa," *The Journal of Negro Education,* XXXI (1962), 531.
2. W. E. Burghardt DuBois, *The World and Africa* (New York: The Viking
   Press, 1947), p. 7.
3. W. E. B. DuBois, "The American Negro and the Darker World," *Freedomways,* VIII (Third Quarter, 1968), 245. This speech was originally
   delivered in New York City on April 30, 1957.
4. Carter G. Woodson, *The History of the Negro Church* (Washington,
   D. C.: The Associated Publishers, 1921), pp. 74-75; John Hope Franklin,
   *From Slavery to Freedom: A History of American Negroes* (New York:
   Alfred A. Knopf, 1950), p. 161.
5. Woodson, *op. cit.,* pp. 75-77; Franklin, *op. cit.,* pp. 161-162.
6. Woodson, *op. cit.,* pp. 78-79; Franklin, *op. cit.,* p. 162. The building
   for the independent black church, according to Dr. Woodson, was not
   erected until 1800.
7. Woodson, *op. cit.,* pp. 86-90; Franklin, *op. cit.,* p. 162.
8. U. S. House, 27th Cong. 3d Sess., Committee on Commerce, *African
   Colonization—Slave Trade—Commerce,* House Report 283 (Washington:
   Gales and Seaton, 1843), p. 195.
9. *Ibid.,* p. 854.
10. *Ibid.,* pp. 853-854; W. E. Burghardt Du Bois, *Dusk of Dawn: An Essay
    toward an Autobiography of a Race Concept* (New York: Harcourt, Brace
    & Co., 1940), p. 195.
11. Hugh Crow, *Memoirs* (London: Longman, Rees, Orme, Brown, & Green,
    1830), p. 306. This source claims that Paul Cuffee visited Sierra Leone
    three times. But practically all other sources contend that he twice visited
    West Africa.
12. American Colonization Society, *The Third Annual Report of the Amer-
    ican Society for Colonizing the Free People of Colour of the United States*
    (Washington: Davis and Force, 1820), pp. 115-120; U. S. House, 27th
    Cong. 3d Sess., Committee on Commerce, *African Colonization—Slave
    Trade—Commerce,* House Report 283, p. 185 and p. 853; P. J. Stauden-
    raus, *The African Colonization Movement 1816-1865* (New York: Colum-
    bia Univesrsity Press, 1961), pp. 9-11.
13. William Jay, *Inquiry into the Character and Tendency of the American
    Colonization, and American Anti-Slavery Societies* (New York: R. G. Wil-
    liams, 1838), p. 27.
14. Robert Campbell, *A Pilgrimage to My Motherland: An Account of a
    Journey among the Egbas and Yorubas of Central Africa in 1859-60* (New
    York: Thomas Hamilton, 1861), pp. 143-145 and also the Preface; Jean
    Herskovits Kopytoff, *A Preface to Modern Nigeria: The "Sierra Leonians"
    in Yoruba, 1830-1890* (Madison: The University of Wisconsin Press,
    1965), p. 216 and p. 347.
15. See Howard Brotz, ed., *Negro Social and Political Thought 1850-1902:
    Representative Texts* (New York: Basic Books, Inc., 1966), p. 110.
16. Frank A. Rollin, *Life and Public Services of Martin R. Delany* (Boston:
    Lee and Shepard, 1883 edition), p. 19.
17. *Ibid.,* p. 20.
18. *Ibid.,* p. 29.
19. The late Richard Wright met one such black Englishman during his
    voyage to Africa. See his *Black Power: A Record of Reaction in a Land
    of Pathos* (New York: Harper & Brothers, 1954), pp. 13-17.
20. Frank A. Rollin, *op. cit.,* pp. 177-179.

21. C. Vann Woodward, *The Strange Career of Jim Crow* (New York: Oxford University Press, 1966 edition), p. 28.

22. "Notes On Negro American Influences On The Emergence Of African Nationalism," *Journal of African History,* I (Second Quarter, 1960), p. 302.

23. See the accompanying letter to a typed copy of Turner's work at the Moorland Library, Howard University, Washington, D. C. The letter was signed by H. M. Turner and was dated Atlanta, Georgia, November 15, 1894.

24. John T. Shuften, "An Outline Of The Oration Delivered By Chaplain Henry M. Turner In Springfield Baptist Church On January 1st, 1866, Being The Celebration Of The First Anniversary Of Freedom," *Colored American,* I, 5 (Jan. 13, 1866); *The Christian Recorder* (July 8, 1915), p. 4.

25. Speech of Bishop H. M. Turner Before the National Council of Colored Men which met in Cincinnati, Ohio, November 28th, 1893. See the Turner file at Moorland Library, Howard University, Washington, D. C.

26. (New York: Random House, 1959), p. 62.

27. This bit of information was found in an A.M.E. Church leaflet—date of publication unknown—and was supplied by Bishop Turner himself. See the Turner file at Moorland Library, Howard University, Washington, D. C.

28. W. K. Roberts, *An African Canaan for the American Negro* (Birmingham, Alabama: Leslie Bros., 1896), pp. 18-19.

29. W. E. Burghardt DuBois, *Dusk of Dawn,* p. 195.

30. The Back-to-Africa movements of Alfred Charles Sam and Marcus Garvey lie outside the scope of this work. Anyone interested in them may profitably consult William E. Bittle and Gilbert L. Geis, "Alfred Charles Sam And An African Return: A Case Study In Negro Despair," *Phylon,* XXIII (Second Quarter, 1962), pp. 178-194; Birgit Aron, "The Garvey Movement: Shadow and Substance," *Phylon,* VIII (Fourth Quarter, 1947), pp. 337-343. The writers of the article on Alfred Charles Sam claimed that none of the African colonization projects which preceded the 1914 exodus "had been Negro conceived and Negro implemented throughout." (pp. 179-180) I can cite at least two such African returns—the ones which were undertaken under the auspices of Paul Cuffee (1815) and Henry McNeal Turner (1896).

31. Alexander Crummell, *The Relations and Duties of free Colored men in America to Africa* (Hartford: Case, Lockwood & Co., 1861), pp. 5-6, p. 19 and pp. 26-27.

32. See p. 10 of his speech at the Cincinnati Convention.

33. *The Christian Recorder* (July 8, 1915), p. 4.

34. "The African in Africa and the African in America," *Africa and the American Negro: Addresses and Proceedings of the Congress on Africa,* J. W. E. Bowen, ed. (Atlanta: Franklin Printing and Publishing Co., 1896), p. 69.

35. W. E. Burghardt DuBois, *Dusk of Dawn,* p. 275.

36. C. G. Woodson's review of *Life in a Haitian Valley* by Melville J. Herskovits in *The Journal of Negro History,* XXII (1937), p. 367.

37. *Remarks of Mr. Calhoun of South Carolina on the Reception of Abolition Petitions* (Washington: William W. Moore & Co., 1837), p. 5.

38. Charlotte Ruth Wright, ed., *The Poems of Phillis Wheatley* (Philadelphia: The Wrights, 1930), p. 18 and pp. 55-57.

39. *A Voyage to Guinea, Brasil, and the West Indies* (London: 1735), pp. 177-178.

40. Martin Robinson Delany, *The Condition, Elevation, Emigration, and Destiny of the Colored People of the United States Politically Considered* (Philadelphia: M. R. Delany, 1852), p. 181.

41. (Boston: Garrison and Knapp, 1832), pp. 9-72.
42. *Ibid.*, p. 19 and p. 42.
43. *Ibid.*, p. 52.
44. *Ibid.*, p. 65.
45. *Ibid.*, pp. 36-37.
46. Charlotte L. Forten, *The Journal of Charlotte L. Forten: A Free Negro in the Slave Era* ed. Ray Allen Billington (New York: Collier Books, 1961 edition), pp. 16-17.
47. William Lloyd Garrison, *op. cit.*, Pt. II, pp. 42-43, p. 46, p. 49 and p. 63; David Walker, *Appeal to the Coloured Citizens of the World* ed. Charles M. Wiltse (New York: Hill and Wang, 1965 edition), p. 56, the footnote on p. 64 and p. 67.
48. Garrison, *op. cit.*, Pt. II, p. 58.
49. (Boston: Allen and Ticknor, 1833).
50. Carter Godwin Woodson, *The History of the Negro Church*, pp. 47-53.
51. U. S. House, 27th Cong. 3d Sess., Committee on Commerce, *African Colonization—Slave Trade—Commerce*, House Report 283, p. 182; Hugh Crow, *op. cit.*, pp. 300-306; P. J. Staudenraus, *op. cit.*, pp. 9-11.
52. *The Negro World* (Dec. 10, 1921).
53. (New York: Oxford University Press, 1966 edition), p. 13.
54. *Appeal to the Coloured Citizens of the World*, pp. 65-66.
55. *Ibid.*, p. 73.
56. *Ibid.*, p. 7, p. 12, pp. 53-54, p. 59 and p. 74.
57. *Ibid.*, pp. 12-13 and p. 53.
58. William Jay, *Inquiry Into the Character and Tendency of the American Colonization, and American Anti-Slavery Societies* (New York: R. G. Williams, 1838), pp. 21-24; William Jay, *A View of the Action of the Federal Government in Behalf of Slavery* (New York: J. S. Taylor, 1839), pp. 23-27.
59. *The Journal of Charlotte L. Forten*, p. 45, p. 47, p. 54, p. 57, p. 64, and p. 74.
60. *Dusk of Dawn*, p. 132.

# 5

## BLACK NATIONALISM

*by*

JAMES TURNER

### 1. A RESPONSE TO THE SOCIAL CONSEQUENCES OF OPPRESSION AND RACISM

The political history of Africans in America is characterized by two predominating themes: attempts to oppress them and their determination to resist and free themselves. They have believed freedom to mean different things at different times and in different places. They thought it was emancipation from being a slave; or sit-ins for equal use of public services and facilities; or a crusading bus ride thru the south for social integration; or voter registration so Black people could vote for the white politicians who were controlling government. All of these thoughts about freedom were basic to the assumptions we accepted about the nature of American society, which were, in fact, derived from white America's description of itself. But being a flexible people and not one to hang on to false goals, each time we arrived at a stage and saw that freedom was not there, the movement pushed onward. The venerable scholar and political analyst C. L. R. James, remarked recently that the African struggle in the Americas "has the richest political heritage, in terms of continuance over time consistency of growth and development thru stages."

Speaking about the failure of assumptions and the dialectic of the Black movement, Brother Rev. C. T. Vivian, an ardent participant in, and maker of the recent fifteen-year civil rights phase in the history of the struggle, writes: "The first and perhaps most fundamental assumption with which we began was that integration would be the route to Black freedom. *And this was an inherent part of all our other assumptions.* The concept of

integration won our allegiance because it fit our understanding
of how the people of a culture *should* relate to one another. It
fit our understanding of the values which *should* determine the
institutions and priorities of a society. It did not, however, fit
American reality. And the measure by which we misjudged that
reality is precisely the measure of the yawning gulf between Black
and whites."

". . . . Altogether, they show how completely the Black subculture accepted the pronouncements of the dominant majority.
But in our actions we proved each of these pronouncements false.
And, as this happened, we came closer to a definition of American
which would allow us to operate effectively. But until this happened, we were impotent. As long as we believed what the nation
said about itself, we chose strategies which were bound to fail. The
fall of these assumptions changed most of our strategies and many
of our tactics . . . . Individual whites of goodwill are as powerless
against this system as we, the excluded. Yet it was not until we
saw the structures in which these men lived and worked reject
their voices that we learned that individuals, Black or white,
cannot effect change in America. The structures of the nation
respond only to amassed power, not to verbal or moral appeals."

". . . . History might have taught us this lesson if we had
listened. . . . . But this was something we came to learn through
our own struggle and failure . . . . America would not give us our
rights just because we pointed out that it was the correct thing
to do. Rights, after all, are potential power. We were looking at
justice and equality before the law as moral, ethical, and human
questions. Those we faced saw more accurately that these were
the coordinates of eventual power . . . . This was too high a price
for America to pay for a mere moral principle. . . . What we had
to learn was that when white America gave it was for its good,
not ours."

". . . . Almost everything we learned in the Movement makes
integration impossible as a goal for the Black community today
. . . . So integration is dead . . . . Integration is dead, but Black
people did not kill it. They could not because they were never
in a position to do so. The Black minority has never had control
of the concept or definition of integration."

"In the integration model, the majority power is always the
broker of the terms . . . . For this reason, the integration model
has always had a built-in obsolescence . . . . Separatism has taken

the place of integration as the strategy and tactic of the Movement."[1]

The shift in the Movement toward nationalism is a coming that was perhaps inevitable. This turn in the Movement rejects integration, because of the irreducible racial contradiction which is a major component in the edifice of the American social system. Black Nationalism is a strategy of survival, and a philosophy of social reality in as much as it recognizes the essential racial dicothomy in American economic organization and its political process, and the fundamental racial separatism in the structure of social institutions and culture in the United States. Commenting in a speech entitled "Beyond the Dilemma," Dr. Kenneth Clark crystalizes racial conditions. "The pathology of the ghetto is now clear and recognized —the statistics of infant mortality, disease, rat infestation, broken plumbing, littered streets, consumer exploitation, riot-burned buildings that have not been replaced, inefficient schools, a discriminatory system of police and court procedures. The litany of pain and despair is the same in every dark ghetto and, despite the anti-poverty programs, Title I funds, Model Cities, and so on, the ghetto is still dark and still desperate.

". . . . Segregated schools, and the tyranny and barbarity of American ghettos, are the institutionalized inescapable immorality of American racism . . . . the knowledge that segregated schools inflicted permanent damage upon [Black] children (and violated their constitutional rights as well)* was not enough to compel the American people to plan and implement a massive and effective program for desegregation of our public schools . . . . The history of racism has prepared many, if not the majority, of Americans psychologically to accept injury to—or the outright expendability of [Black] children."

Unlike the civil rights movement, which focussed on the struggle for legal equality and integration, Black Nationalism addresses itself to the cultural and psychological malaise of the oppression Blacks have had to endure. Nationalism has taken many forms among Africans in America. Some of the most recent varieties are Religio-Nationalism, represented by the Nation of Islam; Cultural Nationalism of Ron Karenga and Ameer Baraka; Marxist Revolutionary Nationalism of the Black Panther Party; Economic Nationalism of the Black Capitalism Advocates; Political Nationalism of the Republic of New Africa; and Pan-African Nationalism of Brother Malcolm X. As a political orientation the

* Parentheses and brackets author's

basic proposition shared by all variants of Black Nationalism*
(though advocating different social blue-prints at times) is that
all things created and occupied by Blacks should be controlled by
Black people, and that the purpose of every effort should be toward
achieving self-determination (variously defined) and a relatively
self-sufficient Black community.

As the Civil Rights movement gave way to the struggle for
Black Power, there was a revival of Black Nationalism which is
now expanding into a revolutionary ideology proclaiming that
the approximately 25 to 30 million African people in America
constitute an underdeveloped nation.[2]

Dr. C. T. Munford, a black political scientist, explains the
Black Nationalist concept of nation . . . . "there is absolutely no
reciprocity of purpose, expectancy and self-definitions between
whites and American Blacks, despite the fact that they inhabit the
same geopolitical space. Social reciprocity must be based on
mutually beneficial economic relations and a recognized equality
of humanity. Nothing of the kind prevails between Black and
White. The only bonds are the historic ones of slavery and
dehumanization and the current confrontation and conflict . . . .

Like other colonized people who have risen to demand freedom, the Black colony in the United States constitutes a nation.
It is different from other emergent nations only in that it consists
of forcibly transplanted colonial subjects who have acquired co-
hesive identity in the course of centuries of struggle against enslavement, cultural alienation, and the spiritual cannibalism of
white racism. This common history which the Black people of
America share is manifested in a concrete national culture with a
peculiar "spiritual complexion," or psychological temperament.
Though the Black nation expresses its thoughts, emotions, and
aspirations in the same tongue as American whites, the different
conditions of existence, the long trail of exploitation and dehumanization at the hands of American white colonial overlords, and
heroic resistance, have, from generation to generation, welded the
bonds of a national experience as different from that of white
existence as day is from night. And what differentiates nations
from one another are dissimilar conditions of life."[3]

Perceived from this perspective liberation can only come when
Black people achieve territorial integrity, plus economic cohesion,

*These varieties of Black Nationalism are not rigidly delineated nor are they
mutually exclusive categories. Any individual or Black Nationalist organization usually assumes any number of combinations of these varieties.

and full ascension of their culture, their dignity, and their nation-
hood, based on political control and social security.

This emerging ideology represents a new awareness of the
radical implications of Black Nationalism (the political implications of which, until now, had usually been rather conservative).
Of necessity, many Black radical movements have been involved
in a cultural revolution, for a man cannot begin to be involved
in the revolutionary process until he looks at himself (and thereby
at others) with new feelings and new ideas. The Black cultural
revolution is thus an important process: it has led to an affirmation
of self, an affirmation of Blackness. For as Julius Lester writes:

> Culture in a revolutionary context must be an instrument of com-
> munication, which serves to raise political awareness . . . as well as
> serving to further intensify the commitment of the people to revolu-
> tion.[4]

From a different perspective, Christopher Lasch similarly points
out that

> the radical implications of Black Nationalism can only emerge once
> the cultural battle has been carried into the sphere of politics, at
> which point it becomes clear that Black Nationalism as a political
> program demands the radical decentralization of American institu-
> tions and perhaps also the socialization of these institutions . . . .
> Indeed, one of the potentially revolutionary aspects of Black Na-
> tionalism is its capacity to demonstrate that cultural and political
> questions are always related.[5]

Thus, economic and social oppression of Blacks cannot be separated
from the spiritual and psychological chaos in their lives due to
subjugation by American racism.

However, reflecting cultural, ideological, and moral bias, most
sociological studies of Black Nationalism have been more descriptive
than analytical, more concerned with outlining characteristics of
Black Nationalist organizations and their members than with
defining the subjective meaning of the movement. Thus, these
studies have ignored the central significance of Black Nationalism:
the emergence of Black group-consciousness, self-assertion, and
cultural identity.

Consensus models and other conservative variants of order
theory define racial strife in pathological terms.[6] Black Nationalism, therefore, has been generally interpreted as not only socially
deviant, but socially dysfunctional. Pluralism, like egalitarianism,
is only entertained within a consensual framework. Pervading the
literature on minority problems is the belief that society, especially
American society, is united by consensus on basic values. This is
largely a consequence of Gunnar Myrdal's influential interpreta-

tion of the "race question" in terms of social will, the notion that society has a common will and a common culture. Hence, the predictable and popular assumption that assimilation into the "superior" white society is the Black man's only solution.[7]

But while consensus models accept the core values of the dominant groups as functional for society, some of these values may in fact be inimical to particular groups, who are thus increasingly led to question the legitimacy of the social system. Proper study of Black Nationalism, on the other hand, employs a conflict perspective. When an aggregate comes to realize itself as a group, a movement will evolve, defining the boundaries of the group and its terms for relations with other groups. Thus, Black Nationalism can be objectively defined as:

(1) The desire of Black people to determine their own destiny through formation, preservation, and control of their own political, social, economic, and cultural institutions.

(2) The determination of Black people to unite as a group, as a people in common community, opposing white supremacy by striving for independence from white control.

(3) The resistance of Black people to subordinate status and the demand for political freedom, social justice, and economic equality.

(4) The development of ethnic self-interest, racial pride, group consciousness, and opposition to and rejection of the dominant ideas of white-defined society perceived to be incompatible with this objective.

(5) The re-evaluation of self and of the Black man's relationship with the social system in general.

### The Genesis of Black Nationalism

Black Nationalism is not new to the American scene. It has been one of the two main trends among Black people in America, even antedating the integration trend. It reached its highest level in this country with the rise of the Garvey movement, the greatest Afro-American mass movement in history, and is a force of widespread influence in contemporary Black society.

The drive toward Black Nationalism has been more than just an occasional silent fit of anger or expression of despair. For the past two centuries, individuals and organizations have emerged periodically to urge Black men to seek solutions other than integration, to use a system of definition of their problems different from that prescribed by the dominant white group. Black Nationalism has sought to establish and express group identity and collective consciousness through conversion of the "Negro" as a socially defined category into a socially determined group of *Black* people.

As early as 1787, the freed slaves of Newport, Rhode Island formed the Free African Society to promote group cohesion and repatriation to Africa. African societies were formed in other parts of the northeast section of the United States, uniting their members on the basis of their African-ness and previous condition of forced servitude, as well as the commonly experienced threat of violence.

In 1815, Paul Cuffee of Boston, a well-to-do entrepreneur, piloted himself and a group of other ex-slaves across the Atlantic to Sierra Leone in West Africa. In 1820 appeared *Walker's Appeal to the Colored Citizens of the World,* by David Walker, which was followed slightly more than a decade later by Henry Highland Garnet's "Address to the Slaves of the United States" and his *Call to Rebellion* in 1843. In 1852, Martin R. Delany, Harvard-educated physician, writer, editor, and theoretician, published his book, *The Condition, Elevation, Emigration and Destiny of the Colored People of the United States Politically Considered,* which was a statement of Black Zionist doctrine. Dr. Delany proposed an expedition to the eastern coast of Africa for purpose of eventual settlement there.

It is worthwhile to quote a few passages from this book, because the sentiments it conveys persist:

> Every people should be the originators of their own designs, the projectors of their own schemes, and the creators of the events that lead to their destiny—the consumation of their desires.

> We have native hearts and virtues, just as other nations, which in their pristine purity are noble, potent, and worthy of example. We are a nation within a nation . . . . But we have been, by our oppressors, despoiled of our purity, and corrupted in our native characteristics . . . leaving us in character, really a 'broken people.' Being distinguished by complexion, we are still singled out—although having merged in the habits and customs of our oppressors—as a distinct nation of people . . .[8]

Faced with the social fact that "Blackness and dignity remain incompatible in American culture,"[9] Black Nationalism has sought to crystallize ambiguous and troubled race feelings into a definite racial consciousness to create a corporate self-awareness and collective response based on shared values.

Hence, the basis for understanding Black Nationalism lies in acknowledgement of the historical by-products of the slave system.

The African and his descendants were conquered, enslaved, de-
meaned, and then converted to accepting their low status. Black
men were told that they had no history, no culture, no civilization;
and for them it was often economically rewarding and socially
advantageous to repeat this litany. Some individuals, however,
began to realize that this was nonsense and sought to dissipate
this lack of self-pride. There has arisen an awareness of cultural
dispossession that rivals concern for problems of material deprivation. From this context Black Nationalism arises, looking inward
to historical and social traditions in order to overcome low status
and prestige, and constructing a new vision predicated upon collective traits of social distinction.

Black Nationalism as a refutation of the racial ideology of
slavery and segregation is a direct challenge to white supremacy.
For slavery and segregated rule were not only a political and
economic affair; they also imposed a specific social framework for
the Black man's experience both of the world and of himself.
Political and economic domination constantly underscored racial
and cultural differences between Black and white men. In turn,
Black Nationalism, by confronting white domination with its own
form of racial protest and zealous partisanship of the Black race,
has done more than draw together sentiments and attitudes of
the collective Black reaction. It has embodied them in a heightened
form that moves toward a racial ideology:

> Anti-white sensibilities among black nationalists operate to supply
> a unifying ideology which transcends the experience of any single
> individual.
> In point of fact, however, black nationalism is much more than a
> response to white outrages (although it of course that too) . . . .
> black nationalism is a sophisticated and pervasive political ideology
> based on a generalized understanding of the history of the black
> man in the United States.[10]

Undoubtedly, such an inclusive ideology directed at the dominant
group in society polarizes feelings and induces conflict between
the two groups. But this external conflict also establishes group
boundaries, promotes group identity, and strengthens group cohesion.[11]

An ideology, when it becomes explicit, is a kind of thinking
aloud on the part of society or a group within it. It is a direct
response to the actual conditions of life and has a social function,
either as a defensive system of beliefs and ideas which support and
justify an established social structure, or as a rational project for
the creation of a new order. The latter type of ideology, even when

it includes a certain degree of idealism, also implies a reasoned program of collective action.

Black Nationalism thus springs from the desire to reverse an intolerable situation; its adherents view the basis of social life as competition between groups for social and economic power. It challenges the legitimacy of the system of white domination imposed on Black men, whose experience of dispersal, humiliation, and subjugation generates social conflict. Against this background it is not difficult to understand that a development like Marcus Garvey's Back-to-Africa movement was not simply atavistic expression; it was presented not as an escape from America, but as a way to confront and overcome the social realities of racism, a positive rather than a negative gesture. Garvey appreciated the psychological needs of his adherents, realizing that freedom from contempt[12] is inextricably linked with political freedom. Garvey's re-evaluation of Africa had the precise function of abolishing the world order created in the minds of Black men by white men. For Garvey saw the Black man is doomed as long as he takes his ideals from the white man, sealing his internal feeling of inferiority and self-contempt.

Two points stand out clearly in the progressive development of Black Nationalism. First, it has been a movement of reaction against white cultural domination concomitant with political domination. Secondly, without the pressure and conflict generated by segregation, without the historical and social factors which dominate the situation of the Black man in America—that is, without the racial factor—the forms of reaction to cultural contact would have had a completely different character. For the cultural position of the Black man in America possesses its own specific characteristics: the Black man lives in a symbiotic relationship with the white man, held in subordinate position by the caste system. Furthermore, the Black man is governed by the white dominant group, especially in the areas of religion and social morality. The wish for independent expression finds a ready springboard in those elements of Black subculture which segregation helped to define structurally.

Thus an ironic aspect of Black popular movements is the way in which white ideas act as catalysts of nationalist feelings. Christian egalitarian teaching, for example, helps show Black converts the fundamental contradiction of white domination and the avowed humanitarian principles of western culture, thereby underscoring the hiatus between objective practice and declared values of white men. The powerful emotional disaffection for the white man that inspires nationalism is borne of judging the white man against his own principles.

As social historian Lerone Bennett has observed, there has been a process of gradual estrangement from the unilaterally subjective mainstream tradition in America since Reconstruction. Since that time, Black men have become real to themselves, acting so as to make themselves real to others as well:

> Parallel with the growth in racial consciousness was a rise in Negro nationalism which should not be confused with specific nationalist movements. The key elements in the nationalist syndrome were: (1) a common sense of oppression, (2) pride in the achievement of Negroes, (3) extreme sensitivity to racial disparagement, (4) a belief in the manifest destiny of Negroes, (5) a feeling of identity with the nonwhite peoples of the world.[13]

Thus the American Black struggle is part of the world-wide struggle for anticipatory and inclusive identities on the part of peasants, workers, and youth. Black Nationalism is precisely about anticipatory and more inclusive identity,[14] and self determination. Self determination always relates to two essential factors—power and control; power to protect vital self interest, and control over immediate social and geographical space occupied by a people (or group). Thus, Black Nationalism refers to the necessity for African people in America to exercise sovereignty over their lives and community.

Ours is a struggle against white racism for national identity and economic liberation; for independence from political manipulation through control of land, and freedom from class oppression and exploitation by developing command of our own means of production for the social well-being of all Black people. Our immediate task is to organize and solidify the Black Colony for control, and increase political awareness by developing caste-class consciousness in order to advance the struggle by systematically confronting and pushing fundamental contradictions in American society.

We must be especially careful to guard against fatalism and frustration during this stage of confusion and reactionary trends and difficulty in implementing our social and political position in the community while continuing to fight reformist-integration deceptions. It is imperative that we develop a perspective of the historical movement of our struggle. Malcolm X is our best model of balance, as a revolutionary Black nationalist with the necessary international scope, and focus on Africa.

## 2. A BLACK PHILOSOPHY OF EDUCATION

With the recent development of Black Studies at Universities with predominantly white enrollments, the very nature of education in relation to the total society has come under serious scrutiny. Black students have begun to question whether school as traditionally conceived is fully beneficial for black people. Historically, the role of education has been viewed as two-fold: first, it aims to prepare individuals for survival in their social environment by developing in them socially useful skills and by making them aware of the structure of social processes (i.e. values and morals) thereby enhancing institutional and individual interactions; secondly, it allows individuals to expand their constructive creativity. Education, therefore, performs both a "tooling" and "socializing" function. Moreover, school has, at all times, the character and direction of the next generation in its classrooms. The point is, that education involves the process of interpretation and definition of learning sources. Reading, writing and arithmetic are not education per se, but are means to an education. Definition determines content and meaning in education. If the primary reason for the existence of an educational structure is to develop potential, to refine and to develop the experience of the society, the question then is—what meaning can this process have for the black community if the only experience recognized as valid is that of the white nation? Thus, educational programs as they now exist are irrelevant and often destructive to the black community because inherent in them is the denial of the legitimacy of cultural and social expressions of black people. There is little in any curriculum which starts with black people as a specially and uniquely cultured people.

For a long time black people have placed a high premium on and great faith in education as a vehicle for reaching higher levels in the society. However, among an increasing number of black educators and students there has emerged the realization that education has a larger societal purpose. By passing on the collective wisdom, education perpetuates a given society. The traditional liberal education has functioned to prepare its subjects, among whom are black people, to accept as valid only the white cultural experience. American education functionally gives total emphasis to "white studies" which have usurped intellectual legitimacy and have been defining the activities and experiences of white western people as the universal yardstick of human existence. Black studies challenge this assumption by assert-

ing that white is not now, nor has ever been either intrinsically
right or complete. However, Whites have attributed universal
value to their own Anglo-American particularism, and have
sought to absorb and distort other cultures in their midst. For
instance, white historians will develop concepts which ignore the
full dimensions of human history. When it comes to human
failings such as greed, barbarity, cruelty, aggression, jealousy and
selfishness they concede that these are attributes common to all
men. But when it comes to recording and acknowledging great
and outstanding activities and works of men, white scholars make
arbitrary distinctions between achievements of one racial group
and another and are not inclined generally to recognize that glori-
ous events in history are all part of the total shared human experience.

It is clear that black people were not ever, and are not now
being educated for the same reasons that whites were and are
being educated. White students are educated to be the rulers
and makers in their society. Blacks, on the other hand, are
taught to synthesize the experiences of another people. One of the
consequences of such an education is that many blacks, if not
most, are inclined to confuse the interests of black people with
those of the white oppressors. Another consequence is the existence
of a situation where Blacks accept not only the white people's
definitions of the problems of Blacks caused by white attitudes
but also solutions proposed by the white oppressors themselves.
Lerone Bennett makes this point eloquently when he says, "In
white-oriented schools, we are educated away from ourselves—
away from our people, away from our rhythm, away from our
genius, and away from our soul . . . . We must abandon the frame
of reference of our oppressor, perceive our own reality . . . George
Washington and George Washington's slaves lived different times
and different reality." Black Studies must contribute to the
development and implementation of a new definition of the ends
towards which black children are to be educated. Bringing
black students to white universities in large numbers was intended to create greater acceptance of the social system by giving
them a vested interest in its benefits. Education, it was argued,
would assure better occupational status and income and expanding social opportunities for Blacks. The long range projection,
however, was that education would be the medium for producing a larger national black bouregeoisie as a stabilizing social
class to counteract the growing alienation and disruptive currents

among the black masses. However, on white college campuses across the country, black students turned out not to be as malleable as was perhaps expected by white administrators and politicians.

Black educators should focus on the development in their students of consciousness and concern for the black community while making sure that the black presence in white schools is not directed against the best interest of black people. Among the most crucial questions at this point are: What do we want to educate black people for? What do we want black students to do? What do we want black students to become? The black community needs a balanced range of skilled personnel if the concept of black self-determination is to even have a chance of becoming a reality. Black Studies programs must move to decolonize young black minds and to reorient them in ways which allow them to establish lasting, positive and creative relationships between young black students and the black community.

The university, in America, like other corporate bodies, is merely a microcosm of the larger society. Black educators and students should understand that in a society made up of oppressors and oppressed, education is fundamentally political in that its major goal is to keep the oppressed in their place. But education also has a political function in societies where circumstances are less oppressive for it also provides individuals with identity, purpose, and direction. Education is not just the development and teaching of factual information, but is also the primary means for imbuing a people with social values, certain political beliefs and a specific cultural character. Furthermore, in any social system teaching is done within definite ideological parameters which are designed to engender a common frame-of-reference and orientation among the people. Anyone making a serious analysis of an educational system must take into consideration the political ideology of the society. Ameer Baraka (LeRoi Jones) makes an important point when he says, "if you accept the white man's definitions you will share his reality." This is particularly significant when you realize that when there are two different racial and ethnic populations whose historical contacts and relationships originate in conflict and continue to be hostile, but who both accept the same social definitions and have similar primary values and entertain a common vision of reality, the case will usually be that one group has been defeated, enslaved, colonized, oppressed, penetrated culturally, and dominated politically and economically by the other group. Such is exactly the fate that African peoples in America have suffered since the Europeans organized and inspired the slave trade in Africa and took her peoples as political subjects for imperialist empire-building. Therefore, African peoples must begin to understand and interpret their historical and cultural experiences in new ways and from their own perspective in order to create new dimensions in their thinking and develop a social philosophy and political direction alternative to those of their oppressors and political enemies. Black education must make students consistently conscious of the need for struggle and commitment. Too often the question of cultural values and political ideology is only superficially perceived. It is necessary at this time to define our long-range goals and our immediate objectives in order to establish an effective system of priorities. Black Studies programs must develop black youth with a revolutionary sense of identity. Therefore, any Black Studies programs which purport to be educating black students for fuller participation in the American mainstream is counterproductive to black people's need for total self-determination. Moreover, it is essential to our liberation that black youth be motivated to resist—not accept—the "mainstream" of a social system which oppresses and destroys our people.

Brother John Churchville, black educator and theorist, has written that "with the increased Black Nationalist consciousness which has developed over the past two or three years among a broad cross-section of our people, a new surge of black activity has erupted. This activity has serious political-directional implications which necessitate definition and analysis in order that we might see clearly what path we must take toward a correct struggle for freedom." It is becoming increasingly clear that the black liberation movement is renewing itself around the basic proposition that black people must control the decisions which affect their lives and shape their destiny. But success in this regard requires more than commitment to idealism and more than bold but non-productive rhetoric. We as blacks must develop a social program and a political plan with which to translate our revolutionary ideas into action. Organizationally, the movement must expand its efforts to resolve the problems of the exploited masses of our people. Too much of what has passed for black consciousness is simply the ritualistic repetition of slogans. Those of us who are concerned with black education recognize that we cannot be apolitical because as an internal colony our people are engulfed by the oppressors' institutions. We must also recognize that control over content and definition of the learning of our young is a pivotal facet of the liberation struggle.

Our task is not only to seek immediate political objectives but also to begin a longer term job of creating a recalcitrant cadre of black students who are committed and equipped to extend the struggle to new levels by establishing institutions which can provide meaningful alternatives for black youth who do not wish to be absorbed into the "mainstream". Independent black institutions of learning should be supported as models of self-reliance, while at the same time we must accept our responsibility to develop the kind of expertise that will make such institutions not only viable but also significant in the lives of our people. A chronic problem in the black community is the dearth of skilled personnel dedicated to developing institutions that will become functionally efficient and socially effective. Such development necessarily requires an unadulterated ideological commitment to the interest of the black community. The question of ideology is no mere intellectual abstraction for all people are influenced by an ideology of one kind or another. Ideology is the view of the world which a particular group has; it is a group's way of seeing its relation to the main processes of the society and understanding the cause of events important to it. However, even a cursory observation of the beliefs held by many of our people reveals the extent to which they have internalized the ideas and concepts of our oppressors. It has been said that "the art of colonization, if it is to succeed, means a colonizer sees to it that the victim is not only colonized politically, but also economically and culturally." In other words, the colonizer must work to develop in the colonized victims a "false consciousness". This in our situation means that black people have absorbed white people's ideology such that it distorts their understanding of their true position in the American social order and severely limits awareness of the ways in which their interests and needs are restricted by the power and social interests of white people. Exploitation and oppression of blacks have developed as a way of life in America, and as a basic mode of its social system. The black historian, Dr. C. J. Munford makes a poignant comment which most whites and many Blacks would like to be able to ignore: "All white people in America are accomplices in inflicting pain and misery on all Blacks. If there were a correlation between justice and objective social conditions, all whites would stand as condemned murderers in the first degree. The original enslavement of Africans is renewed daily in America."

The question of the relationship of ideology to what they teach tends to make many black educators uneasy. They would most likely be inclined to consider the discussion of Black Studies as a subjective approach to learning and a sort of sectarian encroachment that would demean the academic quality of their work. But, we must not become confused by the idea that education is value-free and above the social system when in fact it is the axis for the developing and refinement of ideas that constitute the ideology of the society. Education for Blacks must consider the need to reveal to black people the mechanics of oppression. A serious problem for black educators lies with the most politically concerned black students who are often so socially alienated that they can perceive neither the relevance nor the importance of careful study because of their preoccupation with protest. Such a disposition tends to impede development of political sophistication. In this regard, Albert Memmi has made a salient observation, "the colonized's self-assertion, born out of a protest, continues to define itself in relation to it. In the midst of revolt, the colonized continues to think, feel, and live against and, therefore, in relation to the colonizer and colonization." Consequently, too many black activists are merely vociferous political critics who manage to develop only emotional rapport with our people. But the struggle for liberation has to have a program. At the present time a major consequence of the lack of carefully planned programs geared to protracted struggle is that the black liberation movement tends to cut itself off from many important conflicts and to get caught up in issue-oriented activity where a program seems less important and protest seems sufficient. Thus, the discontent of our people lacks direction and their attention is attached, by default, to liberal reformist programs. We must study in order to be more concise in our social analysis and effective in our political activity. Therefore, Black Studies programs must be characterized by rigorous and demanding discipline and by a fundamental commitment to teaching competence and intellectual development. The integrity of the learning process must be protected through respect for the distinction between student and teacher and the respective responsibilities implicit to each role.

However, we should never delude ourselves into thinking or expecting Black Studies programs to be the incubators of revolution. In fact, we should clearly understand that the essential struggle will not be on the campus but in the communities where the oppressed masses reside. Furthermore, historical circumstances and not classroom lecturers create revolutions and revolutionaries. At the same time, however, guidance can and must be given to those who are serious about struggling for social change. They must be prepared to understand historical circumstances and social conditions that confront black people. The best of Black Studies programs will, at most, only be able to influence the course of study of some black students, but will not be able to control or direct the curriculum they will follow since such programs will not have the power to exact sanctions at white institutions nor at Negro colleges as they presently exist. Nevertheless, the effort must be made to complement the thrust of the Black Liberation Movement by ensuring that some of the necessary educational resources are available for the support of the movement and the development of our people. This is what serving the black community should mean—at least in part.

## NOTES

1. We have taken these extensive quotations from Rev. C. T. Vivian's recent book, *Black Power and the American Myth*. Fortress Press, Pennsylvania; because we believe it is a valuable treatise and deserves attention.
2. In fact, after Nigeria and the Africans in Brazil, the Black people of America constitute the single largest African group in the world.
3. Munford, Dr. C. J., "Black National Revolution in America" in *Symposium*, Utah State University, May 1970, pp. V and VI.
4. Julius Lester, in *Guardian*, January 18, 1969, p. 13.
5. Christopher Lasch, professor of history at Northwestern University. Notes from an unpublished manuscript, 1968.
6. For a discussion of this point, see John Morton, "Order and Conflict Theories of Social Problems as Competing Ideologies," *American Journal of Sociology*, Vol. XXI, No. 6 (May, 1966), p. 712.
7. *Ibid.*, p. 702.
8. Quoted in Bill McAdoo, "Pre-Civil War Black Nationalism," *Progressive Labor*. June-July, 1966, p. 40. Cf. W. E. B. DuBois: "We are Americans, not only by birth and by citizenship, but by our political ideals, our language, our religion. Further than that, our Americanism does not go. At that point, we are Negroes, members of a vast historic race . . . We are the first fruits of this new nation. the harbinger of that black tomorrow which is yet to soften the whiteness of the Teutonic today . . . As such, it is our duty to conserve our physical powers, our intellectual endowments, our spiritual ideals; as a race, we must strive by race organization, by race solidarity, by race unity to the realization of that broader humanity which freely recognizes differences in men, but sternly deprecates inequality in their opportunities of development" (quoted in E. U. Essien-Udom, *Black Nationalism* [New York, 1962], pp. 28-9).

9. Sethard Fisher, "Essay Review—Negro Life and Social Process," *Social Problems*, Vol. 13, No. 3 (Winter, 1966), p. 344.

10. Frank Kosfsky, "Malcolm X," *Monthly Review*, September, 1966, p. 44.

11. Lewis A. Coser, *The Functions of Social Conflict* (New York, 1964), pp. 87-8.

12. E. Franklin Frazier, *Race and Culture Contacts in the Modern World* (New York, 1957), p. 311.

13. Lerone Bennett, *Confrontation: Black and White* (Baltimore, 1965), p. 10.

14. Cf. Erik H. Erikson, "The Concept of Identity in Race Relations," in Talcott Parsons and Kenneth B. Clark (eds.), *The Negro American* (Boston, 1966), p. 247.

# 6

# THE EVOLUTION OF BLACK NATIONAL-
# SOCIALIST THOUGHT:
# A STUDY OF W. E. B. DuBOIS

*By*
Wilson J. Moses

## PREFACE

This paper deals with W. E. B. DuBois' darker side, his National-Socialist or proto-Fascistic thought. DuBois relates to the present-day black radical right in the same way that Herder, Schleiermacher, Neitzsche, while not Fascists themselves, relate to Fascism. DuBois and other black scholars, working at the turn of the century, men like Edward Wilmot Blyden, Alexander Crummell, and Orishatukeh Faduma, originated the conceptions of racial solidarity and black power which were to find expression in the Pan-Africa movement and later in the Garvey movement, although Garvey would have angrily denied that he was in any way indebted to DuBois.

The purpose of this paper is not, however, to discuss the influences of DuBois upon other persons, but to outline, briefly, the development of a right wing tendency in his thinking from the late 1890's till his death in 1963. Such terms as proto-fascist, National-Socialist, and right-wing are not used here in a pejorative sense. Black political thought is just beginning to come into its own and only time will tell whether a rightist or a leftist philosophy is best suited to the world's black African peoples.

It has been common practice, since the turn of the century, to describe black leaders as if all were either radical or conservative,

as if all were either militants or capitulationists. Earl E. Thorpe
is typical of historians who have viewed black leadership in this
way.

> Those whose convictions have led to permanent or temporary
> acceptance of the planter's preachments of the inferiority of their
> race have thought and acted in the accommodation relationship
> which was popularized by Booker Washington.
>
> The band of slaves who surreptitiously or openly rebelled against
> the institution and the colored abolitionists, adhered vigorously to
> tne equalitarian picture. This includes the Beginning Group of
> Negro historians who were mostly abolitionists. Until 1895 Fred-
> erick Douglass was the best-known protagonist of his race's equali-
> tarian sentiments and efforts. He died that year and soon W. E. B.
> DuBois and the NAACP assumed the position which Douglass
> had held.[1]

Such a view is correct only in the most general sense. It is true that
Frederick Douglass and later the NAACP advocated an equal-
itarianism which was to be realized only by militant agitation for
social equality with whites. It is also true that Booker T. Washington discouraged open confrontation with whites over the issue of
immediate social equality. But it is not true that Booker T. Washington and others who accepted a separate but equal philosophy
accepted the racist view that black people were inherently inferior
to whites. Marcus Garvey, for example, who was a disciple of
Washington, opposed those black organizations and leaders who
advocated racial "agitation and aggression,"[2] and Garvey was
certainly no believer in white superiority.

It is also incorrect to see DuBois as the inheritor of Douglass'
position. During the years that he edited the *Crisis*, DuBois was
a crusader for integrationist principles, particularly in the areas
of employment and politics, but DuBois was the product of an
altogether different tradition in Afro-American thought than that
represented by Douglass and the equalitarian radicals of the
abolitionist school.

Some serious misunderstandings of Afro-American intellectual
traditions have persisted through the years because it has been
customary to view the Washington-DuBois controversy as the
central debate in Afro-American thought. It is not my purpose in
this paper to discuss that controversy once again. There is reason
to believe that DuBois and Washington were never very far apart
in their attitudes as to what was best for black people. DuBois,
himself, admitted this in his later years.[3] I believe that we can
best understand the philosophy of DuBois, not by continuing to
contrast him with Booker T. Washington, but rather by understanding the intellectual tradition of which he was a part and by

seeing how his early experiences with this tradition influenced his later development.

Throughout the nineteenth century, Afro-American intellectuals were divided into two camps. On one side were the black nationalists among whom were the emigrationists Alexander Crummell and Martin R. Delaney as well as the institutional separatist, Bishop Daniel Alexander Payne. On the other side were the equalitarian radicals, men like Frederick Douglass, William Wells Brown, and Henry Highland Garnet, who from time to time displayed strong sympathy with nationalist sentiment.

The equalitarian radicals, whose most important spokesman was Frederick Douglass, were liberal in outlook. They were similar in some respects to the Jacksonian Democrats with their strong belief in the natural goodness of the common man and a corresponding fear of powerful institutions which they felt might corrupt that natural goodness. Douglass' favorite argument against the powerful institution of slavery was that it tended to corrupt the natural goodness not only of black bondsmen but of white masters as well. Douglass and the other black equalitarians differed, of course, from the Jacksonian Democrats in their extension of the rights of man to American people of color. The black equalitarians were individualists with a love of personal freedom above all things. They believed in self-evident truths and inalienable rights and they conceived of all mankind as brothers, essentially equal. They did not see themselves as a separate "imperium in imperio," a nation within a nation possessed of a destiny separate from that of other Americans. They conceived of themselves as "darker brothers," denied their rightful places at the banquet table but having a right to all the benefits of United States citizenship that any white American enjoyed. They sought to solve the Negro problem through appeals to the conscience of society at large and through agitation, either violent or non-violent, to focus on the issue of social equality. The equalitarian radicals thought of the race problem as a problem for all Americans to solve and sought to revolutionize or reform society to such an extent that blacks would receive any and all rights enjoyed by American citizens.

The black nationalist tradition had as its most influential spokesman Alexander Crummell who was later to inspire W. E. B. DuBois.[4] The nationalists were possessed of conservative values and, while they were not anti-democratic, tended to be more authoritarian than the equalitarian radicals. The nationalist conceived of the race as an organism and saw the welfare of the individual as inseparable from the future of the race. While they did not deny the equality of man, the nationalists were opposed to assimilationist doctrines and especially hostile toward talk of racial amalgamation. Each race was seen as having its own genius or set of aptitudes and abilities and each race, they believed, ought to be preserved as a distinct entity. Black nationalists did not seek to solve the black man's problems through agitation for racial equality. They did not seek to revolutionize or even to reform American society as a whole but were concerned primarily with the predicament of the black man. Through self-help and the formation of political, moral, and economic institutions they hoped to create a self-protecting black culture either within the United States or elsewhere. The nationalist was often a sort of mystic who spoke of divine decrees applying to races. He was opposed to individualism and insisted that there was no conflict between what was good for the individual and what was good for the race.

W. E. B. DuBois was in some respects very similar to Frederick Douglass and the other radical assimilationists, but then so was Booker T. Washington, as Howard Brotz has observed.[5] Douglass was hostile to the idea that race as a concept had any value or validity at all. Race pride, he felt was "ridiculous."[6] The concept of race was only a means of oppression.[7] So thoroughly assimilationist was Douglass that he even endorsed intermarriage. Washington, who unlike Douglass, opposed racial amalgamation, nonetheless hoped that blacks would ultimately be integrated into the "mainstream of American life." Kelly Miller, Washington's contemporary, seems to have believed that Washington was committed to integrationism but refused to speak up because it would have been impossible for a more radical policy to have had any effects at all.[8] More recently, August Meier has made a scholarly attempt to show that Washington was a silent but effective opponent of segregationist legislation.[9] And Washington publicly expressed opposition to segregation on more than one occasion.[10]

W. E. B. DuBois sounded very much like Douglass, at times, but unlike Douglass, DuBois believed in race pride. He was not a radical assimilationist; he wished, on the contrary, to conserve racial traits. In this sense, at least, he was a conservative. Unlike either the equalitarian Douglass or the practical Washington, DuBois was fascinated by race which he conceived of as a mystical cosmic force. He saw race as a very real thing, not simply as a figment of depraved imagination, not simply as the creation of a group of oppressors bent on degrading a portion of mankind. Though DuBois was an agitator for racial equality, he believed that the assimilation of the black race would have been a great tragedy. He was a cultural nationalist, then, and his roots were in the nineteenth century black nationalist tradition. Something more ought to be said about nineteenth century Afro-American nationalism and its adherents before we go on to describe DuBois' place in that tradition.

In black nationalist thought of the period there was a recurrent religious mysticism, so Martin Delaney in 1861 quoted scripture to encourage Afro-Americans in their search for a new land:

> "Princes shall come out of Egypt; Ethiopia shall soon stretch out her hands unto God."—Ps. lxviii. 31. With the fullest reliance upon this blessed promise, I humbly go forward in—I may repeat—the grandest prospect for the regeneration of a people that ever was presented in the history of the world. The disease has long since been known; we have found and shall apply the remedy. I am indebted to Rev. H. H. Garnet, an eminent black clergyman and scholar, for the construction, that "soon," in the Scriptural passage quoted, "has reference to the period ensuing *from the time of the beginning.*" With faith in the promise, and hope from this version, surely there is nothing to doubt or fear.[11]

When Delaney and Garnet spoke of emigration to Africa as a divinely appointed mission they were echoing earlier supporters of emigration such as Paul Cuffe and Lott Carey who saw themselves as instruments of God's will in attempting to Christianize the black population of Africa. But religious mysticism was not related solely to missionary proposals. The nationalists tended to see race itself as a divine institution. The nationalists echoed the sentiments of the great German nationalist preacher, Friedrich Schleiermacher who wrote:

> Every nation is destined through its peculiar organization and its place in the world to represent a certain side of the divine image . . . . For it is God alone who directly assigns to each nationality its definite task on earth and inspires it with a definite spirit in order to glorify himself through each one in a peculiar manner.[12]

The following statement could very well have been written by the author of the one above:

> As in every form of the inorganic universe we see some noble variation of God's thought and beauty, so in each separate man, in each separate race, something of the absolute is incarnated. The whole of mankind is a vast representation of the Deity. Therefore we cannot extinguish any race either by conflict or amalgamation without serious responsibility.[13]

So spoke Edward Wilmot Blyden in an address before the American Colonization Society in 1890. He had come to America in

1889 at the invitation of that group to encourage the emigration
of educated and Christian blacks to Liberia. During the months
that he remained in the United States, Blyden addressed blacks
in numerous cities, often speaking on the subject of racial pride.
"As a race," he told them, "you are independent and distinct,
and have a mission to perform."[14] One scholar has already observed that, "In an age of nationalism, Blyden adapted the current racial ideas of the German philosophers—Hegel, Herder, and
Fichte—to his own people and continent . . ."[15]

The similarities of Black nationalism of the nineteenth century
to German nationalism of the same period are apparent not only
in the writings of Blyden but also in those of Alexander Crummell.
An Episcopalian priest, Crummell had emigrated to Africa in
1850 under the auspices of the American Colonization Society,
after taking a degree from Queen's College, Cambridge. He had
accompanied Blyden on a trip to the United States in 1862 as an
official representative of the Liberian government to encourage
emigration to Liberia. Crummell was occupied throughout his
life with racial ideas, in some respects, similar to those of Blyden.
"Races, like families, are the organisms and the ordinance of
God," Crummell wrote in 1888, "and race feeling, like family
feeling, is of divine origin."[16] Clearly, he was influenced, as was
Blyden, by conceptions of nationalism then prevalent. His ideas
of nationalism, like those of Herder, Schleiermacher and Fichte
emphasized a conception of each nationality as "destined through
its peculiar organization and its place in the world to represent
a certain side of the divine image."[17] Indeed, there is in Crummell, as in the German nationalists of the late 19th century a
hint of the doctrine of racial superiority. One ought to notice in
the following statement a theme which recurs in DuBois, the idea
that while other civilizations are on the decline, the Black Star
is ascending:

> Amid the decay of nations, a rekindled light starts up in us.
> Burdens under which others expire seem to have lost their influence
> upon us; and while *they* are 'driven to the wall,' destruction keeps
> far from *us* its blasting hand. We live in the region of death,
> yet seem hardly mortal. We cling to life in the midst of all reverses;
> and our nerveful grasp thereon cannot easily be relaxed. History
> reverses its mandates in our behalf: our dotage is in the past.[18]

The similarities of William Edward Burghardt DuBois to the
German nationalists have been commented upon by A. Norman
Klein who sees his rhetoric as similar to the "superheated prose
of central European nationalism . . . that is [to Klein] more in
harmony (especially in the context of 1923-24) with a utopian

*Volksgeist* and a German nationalist tradition than with the political rhetoric of a Garvey or any later American black-nationalist leader."[19]  (Klein, of course, overlooked the fact that Garvey, too, resembled a German nationalist, not only in his rhetoric, but in his behavior as well. In fact, he represented, even more so than DuBois, the culmination of a tradition that conceived Black nationalism in European terms.) In DuBois' 1897 essay "The Conservation of Races," the tendency to think of Black nationalism in Germanic terms, as did such earlier nationalists as Blyden and Crummell is easily seen. Published two years after Booker T. Washington's "Atlanta Compromise," it reveals that DuBois had not yet emerged as an uncompromising integrationist and did not advocate "such social equality between [the] races as would disregard human likes and dislikes."[20]  In this essay DuBois placed the responsibility for racial elevation upon the blacks themselves and strongly discouraged individualism because of his belief that:

> The history of the world is the history, not of individuals, but of groups, not of nations, but of races, and he who ignores or seeks to override the race idea in human history ignores and overrides the central thought of all history. What, then, is a race? It is a vast family of human beings, generally of common blood and language, always of common history, traditions and impulses, who are both voluntarily and involuntarily striving together for the accomplishment of certain more or less vividly conceived ideals of life.
>
> Turning to real history, there can be no doubt, first, as to the widespread, nay universal prevalence of the race ideal, and as to its efficiency as the vastest and most ingenious invention for human progress.[21]

Howard Brotz calls DuBois a cultural nationalist and considers the nationalist current in his thought more important than the integrationist.[22] Neither Frederick Douglass nor Booker T. Washington, he argues, was preoccupied with current doctrines about white racial superiority. As far as they were concerned, Social Darwinism was an academic doctrine and, as practical men, they did not waste much energy in debating their equality. DuBois, an academic himself, devoted much of his early scholarly life to studies that were to prove the equality of black folk. In his essay "The Conservation of Races", DuBois launched an abstract and theoretical attack on the idea that Blacks were inferior as a group. This indicates that for DuBois, "not unlike the contemporary proponents of Negritude, the problem was that Negroes, in order to validate themselves as a civilized race, had to contribute an original message to the world."[23]

The writings of the young DuBois are in harmony with a German *Volksgeist* tradition, as we have seen. It has been suggested that DuBois "serious study of the concept of race could hardly have remained insulated after his two formative years (1892-94) of study in Berlin and travel in Europe."[24] DuBois studied with Treitschke and seems to have had a strangely affectionate regard for the "fire-eating Pan-German," whom he called the "most interesting of the professors."[25] But while it is probably true that DuBois was influenced to some extent directly by German nationalism, it is just as likely that his ideas on race derived directly from such 19th century Christian Black nationalists as Edward W. Blyden, and Alexander Crummell, both of whom possessed rather Germanic ideas concerning race and nationality.

DuBois first met Crummell during his tenure at Wilberforce, University, (1894-96):

> Instinctively I bowed before this man, as one bows before the prophets of the world. Some seer he seemed, that came not from the crimson Past or the gray To-come, but from the pulsing Now . . . .[26]

Crummell and DuBois were among the forty black intellectuals who founded the American Negro Academy of which Crummell was the first president. Along with the other members of the academy they began to work out "an elitist conception of racial solidarity."[27] In the academy's Occasional Papers, No. 2 Crummell anticipated DuBois' call for a "Talented Tenth." In No. 3, DuBois published his Crummellian "The Conservation of Races." What all this seems to indicate is that DuBois was strongly influenced by the American Negro Academy which was, according to William H. Ferris, a cultural nationalist organization.[28]

In appraising DuBois, one ought to remember the sincere reverence which he felt for the Grand Old Men who became involved in the abolitionist and nationalist causes before the Civil War. He spoke with the deepest respect, not only of Crummell but also of the nationalistic A.M.E. Bishops, Henry McNeal Turner, the "firebrand," and Daniel Alexander Payne, the "saint." DuBois encountered and was influenced by these men with their strong racial pride and belief in self-help before he reached the age of thirty. He was an impressionable and romantic young man and the things that affected him before 1900 exerted a lasting influence upon his later life.

During the late 1890's, DuBois followed in the tradition of such Christian black nationalists as Crummell, rather than in the radical integrationist tradition of Frederick Douglass. He seems to have had, like the nineteenth century nationalists, an organic conception of race, as well as mystical beliefs concerning the destinies of races. But the maintenance of nationalist attitudes was not confined to DuBois' youth. He invented, in 1899, the phrase, "The problem of the twentieth century is the problem of the color line," and he had repeated that statement in 1903 in *The Souls of Black Folk.* His essay in *The New Negro* reveals that in 1924, at the age of 56, he still considered the problem of the twentieth century to be the problem of the color line, still looked at world history in terms of race. This is very important because DuBois had become, by 1924, a socialist, yet he refused to view labor as "the present problem of problems."

As editor of *The Crisis*, DuBois became known as America's foremost advocate of integrationism. Rarely has anyone commented upon the nationalist current in his thinking during those years. Yet race pride and cultural nationalism are consistently present in his work during the years of his *Crisis* editorship, (1910-34) and afterwards. Occasionally, his writings exhibit a racial chauvinism as powerful as Garvey's. So, in *The Souls of Black Folk,* we read:

> After the Egyptian and Indian, the Greek and Roman, the Teuton and Mongolian, the Negro is a sort of seventh son, born with a veil, and gifted with second-sight in this American world . . . .[29]

And he refers to his people as "the sole oasis of simple faith and reverence in a dusty desert of dollars."[30] Throughout *The Souls of Black Folk,* he reveals a mystical conception of the destiny of the black people, who must not be destroyed either by conflict or amalgamation, because of invaluable gifts they had already given and were yet to give to the world.

*The Quest of the Silver Fleece*, DuBois' first extended fictional work is in many ways a typical progressive-socialist novel, but it can also be seen as one of the important documents of cultural nationalism. In some ways it resembles the work of Frank Norris, although I do not believe that Robert Bone is correct in his assertion that DuBois borrowed the "germinal idea" from *The Epic of Wheat.*[31] The germinal idea is Black Magic, Obe worship, the mythic spirit which is shared by Greek mythology and Voodoo. Published before either Joyce's *Ulysses* or Eliot's *The Waste Land,* it is one of the first works representing the twentieth century rediscovery of interpretive mythology. In some ways, of course, *The Quest of the Silver Fleece* does resemble *The Epic of Wheat.* In it DuBois expressed the socialist novelist's usual

concern for the problems of the working classes, but he went
further than any other socialist literary figure in showing a concern for people outside his own race. In one chapter he described
a cotton mill's exploitation of white child labor:

> It seemed to devour children, sitting with its myriad eyes gleam-
> ing and its black maw open, drawing in the pale white mites, suck-
> ing their blood and spewing them out paler and ever paler.[32]

But alongside this universal humanitarianism there is an almost
contradictory element of racial chauvinism which usually appears
in relation to the main female character, Zora, the "half devil and
half child." Zora early expresses her contempt for whites:

> "No, no. They don't really rule; they just thinks they rule. They
> just got things,—heavy, dead things. We black folks is got the *spirit*.
> We'se lighter and cunninger; we fly right through them; we go and
> come again just as we wants to. Black folks is wonderful."[33]

Zora soon grows to womanhood and whites are quite often awed
by her Abyssinian regality.

> "I never realized before just what a lie meant," said Zora.
> The paper in Mrs. Vanderpool's hands fell quickly quickly [sic.]
> to her lap, and she gazed across the toilet-table.
> As she gazed that odd mirage of other days haunted her again. She
> did not seem to see her maid, nor the white and satin morning-room.
> She saw, with some long inner sight, a vast hall with mighty pillars;
> a smooth marbled floor and a great throng whose silent eyes looked
> curiously upon her. Strange carven beasts gazed on from a setting
> of rich, barbaric splendor and she herself—the Liar—lay in rags
> before the gold and ivory of that lofty throne whereon sat Zora.[34]

In contrast to Zora, DuBois created Miss Carolyn Wynn, a
mulatress who has noble bearing, like Zora's, but has lost her
African sensuousity and can be mistaken for a white woman.

> While Bles Alwyn in the outer office was waiting and musing,
> a lady came in. Out of the corner of his eye he caught the curve
> of her gown, and as she seated herself beside him, the suggestion of
> a faint perfume. A vague resentment rose in him. Colored women
> would look as well as that, he argued, with the clothes and wealth
> and training. He paused, however, in his thought: he did not want
> them like the whites—so cold and formal and precise, without heart
> or marrow.[35]

At no time is DuBois' racial pride stronger than when he is
praising black womanhood "whose strength lies in freedom and
whose chastity was won in the teeth of temptation and not in
prison and swaddling clothes."[36] His sexual attitudes were progressive for 1919 and in *Darkwater* he reveals what is even today
an essentially black attitude toward motherhood.

> God send us a world with woman's freedom and married mother-
> hood inextricably wed, but until He sends it, I see more of future
> promise in the betrayed girl-mothers of the black belt than in the
> childless wives of the white North, and I have more respect for
> the colored servant who yields to her frank longing for motherhood
> than for her white sister who offers up children for clothes.[37]

It was in *Darkwater* that DuBois assembled together his melanomorphic deities, black gods and goddesses who smybolized the spirit of the race. "Surely Thou, too, art not white, O Lord," he had written during the Atlanta pogrom of 1906, "a pale, bloodless, heartless thing!"[38] And, for the most part, there is in DuBois' poetry a stubborn insistence on creating God in the image of the black man. So, in "The Second Coming", he tells the story of three bishops who are summoned to "Valdosta in the land of Georgia," on Christmas Eve. Eventually, they find themselves in an "an old, black, rickety stable," where a light skinned, almost-white girl crouches holding a baby in her arms. The baby is black.

"Children of the Moon," which I consider one of DuBois' better poems, appeared in *Darkwater*, but was written somewhat earlier than 1920. It is a mystical narrative, six pages in length, revealing DuBois competency and occasional brilliance as a poet. The poem creates a mythic cosmos, built upon the racial consciousness and historical sensitivity of the author. Like a Blakean vision, it must be discussed in terms of Christian mythmaking, political philosophy, artistic consciousness and race pride. In this poem DuBois draws upon his knowledge of Christian doctrine and Egyptian mythology in order to create a mythic cosmos. The principal figure is an afflicted Harlem woman, apparently on the brink of suicide, who is saved when a pathway into the sky appears at her feet. She performs Herculean feats beneath a blazing sun and brings to the Children of the Moon, "freedom and vast salvation." She is reminiscent of Isis, the Egyptian goddess who ascended into the heavens while she was still only a woman, and forced the Sun God to reveal his secrets. The Children of the Moon represent black people in the past, present, and future, and the Isis-like narrator represents the racial soul. "Isis, the mother, is still titular goddess, in thought if not in name, of the dark continent," DuBois wrote elsewhere in *Darkwater*. "Nor does this all seem to be solely a survival of the historic matriarchate through which all nations pass,— it appears to be more than this,—as if the great black race in passing up the steps of human culture gave the world, not only the Iron Age, the cultivation of the soil, and the domestication of animals, but also, in peculiar emphasis, the mother-idea."[39]

The poems and essays that make up *Darkwater* are excellent examples of the "literary Garveyism" that characterized the Harlem Renaissance.

DuBois could be anti-white as well as pro-black and in "The Riddle of the Sphinx" his "black rage" is just as violent as that of his successors in the 1960's.

> The white world's vermin and filth:
>     All the dirt of London,
>     All the scum of New York;
>     Valiant spoilers of women
>     And conquerors of unarmed men;
>     Shameless breeders of bastards,
>     Drunk with the greed of gold,
>     Baiting their blood-stained hooks
>     With cant for the souls of the simple;
>     Bearing the white man's burden
>     Of liquor and lust and lies!
> Unthankful we wince in the East,
> Unthankful we wail from the westward,
> Unthankfully thankful we curse,
> In the unworn wastes of the wild:
>     I hate them, Oh!
>     I hate them well,
>     I hate them, Christ!
>     As I hate hell!
>     If I were God,
>     I'd sound their knell
>     This day![40]

DuBois was, in fact, even more chauvinistic in 1920 than LeRoi Jones and Ron Karenga are today; for, while they denounce white culture and extol that which is black, DuBois denied, in his more passionate moods, the very existence of a European culture. "Africans," he said, and peoples of African stock, "form the largest and often the only group of human beings successfully advancing from animal savagery toward primitive civilization."[41] The world's cultures originated among its colored peoples.

> Who raised the fools to their glory
> But black men of Egypt and Ind,
> Ethiopia's sons of the evening,
> Indians and yellow Chinese,
> Arabian children of morning,
> And mongrels of Rome and Greece?[42]

This, then, is one of the most powerful examples of the glorification of things black—DuBois' *Darkwater*, published during the high period of his alleged "treason" as editor of *The Crisis*.

But even more important than the publication of *Darkwater* was his involvement in the Pan-African Conferences. This, more than anything else, reveals that DuBois was a Black nationalist even in the 1920's. Because of his leadership in the Pan-African Conferences of 1900, 1919, 1923, 1927 and 1945, DuBois has been called The Father of Modern Pan-Africanism. The conferences which he helped to organize have been hailed by such leaders as Jomo Kenyata, Kwame Nkrumah, and Nnamdi Azikiwe as a source of inspiration in the struggle for African independence. DuBois conception of Pan-Africanism was more modern and more democratic than Marcus Garvey's. Garvey's concept of African nationalism was obviously modeled on central European National-ism, so he rode around in open limousines, bedecked with ostrich plumes, just as if he were an Austrian Archduke. "Where is the black man's Government?" he asked. "Where is his King and his king—dom?" "Where is his President, his country, and his am-bassador, his army, his navy, his men of big affairs?" And then, he declared, "I will help to make them."[43] DuBois African nationalism was to be democratic and socialist. More importantly, it was to be African, that is, it was to be based on African patterns. The structure of the family among certain Gold Coast tribes, and the position of women within that structure were hailed as possible patterns for a modern African state. The native African village was to be the model for the Neo-African culture, and in his essay "What is Civilization? Africa's Answer," he calls the native village "a perfect human thing." It was DuBois philo-sophy, and not Garvey's which was ultimately to form the basis for twentieth century Pan-Africanism. The following statement, quoted from *The Crisis* of February, 1919 would be acceptable to the majority of young Pan-Africanists in the United States today.

> The African movement means to us what the Zionist movement must mean to the Jews, the centralization of race effort and the recognition of a racial front. To help bear the burden of Africa does not mean any lessening of effort in our own problem at home. Rather it means increased interest. For any ebullition of action and feeling that results in an amelioration of the lot of Africa tends to ameliorate the condition of colored peoples throughout the world. And no man liveth to himself.

By 1934, however, DuBois opinion on how blacks should con-front the problem at home had changed considerably from what it had been during the earlier part of the century. In 1934 he returned to his former position, that blacks were responsible for their own uplift, and that integration, in itself, was not an im-portant issue. "The opposition to segregation," he argued, "is an opposition to discrimination."[44] And desegregation had only been a means to an end, not an end in itself. If freedom and equality could be worked for through separate black institutions, he was willing to make the attempt. Segregation was a fact of life and was certain to remain so for the rest of the century. Concerning segregation, DuBois had recognized, for many years, "a curious paradox." "Unless we had fought segregation with determination, our whole race would have been pushed into an ill-lighted, unpaved, unsewered ghetto. Unless we had built great church organizations and manned our own Southern schools, we should be shepherdless sheep . . . . Here is a dilemma calling for thought and forbearance. Not every builder of racial co-operation and solidarity is a Jim Crow advocate, a hater of white folk. Not every Negro who fights prejudice and segregation is ashamed of his race."[45]

That was in 1919. But in 1934 when DuBois decided to support voluntary segregation, he denounced the integrationists in no uncertain terms. His attack on Walter White was in exceptionally poor taste.

> The arguments of Walter White, George Schuyler, and Kelly Miller have logic, but they seem to me quite beside the point. In the first place, Walter White is white. He has more white companions and friends than colored. He goes where he will in New York City and naturally meets no Color Line, for the simple and sufficient reason that he isn't "colored"; he feels his new freedom in bitter contrast to what he was born to in Georgia. This is perfectly natural and he does what anyone else of his complexion would do.[46]

This was destructive and unfair criticism, as DuBois was well aware, since Garvey had subjected him to the same sort of abuse in 1923.[47]

DuBois separatist program of the 1930's was considerably different from the program of self-help through separate institutions that he had advocated at the turn of the century. In *The Souls of Black Folk*, he had called for a Talented Tenth, including a black captain of industry, to uplift the masses of his people; now, he was to urge a communal effort. In *Dusk of Dawn*, published in 1940, he outlined a plan, similar in many respects to that of The Honorable Elijah Muhammad, who was then, of course, virtually unknown.

> Already Negroes can raise their own food, build their own homes, fashion their own clothes, mend their own shoes, do much of their repair work, and raise some raw materials like tobacco and cotton. A simple transfer of Negro workers, with only a few such additional skills as can easily be learned in a few months, would enable them to weave their own cloth, make their own shoes, slaughter their own meat, prepare furniture for their homes, install electrical appliances, make their own cigars and cigarettes.

> Appropriate direction and easily obtainable technique and capital would enable Negroes further to take over the whole of their retail distribution, to raise, cut, mine and manufacture a considerable proportion of the basic raw material, to invent and build machines.[48]

And it was not to be a capitalist or an elitist scheme. On the contrary, "All this would be a realization of democracy in industry led by consumers' organizations and extending to planned production." The plan also called for socialized professional services which would, "mutualize in reality and not in name, banking and insurance, law and medicine." Black people, he reasoned, might easily constitute the vanguard of a new movement toward complete socialization and democratization of the American economy. It can be seen, then, that he was not conceiving of segregation as an ultimate goal, and, indeed, when Stalin proposed in 1930 that black Americans living in the southern black belt be dealt with as a nation, DuBois made no rush either to join the party or to endorse its separatist proposal. The scheme which he set forth in *Dusk of Dawn* contained nothing whatsoever of a nationalist rhetoric. I see no reason to assume, as Earl Ofari does, that DuBois nationalist expression reached a high point in *Dusk of Dawn;* actually, it was one of his least nationalistic works.[49]

In recent years, people have begun to raise the question of how much the leftist DuBois really was. Harold R. Isaacs, for example, feels that it was an abiding reverence for power, taking numerous forms throughout his life, that attracted DuBois to the Communist Party.[50] Soviet Russia had become, by 1960, almost a synonym for power, and the party was—at least on paper—an avowed foe of racism and imperialism. Also, communism was beginning to be associated with the emergent nationalism of the world's darker peoples.

Ralph McGill, in his assessment of DuBois, sees racial chauvinism as the dominant force in DuBois life. He draws attention to a "typical" editorial comment in *The Crisis* stating that "the most ordinary Negro is a distinct gentleman, but it takes extra-ordinary training and opportunity to make the average white man anything but a hog."[51]

Irving Howe sees DuBois as ending his life by "lapsing into Stalinism." Unlike Isaacs and McGill, whose opinions are based on personal contact with DuBois, Howe sees DuBois life as inconsistent.[52] Howe does not recognize that love for power and authority and an aristocratic tendency—the ninety-two year old DuBois still wore a Phi Beta Kappa key—were at the base of his embracing totalitarianism in its Stalinist and Maoist forms.

How leftist was DuBois, really? A brief outline of the development of his socialistic thought seems to be in order. I am suggesting that he was not so much the radical socialist as the conservative anti-capitalist. No one who reads *The Souls of Black
Folk* can help but be impressed by DuBois contempt for the upstart burgher class which he felt was represented in the black world
by Booker T. Washington who had,

> by singular insight . . . intuitively grasped the spirit of the age which
> was dominating the North. And so thoroughly did he learn the
> speech and thought of triumphant commercialism, and the ideals of
> material prosperity, that the picture of a lone black boy poring over
> a French grammar amid the weeds and dirt of a neglected home
> soon seemed to him the acme of absurdities. One wonders what
> Socrates and St. Francis of Assisi would say to this.[53]

DuBois, and others members of the American Negro Academy
did not oppose Booker T. Washington because they felt he had
capitulated to racism. Some of the members of the academy, and
some readers of papers before that body, held mystical beliefs concerning the destinies of races. For this and for other reasons, they
were not outspoken integrationists, by any means, nor was DuBois,
himself, an integrationist, and, as Francis L. Broderick has observed:

> On universal suffrage DuBois was no more outspoken than
> Washington. When Georgia considered the Hardwick bill for
> effective Negro disfranchisement in 1899, DuBois endorsed educa-
> tional and property qualifications for voting, thus protecting the
> ballot for the few at the expense of the many. DuBois was more
> insistent than Washington in applying the standard equally to both
> races, but on the basic issue of universal suffrage, neither took a
> particularly democratic view.[54]

The Washington-DuBois debate did not take place simply
because DuBois was an integrationist and Washington a capitula-
tionist to racism. DuBois' opposition to Booker T. Washington
might just as well be seen as a conservative acadamician's dislike
for the "speech and thought of triumphant capitalism." As DuBois
saw it, the new century had brought with it a new system of
values and had replaced the lofty idealism of the abolitionist and
reconstruction movements with crass materialism and mundane
utilitarianism. True, DuBois had proposed, even before Washington had, a national black business organization,[55] but he certainly
did not wish to see black leadership pass from the educated
ministers and professionals to the businessmen and administrators.

> The old leaders of Negro opinion, in the little groups where there
> is a Negro social consciousness, are being replaced by new; neither
> the black preacher nor the black teacher leads as he did two decades
> ago. Into their places are pushing the farmers and gardeners, the
> well-paid porters and artisans, the businessmen,—all those with

property and money. And with all this change, so curiously parallel to that of the Other-world, goes too the same inevitable change in ideals. The South laments today the slow, steady disappearance of a certain type of Negro,—the faithful, courteous slave of other days, with his incorruptible honesty and dignified humility. He is passing away just as surely as the old type of Southern gentleman is passing, and from not dissimilar causes,—the sudden transformation of a fair far-off ideal of Freedom into the hard reality of bread-winning and the consequent deification of Bread.[56]

We can see, then, that when he wrote *The Souls of Black Folk* DuBois was capable of mythologizing the old South, even if only as a rhetorical device. DuBois was an anti-capitalist long before he was a socialist. Only late in life did he come to believe "that private ownership of capital and free enterprise [were] leading the world to disaster." [57] DuBois is remembered as one of the great socialists of the twentieth century and it is easy to forget the conservatism of his intellectual origins. He became a socialist by gradual stages. An imperious intellectual, a graduate of Harvard, with a sense of *noblesse oblige* and a conservative, classical view of education, he was not ready to accept in 1903 what he called "a cheap and dangerous socialism."[58] In 1907 he called himself a "Socialist-of-the-Path," meaning that he favored the socialization of certain industries which he felt were "no more private than God's blue sky."[59]

In 1911 DuBois abandoned the Socialist Party to which he had belonged for about one year hoping to support the Progressive Party of Theodore Roosevelt, who was hardly a radical. He proposed a plank for the party platform, which he sent to Chicago, and asked the party to demand for American blacks, "the repeal of unfair discriminatory laws and the right to vote on the same terms on which other citizens vote."[60] It was taken to Chicago by Joel V. Spingarn, advocated by Harry Moskowitz and Jane Adams. "Theodore Roosevelt would have none of it. He told Mr. Spingarn frankly that he should be 'careful of that man DuBois,' who was in Roosevelt's opinion a 'dangerous' person."

Angered by Roosevelt's rejection, DuBois had thrown the weight of the *Crisis* behind Woodrow Wilson, although he preferred the Socialists with their "manly stand for human rights irrespective of color."[61] We can see that even by 1912 at the age of 44, DuBois had not become a committed radical, but was still an optimistic Progressive. He claimed in his autobiography that Marxism began to influence him during WWI, but in 1919 with publication of *Darkwater*, DuBois continued to display a fear of the mob and a belief in the right of the educated to exclusive exercise of voting rights. This would be acceptable, at least temporarily, "until the ignorant and their children are taught, or to avoid too sudden an influx of inexperienced voters."[62] When he speaks of socialism, he removes it from the context of unqualified democracy, and expresses fear of a "tyranny of the majority." If he favors democracy at all, it is a technocratic democracy resembling that advocated by Frederick Winslow Taylor or Thorstein Veblen. His socialism is still cautious; the transformation of society will not be effected by instant revolution but will be effected step by step.

In 1919, at the age of 51, DuBois was still a Progressive, not a radical Marxist. His position could be described as leftist in that it attacked capitalist business enterprise which preyed on the black peasantry, but it was not radical or revolutionary. Indeed he cautioned Americans lest they "force moderate reformers and men with new and valuable ideas to become red radicals and revolutionists."[63] It seems to me that what DuBois found most appealing about socialism was neither its opposition to private ownership, nor its advocacy of egalitarianism, but rather its war on the values of upstart bourgeois culture. Also agreeable was socialism's insistence on rigid planning and control.

When DuBois began to speak, in 1934, of a planned separatist economy for the black community which would exercise, in Earl Ofari's words, "total control over every aspect of their community life,"[64] he was far outside the radical leftist tradition of Frederick Douglass, who prized personal freedom above all things. But Douglass, who had escaped from slavery knew much better than Crummell or Blyden or DuBois or any other black nationalist what personal freedom really meant, and perhaps that was why Douglass could never accept the idea of subordinating individual will to racial duty.

DuBois was obviously successor to the conservative principles of Crummell, not the liberal principles of Douglass. Even when he urged socialism, the aging DuBois did so on Black Nationalist, rather than on Marxist grounds. He was similar, in this respect to Crummell who had encouraged Victorian morality with a Black Nationalist rhetoric.

> I have no hesitation in the generalization that, in West Africa, every female is a virgin to the day of her marriage. The harlot class is unknown in all their tribes. I venture the assertion that any one walking through Pall Mall, London, or Broadway, New York, for a week, would see more indecency in look and act than he could discover in an African town in a dozen years.[65]

It was in such a spirit that DuBois referred in *The Souls of Black Folk* to "ancient African chastity" and it was in such a spirit that he spoke in 1954 of "the ancient socialism of Africa,"[66] and said of Ghana in 1962 that:

Socialism blossoms bold
On Communism centuries old[67]

DuBois became a citizen of Ghana in 1963; that was, perhaps, the most significant act of his later life. He explained his emigration in 1962, employing a classical Crummellian rhetoric. Crummell had said in 1848 that, "Amid the decay of nations, a rekindled light starts up in us." DuBois said in 1962:

I lifted my last voice and cried
I cried to heaven as I died:
O turn me to the Golden Horde
Summon all western nations
Toward the Rising Sun.

From reeking West whose day is done,
Who stink and stagger in their dung
Toward Africa, China, India's strand
Where Kenya and Himalaya stand
And Nile and Yang-tze roll:

\* \* \* \* \*

Awake, awake, O sleeping world
Honor the sun;
Worship the stars, those vaster suns
Who rule the night
Where black is bright
And all unselfish work is right
And Greed is sin.

And Africa leads on
Pan Africa![68]

## SUMMARY

DuBois is remembered as a radical liberal; certainly he possessed certain traits of mind and character which make it reasonable to place him within this tradition. Such traits were his life-long commitment to free thought and common sense, his hatred of military "tinsel and braggadocio," his reverence for life. DuBois campaigned, while he was editor of *The Crisis*, for open housing and he believed in the right of every man to choose his own friends. He defended the right to interracial marriage, although, he had a strong sense of race pride and often expressed open contempt for white women. DuBois supported the white working class in their quest for social reform, in spite of the racism endemic to American unionism. Like his predecessor, Alexander Crummell, he was an early fighter for women's rights. And although he became an atheist in his later years, he was always capable of genuine religious tolerance.

But DuBois had his darker side, which was conservative, elitist, formal, authoritarian. These tendencies were partially inherited from Alexander Crummell and *The American Negro Academy*. Crummell, who influenced the young DuBois greatly, was called "a born autocrat, a man born to command."[69] The Academy existed in order to dictate literary and artistic standards to black America, as well as manners and morals, and "to do for the Negro race what the French Academy did for France."[70] DuBois was as much a "racial chauvinist" as Marcus Garvey. At times he became involved in a black "aryanism" tracing every civilized worldly thing to an African origin.

> The primitive religion of Africa, as developed by the African village, underlies the religions of the world. Egyptian religion was in its beginning and later development of purely Negro character, and mulatto Egyptian priests on the stones of Egypt continually receive their symbols of authority from the black priests of Ethiopia.

> \* \* \* \* \*

> The religion of the black man spread among all the Mediterranean races. Shango, god of the West Coast, hurler of thunderbolts and lord of the storms, render of trees and slayer of men, cruel and savage and yet beneficent, was the prototype of Zeus and Jupiter and Thor.[71]

DuBois often argued that all the culture of the Western world had originated in the region of the Nile-Congo watershed, because all Egyptian civilization was black in origin and all Western civilization originated in Egypt.

Like most black cultural nationalists, DuBois desired that America would evolve into a truly pluralistic society, yet like the majority of black cultural nationalists of the past seventy years, he was reluctant to allow pluralism within the black community. He apologized, in his autobiography, for Stalinist totalitarianism and he came to reject totally the concept of individual freedom.

> But what is Socialism? It is disciplined economy and political organization in which the first duty of a citizen is to serve the state . . . the African tribe, whence all of you sprung, was communistic in its very beginnings. No tribesman was free. All were servants of the tribe of whom the chief was father and voice.[72]

W.E.B. DuBois was the first black National-Socialist. He was among the first men to conceive of a Black Nationalism based on African rather than Western concepts. He is the father of Pan-Africanism, as it exists today, a National-Socialist doctrine.

## NOTES

1. Earl E. Thorpe, *Negro Historians in the United States*, (Baton Rouge, La., 1958), pp. 14-15.

2. Marcus Garvey, *Philosophy and Opinions*, (New York, 1925), II, p. 38.

3. Ralph McGill quotes DuBois in *The Atlantic Monthly*, (November, 1965), p. 79, "The controversy developed more between our followers than between us . . . . In the early years I did not dissent entirely from Washington's program." See also Francis L. Broderick's discussion of similarities between the two in *W.E.B. DuBois: Negro Leader in a time of Crisis*. (Stanford, Calif., 1959), pp. 64-70.

4. Harold Cruse in *The Crisis of the Negro Intellectual* tends to emphasize the importance of Martin R. Delaney in black intellectual history. I do not disagree with Cruse, Theodore Draper or anyone else who considers Delaney important, but Crummell is the father of the tradition I am discussing and he had considerably more influence on DuBois, and consequently on Pan-Africanism, than did Delaney or anyone else living at the time.

5. See the Introduction to his *Negro Social and Political Thought, 1850-1920: Representative Texts*, (New York, 1966).

6. Frederick Douglass, *The Nation's Problem*, (Washington, D.C., 1889), reprinted in Brotz, op. cit. p. 311.

7. See Frederick Douglass, "The Future of the Negro," also anthologized in Brotz, pp. 307-310.

8. See Kelly Miller's essay, "Radicals and Conservatives," reprinted in Miller, *Radicals and Conservatives and other Essays on the Negro in America*, Schocken Books (New York, 1968), p. 34.

9. August Meier, "Booker T. Washington: An Interpretation," in *Negro Thought in America, 1880-1915*, (Ann Arbor, Mich., 1963), p. 100 ff.

10. See, for example, his essay "My View of Segregation Laws," *The New Republic*, (December 4, 1915), pp. 113-114.

11. Martin R. Delaney, *Official Report of the Niger Valley Exploring Party*, (New York, 1861). This passage quoted in Brotz, op. cit. p. 111.

12. Quoted in Louis L. Snyder, ed., *The Dynamics of Nationalism*, (New York, 1964), p. 138.

13. Edward Wilmot Blyden, *The African Problem and the Method of its Solution*, (Washington, D.C., 1890), reprinted in Brotz, op. cit. p. 138.

14. Edwin S. Redkey, *Black Exodus: Black Nationalist and Back to Africa Movements, 1890-1910*, (New Haven, 1969), p. 52.

15. Ibid.

16. Alexander Crummell, *Africa and America: Addresses and Discourses*, (Springfield, Mass., 1891), p. 46.

17. Ibid.

18. Quoted in William Wells Brown, *The Black Man*, (New York and Boston, 1863), 167, 168.

19. A. Norman Klein, Introduction to the Schocken edition of W. E. B. DuBois, *The Suppression of the African Slave-Trade*.

20. W. E. B. DuBois, "The Conservation of Races," *The American Negro Academy Occasional Papers*, No. 2, 1897, p. 15.

21. DuBois, op. cit. p. 7.

22. Brotz, introduction to *Negro Social and Political Thought.*

23. Ibid.

24. Klein, op. cit.

25. *The Autobiography of W. E. B. DuBois,* (International Publishers, 1968), p. 164.

26. W. E. B. DuBois, *The Souls of Black Folk,* in John Hope Franklin, ed., *Three Negro Classics,* (New York, 1965), p. 355.

27. John H. Bracey Jr., August Meier, and Eliott M. Rudwick, *Black National-ism in America,* (Indianapolis and New York, 1970), p. 124.

28. There is much information on DuBois and Crummell in William H. Ferris, *The African Abroad,* (New Haven, 1912), and in his essay on Crummell in No. 20 of *The American Negro Academy Occasional Papers.*

29. *The Souls of Black Folk* in John Hope Franklin ed., Three *Negro Classics,* p. 214.

30. Op. cit. p. 220.

31. Robert Bone, *The Negro Novel in America,* revised edition, (New Haven, 1965), p. 43.

32. *The Quest of the Silver Fleece,* (Chicago, 1911), p. 391.

33. *The Quest of the Silver Fleece,* p. 46.

34. *The Quest of the Silver Fleece,* p. 326.

35. *The Quest of the Silver Fleece,* p. 235.

36. *Darkwater: Voices from Within the Veil,* (New York, 1920) p. 173.

37. Darkwater, p. 184.

38. DuBois, "A Litany of Atlanta," in Darkwater.

39. Darkwater, p. 166.

40. "The Riddle of the Sphinx," in *Darkwater.*

41. DuBois, "What is Civilization? Africa's Answer," in *Forum,* (February, 1925), reprinted in Meyer Weinberg, ed., *W. E. B. DuBois: A Reader,* p. 374.

42. "The Riddle of the Sphinx."

43. Marcus Garvey, "The Negro's Greatest Enemy," in *Philosophy and Opinions,* II, p. 126.

44. DuBois, "Segregation," *The Crisis,* XLI, 1, (January, 1934), p. 20.

45. *The Crisis,* (January, 1919).

46. *The Crisis,* (April, 1934), p. 115.

47. See Garvey's critique of DuBois in *Philosophy and Opinions,* "W. E. B. DuBois—A Hater of Dark People," Vol. II, pp. 310-320.

48. DuBois discusses the separatist program in his *Dusk of Dawn,* Chapter 7, "The Colored World Within."

49. See Earl Ofari's Summary of "The Colored World Within," important because it publicizes the nationalist side of DuBois and defends him from the attacks of ultra-blacks, in *Black World,* (August, 1970), Vol. XIX, No. 10, p. 26.

50. Harold R. Isaacs, "DuBois: A Contemporary Assessment," from a chapter, "DuBois and Africa," *The New World of Negro Americans,* (New York, 1964), pp. 197-230.

51. Ralph McGill, "W. E. B. DuBois," *The Atlantic Monthly,* (Nov. 1965), pp. 78-81.

52. Irving Howe, "Remarkable Man, Ambiguous Legacy," *Harper's Magazine,* (March, 1968), p. 143-149.

53. Quoted from *The Souls of Black Folk,* in Franklin, op. cit. p. 241.

54. Broderick, op. cit., p. 66.

55. Louis R. Harlan, "Booker T. Washington and the National Negro Business League," in William G. Shade and Roy C. Herrenkoll, *Seven on Black: Reflections on the Negro Experience in America,* (New York, 1969), pp. 76-91. DuBois originated the idea of a business league as a Black Nationalist proposal. He reiterated the cry of "Negro Money for Negro Merchants," p. 77. He and others accused Washington of stealing the proposal, p. 77.

56. *The Souls of Black Folk,* in Franklin, op. cit. p. 265.

57. *The Autobiography of W. E. B. DuBois,* p. 57.

58. *The Souls of Black Folk,* in Franklin, op. cit. p. 311.

59. *Horizon,* I, 2, (February, 1907), p. 7.

60. *Autobiography* pp. 263, f.

61. *The Crisis,* 1912, vol. 4, Quoted from DuBois, *An A B C of Color,* (Berlin, 1963), p. 50.

62. *Darkwater,* p. 147.

63. *Darkwater,* p. 208.

64. Ofari, op. cit.

65. Alexander Crummell, *The Future of Africa,* p. 87.

66. Weinberg, op. cit., p. 402.

67. *Freedomways,* (Winter, 1962), p. 100.

68. Ibid.

69. William H. Ferris, "Alexander Crummell," in *American Negro Academy Occasional Papers,* No. 20, p. 1.

70. Ferris, *Academy Papers,* No. 20, p. 9.

71. "What is Civilization? Africa's Answer," in Weinberg, op. cit., p. 377.

72. *Autobiography,* pp. 402-403.

# 7

# THE RE-AFRICANIZATION OF THE BLACK AMERICAN

*By*

RONALD WALTERS

## INTRODUCTION

All the talk about a Black Revolution and the necessity for rapid social change has made this observer stop and question the end result of the process we are now going through. I pose the all-important question—revolution into what? In the April 6, 1970 issue of *Time* which purported to analyze the current phase of the black social process, Bobby Seale of the Black Panthers said that we "must civilize America." There is a powerful message in that sentence. I am sure that he was not thinking of the traditional view of civilization as being synonymous with whiteness but rather was thinking of the process of humanizing white America by teaching her of the pain, the struggle, the suffering and the survival of black people, a dignified people despite the continuing attempt to destroy them. With the above in mind, I believe that more than this, it is essential that every effort be made to prevent the black revolution from degenerating into a blind search for counter-destructive capability. Truly meaningful change in our existence and the revival of a strong relationship to our forefathers should be the primary goals of the black revolution.

The history of black soul force must, of necessity, begin in the heart-land of Africa which gave us our cultural richness and our cultural continuity. Rooted in what white western civilization calls superstition is the African "will to celebration" which is functional in the sense that in it there is the constant merging of the religious and the secular aspects of life. This fusion is in itself the force which moves and shapes African culture. Spiritual communion with the gods and with the departed loved ones in a complex yet constant system of identity is an integral part of African tribal cultures and properly represents a philosophical system that is at least as universal as those of the Western world.

Did any of this survive America? Writers on slavery, both black and white, tell us that in America the African was stripped of his culture and that what he now possesses is an American culture that is essentially European. I want to remind them of the difficulty and cruelty of slavery and how the "will to celebration" was critical in helping many black men and women survive—men and women who could not possibly have forgotten what it was like to be human beings—African human beings. If they had forgotten their humanity, black people would not have been capable of taking the religion of the white man and transforming it into an instrument for social, political and cultural organization. There are writers like James Washington who claim that black people never developed a theology, and that the form of their religious expression is European. The fact, however, is that the essence of the religious expression of black people is not European[1] but rather is from African tradition.

## BLACK RELIGION

The internal theology of how African men relate to each other in situations which require holiness and reverence for the gods is again a functional quality of African culture, and of the African transplanted into the new world. When black people cried "Oh God" they were talking about the ancient spirit god Sango, still rooted in their very souls, impossible to destroy. Let us examine the following lines:

> O God of the gods and me,
> shall I not heed
> this prayer-bell call,
> the noon angelus,
> because my stork is caged
> in singed hair and dark skin?[2]

This poem focuses on the dilemma of an African who has to answer to a European form of "religious" worship after he has been taken out of the context of his daily business; in this sense the acute artificiality of it all hangs heavy over the adopted religious act. Also, his address, "O God of the gods and me", informs us that he has not forgotten his own gods and personal reference to himself in the same phrase tells us once again how personal god is to him.

This functionality—this same personalism—is in the act of a mother who has had to kill her baby to keep it from being taken away and sold into slavery by the white man. Its presence is in the human drums which carried the news of liberation and of safety hundreds of miles down into the cotton lands and through the swamps to the edge of the great waters. Its driving spirit is in the spreading of new black towns across the land after emancipation, towns ringed for one hundred years by hostile Europeans— towns with names like Boley, Mound and Bayou that had to have been inspired by black humanism in order to have survived. The institutions which developed in the black community during and after slavery, though they may have had a specific function for the community, nevertheless performed the generalized function of mutual assistance as though it were a ritual.

The ethic of black humanism came with the people who were brought here as slaves and is now part of our situation in America. When we are made aware of the tremendous burst of energy which fueled the Harlem (in fact the nationwide) Renaissance we are made aware of the "will to celebration" all over again. Countee Cullen must have been turning joy to jubilation when he reveled in the African past in his poem "What is Africa to Me?" It is possible to understand the depth of spiritual freedom which led Langston Hughes, who was ever so keenly aware of the low road which the black man had taken in this society, to write "I Too Sing America." There were those who understood the pain too well, and did not neglect the human feelings of suffering in their art. Such an artist was Claude McKay, who wrote *The Negro's Tragedy*. The possibility that even after such tragedy, black humanity could still entertain feelings of gentleness and humility, as seen in the poem by Arna Bontemps, "A Note of Humility" is indeed fascinating.

The black humanism is evident not only in poetry, but also in other forms which blacks have used to express themselves aesthetically. One marvels at the extent to which the notion of unity, or the symbiotic expression of culture resulted in the union of song and dance in the musical by Noble Sissle and George Blake, *Shuffle Along*, which revolutionized the theatre. One also marvels at the attempts of Duke Ellington to "civilize" European music, or those of other musicians to bring a wholly new form of musical expression to this land in the form of spirituals, jazz and blues. Some folks even forget that these attempts are in effect functional extensions of the black self.

The wholistic effects of black humanism must surely extend to other realms of black life. (This is not in the sense meant by

Janheinz Jahn, who has imputed to African humanism the German meaning of *Weltanschauung,* or "life force," which is not to characterize the implicit ethics of the African humanism, but to generalize them.) It seems that there are perfect expressions of the ethics of black humanism in what some black-oriented groups have set for their standard code of behavior. An examination of the Black Laws of the Republic of New Africa says a great deal about the human qualities which its proponents would wish a black nation to uphold as a standard for its people; they include the mutual aid ethic, secrecy and mutual safety, humility in punishment for wrongs, courage in defense of black people, courtesy and respect for one another and selflessness in service to the nation (appendix I). The platform of the Black Panther Party also gives some notion of black humanism in its concern for sharing the money owed black people with all black communities; the destruction of capitalism; decent housing and shelter; education which will tell us something of the black man's role in history; imperatives for every-day survival; an end to police brutality and murder of black people; finally, a concern with equal justice in a total sense (appendix II). Then, the Nguzo Sabaa developed by US through Maulana Karenga, gives us the principles of unity, self-determination, collective work and responsibility, cooperative economics, purpose, creativity and faith. Brother Ameer Baraka has commented upon these in the November, 1969 issue of *The Black Scholar,* "A Black Value System". He calls the Nguzo Sabaa the "key to the new nationalism," and in his view, as in mine, if the nationalist period which we are currently building becomes intensified and leads to "rapid social change," then these principles of black humanism should permeate all aspects of whatever the revolution brings to our people.

Finally, if one examines the Muslim program, one discovers that what the Muslims want is strikingly similar to the Panther credo. In particular, they want freedom, justice, education, land and a chance to work out the logic of the Muslim religion for black people in a separate state or land area. Some brothers and sisters have interpreted the Muslim program for economic achievement negatively because it was compared to "Black Capitalism." However, although Muslims respect American laws, desire equal employment immediately, and believe to a great extent in Black enterprise,[3] the final test of their allegiance to this concept should be in how they utilize the wealth that flows into Islam. Here again is testimony to the ethics of black humanism, and through it the ability to share. Have you ever seen a Muslin hungry? (appendix III)

Seen in broad perspective, then, the laws of black humanism must relate not to empty principles, which these could be if they were not tied to a specific cultural context, but to a remembrance of and respect for our African past and our African future. In that sense our present attempt to reorient the values of black people away from Europe is the process of re-Africanization. The next section will point up this task more vividly by showing the contradiction between the individualistic and collectivistic ethics. In short, it is the choice of identity we must make if we truly desire to build a black nation.

## THE POSSIBILITY OF A BLACK HUMANISM:
*the individual and the group ethics*

Accompanying the slow, tortuous path to progress in America has been the gradual acceptance by Blacks of the fact that the rhetoric of democracy and *individual freedom* was not intended to apply to black people here or internationally. From the founding of the nation, and that moment when the rights of all men were delineated, to the First World War and the enunciation of the principles of self-determination, to the Second World War and pronouncements of the Four Freedoms and others embedded in the Atlantic Charter, the audience in mind was one other than the oppressed black peoples of the United States or Africa. Blacks tactically seized upon these pronunciamentos at many points in history in order to adapt them to the cause of indigenous freedom. They had to point out the obvious meaning of these phrases to those who uttered them. Nevertheless, those who made the high-sounding statements in the Declaration of Independence and the Constitution continued to maintain both slaves and support the institution of slavery in their states. Woodrow Wilson was known to the oppressed peoples of Europe as a champion of freedom and a saviour, but in a period when the same principles of freedom would have been thought to apply at home, he was chasing those Blacks out of the White House who would remind him of his words, and was branding their reminders as "insulting."

Lastly, when Roosevelt and Churchill were reminded that perhaps freedom and independence should also extend to the colonized peoples of Africa and to Blacks in America, they replied by either silence or by saying that the words were not intended to dissolve the British Empire.

Faced with this anachronism, Blacks have tended to persist in demanding that the rights to which they are entitled be extended to them. When this country asked for military service from the black community, we have always replied in spite of the lack of equal status with whites who also were fighting for their country. We saw in this activity an assurance that we would subsequently have a stake in the nation which the strictures of race had not afforded us. Black leaders counseled time and again that in spite of harsh treatment, this was a time-honored way to gain dignity not only for one's family, but for the race. Needless to say, even though Blacks enlisted in the military service in great numbers, they were sometimes fought more vigorously by white Americans than by the enemy. When the war was over they continued to suffer violence at the hands of their supposed comrades. In other words, even this sure way for Blacks to gain *collective dignity* and *personal distinction* was usually vitiated by the centrality of race. This was as true in other areas of life in America, but it is more graphically portrayed by this example.

Still black leadership had continued to counsel patience and cooperation. In the early 1920's, the philosophy of Booker T. Washington was well known to support the strategy of *personal example*, of honesty and industry as the eventual road to racial integrity and equality. Other more militant members of the black leadership elite supported the acquisition of political rights as the surest road to social and economic equality and individual integrity. In many ways these techniques merged and mattered less, once it became clear that they were all fighting for the same principles of American Democracy. The essential problem was which to advocate first—*individual* or *collective methods*. The question of the purpose for which the United States exists had been settled by the forefathers who affirmed that the union existed to protect the *individual rights of citizens*. The most important of these rights was the right to property, and that included chattel slaves. It was, thus, only natural that when slaves struck for freedom, they had in mind not so much freeing *all Blacks* as freeing themselves so that they could better their individual condition. When they formed civil rights movements, even though they utilized group techniques involving the dramatization of community issues, there was still the vision of the individual, *personal* freedom which was the overriding objective.

The great anachronism stems from the fact that whenever Blacks believed they had been in a position to exercise the full range of personal and individual rights which white Americans possessed, they were always stifled by the strictures of racism. In this sense, it did not matter how much money one possessed; the scene of moneyed freedmen losing their freedom is poignant in the decades before 1860. Also, in many cases it did not matter that one might be protected by the shield of social class or color. If it could be proven at any time that an individual was even potentially of black heritage, the same strictures applied.

Some writers have wrestled with the problem posed by a nation advocating democracy and christianity and still holding fast to the institutions of slavery and racism.[4] If this has been painful for Whites in the sense that it wrung out of them irrational and deceitful justifications, it was also painful for the progress of Blacks in American society. In order to adopt a strategy of acculturation which would in fact result in Blacks becoming a part of this society, Blacks had to know what was intended—what was possible. Thus, there emerged in the black community many strategies historically predicated on the possibility of full equality and citizenship, which essentially meant that Blacks would be able to live as Whites lived. These strategies eventually died once it was demonstrated that the goal for which they were employed could not practically be attained.

In one sense this has nothing to do with the objective qualities of either democracy or christianity, because both point toward the type of society which would certainly be acceptable to Blacks. It does, however, point up the fact that so many Blacks have made christianity a way of life and democratic government a lifetime pursuit, only to find that the *subjective expression* of these great concepts in America makes their fulfillment all but impossible. It was James Baldwin who expressed the notion that one of the tragedies of America was its inability to use christianity as a redeeming force in the lives of its people because dishonesty with its history (which has contained the tendency and capacity for cruelty to others) has effectively violated one of the main tenets of that same ethic. The same could be said about democracy as a governing principle. What Americans have today is closer to the Roman style of democracy, which, it will be recalled, did not include *all* people in the category of citizen, and which deteriorated in no small measure due to the maltreatment of its slaves.

One of the great insights of W. E. B. Du Bois was his affirmation that the problem of color would be central to the twentieth

century. It is possible to divide the world on the basis of rich
and poor, but it is also possible to do it on the basis of who are
colored and who are not. This fact of the centrality of color is
also present in this country, and though it is not honored, the
range of critical abiding problems which the country has historically faced internally has come from the presence of black people in
the land.

Thus, it was that in 1940 Du Bois became uneasy with the
singlemindedness of NAACP strategy in this regard, and began
to advocate some new directions in which the black community
should go in order to achieve full citizenship. His thought was
that the organization for which he had worked from its inception
had been dominated by the philosophy of white liberal philan-
thropy and that this had fostered a legalistic attack on the status
of Blacks. Although there were as many victories as defeats from
involvement by the organization in cases such as lynching and
other forms of violence and inequality, he had the feeling that
somehow things still had not changed very much. What he came
to see was the overriding need for a physical transformation in the
black community which could not necessarily be accomplished by
the courts but which could indeed have been accomplished by an
economic rather than a political strategy. Strangely enough, his
economic determinism encompassed some of the tenets of black
separatism which currently is in vogue. Du Bois also believed, as
he said on one occasion, that the black community always has been
segregated. Today he would use that concept to build a floor of
economic security under the group. All the ways in which this
would be accomplished have resembled current methodologies such
as black capitalism and black co-op movements, but DuBois added
many other things to his general concept of the socialization of
wealth in the black community.[5]

What Du Bois did was as simple as it was controversial. He
simply posited the existence of racism for at least another 100 years
and then asked under those constant conditions what should be the
strategy which would at least result in satisfying the minimum
need for survival of the black community. The chief reason he
discredited much of his Marxian theory was that Marx did not
anticipate the vertical cleavage between Black and Whites which
was getting larger in economic, political and social terms. His
advice to the NAACP was for it to be a realistic organization. To
a great extent the loss of prestige which that organization has

suffered in the black community has resulted from the fact that it failed to follow his charge.

The other philosophical problem raised by the central fact of racism is the desire on the part of many Blacks to posit their essential humanity without reference to racial origin. In a sense, this situation goes closer to the question of identity because it represents the urge to underscore oneness of man and is not necessarily tied to any question of politics until one tries to operationalize humanity. When one tries to invoke his humanity, he suddenly discovers that it has a great deal to do with culture, rights under a given political system, economics, etc. In the absence of the need to use one's humanity for any given end, such as valuating human life in two different countries, in times of crises, it may be simply assumed.

One does not have to look far to discover all the ways in which the essential humanity of any one black man in America has been violated. One has only to start with the institution of slavery. This is an important question because of the primary difference between the institution of slavery which grew up under the Western states and that which had existed for many thousands of years in the Mediterranean and in Africa itself. Even the humanity of the slave in Roman times was not negated and there were many common occasions when when one is led to believe, by the behavior of the slave to the master, that the basic humanity of the slave was well intact.

Of course, it was on this basis that the opposition to slavery first began to take shape. In America, before the 18th century, it had been codified that a slave was not a whole man; in fact, he was "3/5ths of a man" for purposes of taxation. Under these conditions, and certainly under the harsh systems of control which the slave institutions evolved, slaves in America lost all claim to their humanity (even though in full possession of a private humanity) except at rare moments in history, and usually when they forced a recognition of it upon unwilling masters by some extraordinary deed.

The methodology of the black man who was supremely interested in either his individuality or his humanity was to objectify it by placing himself in a situation which truly would illuminate his individual qualities, and which would surely beg the question of his relationship to other humans of different qualities—that is, he would leave the country—usually for Europe or Africa. Literally thousands of Blacks have used Europe for this purpose. William Gardner Smith says that this is because there is a facade (at least) of acceptance on individual merit in Europe, and for a while Blacks who respond to the facade can feel freer there than in America. Part of the climate of acceptance has to do with the pity Europeans feel for the persecuted Blacks in America, and part of it stems from the Europeans' contempt for the rich, obnoxious Americans. In any case, this places the black man in the temporary position of being esteemed or degraded for his human qualities; the author is quick to remind us that, even though one is careful, even in Europe he may discover both familiar and newer forms of discrimination.

Novelist John Williams supports the general position of the existence of a refuge in Europe. The important differences in the degrees of freedom available have to do with the truly individual aspects of personal adjustment. He says, for example, that black and white people see different worlds of social existence in America. Is that to say that they should go to Europe and suddenly be objective about humanity? In this sense, therefore, the degree of humanity one feels has a great deal to do with his prior socialization to racist experiences.

Perhaps the most important and influential group of Blacks who have gone abroad have been the artists, for, as previously stated, what one produces is but an extension of the self and in that sense part of his humanity. In America it is a fact that the creative work of Blacks—be they intellectuals or artists—has not been accepted on the same basis as the work of other intellectuals or artists, but rather has been accepted first on whether or not their authors were black people. Usually, if it can be immediately established that they are black, the automatic reflexes of racism become operative and the work is rejected—often before it is even evaluated. In Europe, black American artists report that they are able to have their work evaluated more fairly, based on their individual qualities rather than their membership to the black race. This state of affairs has led Blacks like Richard Wright to conclude that in this atmosphere, what one produces as an artist is more natural and therefore, on the whole, one is able to be more creative.

James Baldwin also went to Europe and almost immediately experienced what he thought was race prejudice when he heard children shouting the word *Neger, Neger!* Baldwin soon began to understand that this was an expression of surprise and curiosity rather than an expression with the connotation which the epithet "nigger" carried with it—the prejudged attitude of contempt and hostility toward black people. He went on to say:

> For the history of the American Negro is unique also in this: that the question of his humanity, and of his rights therefore as a human being, became a burning one for several generations of Americans, so burning a question that it ultimately became one of those used to divide the nation. It is out of this argument that the venom of the epithet Nigger! is derived.[6]

Baldwin also felt that Europe had never had the problem of having to deal with the humanity of the black man, and doesn't understand why it is such a problem to white Americans. Nevertheless, there is some indication that the more Europe comes in contact with black people (and perhaps white Americans), the more it is beginning to change its attitude toward Blacks. Both William Smith and John Williams have noticed that Europe is not the color-blind Shangri La which it has traditionally been reputed to be. Increasing numbers of the same barriers erected to black humanity in America have become part of the landscape in many European countries. Perhaps, as Europeans become more accomplished racists, this will have the ultimate effect of raising the worldwide question of objective humanity.

When the world-wide question *is* raised, central to the discussion will be the 200 million black people of Africa who do have an historic connection with Europe, but a more intimate one with Blacks in America. There are many Blacks in America who, through the renaissance of black awareness, have again discovered African ties of culture and history. It had been traditionally very difficult for Blacks in America and Africa to witness the same qualitative sense of humanity. If one is to believe the experience of Richard Wright and other black Americans in Africa, the problem seems to be that in the absence of any virile racist tradition indigenously grown, Africans have not developed continental or cultural strictures to their humanity. On the contrary, African culture has provided a great shield for the continuity of African life even under the most harsh conditions of colonialism.

The point here is that it is difficult for black Americans to have the same sense of humanity that their African brothers have because of the serious differences in culture. Even if one starts with individuality, the problem is compounded by the fact that African cultural systems are rarely structured with the individual alone in mind—since the individual is seen as a part of the group. On the other hand, because of the more similar aspects of one African culture to another, rather than to European or American

cultures, naturally Africans are able to look for their humanity—
the degree to which they are related to other men. And, without
the strictures of race prejudice and discrimination embedded in
the culture, they are able to simply assume their Africanness and
highlight the individual human differences. This fact is sometimes puzzling to Africans who come to America looking for human
experiences, often to find that they are limited by a factor wholly
foreign to them and their indigenous environment—white racism!

The way in which African culture helps the black man in
America to solve the problem of his basic identity is to help him
understand the foundations of his existence—his culture and
history. Man is, therefore, free to be more human when he under-
stands the basic elements of his peculiar form of humanity. Because of the fact of color and race prejudice, it is folly for black
people (or any other people, for that matter) to define their basic
humanity apart from the environment in which they interact in
order that they may be able to utilize it for positive orientation
within the framework of their society. The longevity of racist
institutions in America is testimony to the fact that the power of
the American people has been used to enforce and support their
particular definition of black people. The subjective content of
black people, therefore, is rooted in all the things which can be
said to operate on them: on the one hand, the basic humanity
of Blacks in America is defined by the strictures placed upon it by
whites. On the other hand it is defined by the positive aspects of
the black experience.

There has, then, been a sort of liberation of the spirit, from
a yearning which the black people have had to be able to express
an objective sense of their humanity to a realization that there was
positive value in the human experiences which they possessed as
black people in this country at this and earlier periods in history.
Because of the context in which events take place in this country
black humanism is not a pure expression of African humanism,
it has been significantly intermingled with European culture. That
I hesitate to call it European humanism is testimony of the extent
to which I feel a party to inner substance of that experience; I
prefer to believe that black people in America have adopted, because
of their interaction with Whites in this country, the style of that
interaction, but that they, in spite of this environment, transmit
a basically unique humanism.

It must be a numbing experience for some black people in
America to yearn to be individuals in the pure objective sense of

the word. For to do this means to negate those factors, like race, which give to individualism its most poignant meaning. One suspects, therefore, that what Blacks mean when they say they want to be known as "individuals" is that they want to be known as individuals in a white context. Other meanings of such a plea are readily discernible. Blacks who engage in the existentials of humanitarian identity are indulging in excessive chauvinism and have little to give to that black humanism which is becoming the foundation of a nation in being.

## NOTES

1. *Black Religion: The Negro and Christianity in the United States,* Beacon Press, 1964. But for a sign that there is a developing theology, see *Black Theology and Black Power,* James H. Cone, Seabury, N. Y., 1969.
2. From Gabriel Okara, "Spirit of the Wind" in *An African Treasury,* ed. by Langston Hughes, New York, 1961.
3. *Muhammad Speaks,* April 17, 1970: "Black Enterprise," by the Honorable Elijah Muhammad, p. 17.
4. See for example, *White Over Black: American Attitudes Toward the Negro 1550-1812,* Penguin, 1969, Part II.
5. *Dusk of Dawn: The Autobiography of a Race Concept,* W. E. B. DuBois, International Publishers, New York, 1939, p. 303; also see *W. E. B. DuBois:Propagandist of the Negro Protest,* Elliot Rudwick, Atheneum, 1968, pp. 276-283.
6. *Harper,* May, 1963.

## APPENDIX I

BLACK LAWS AS ACCEPTED AND VOTED ON BY BROTHERS AND SISTERS IN ATTENDANCE AT THE "BLACK LAWS" CONFERENCE, NOVEMBER 2, 1969 — URBAN LEAGUE BARN.

1. A Black Brother or Sister must aid one another in trouble with the enemy authorities representing the controllers, enslavers, oppressors and exploiters of our people.
2. A Black Brother or Sister must not knowingly reveal one another's name, ever, to any authorities representing enemies or exploiters of Black People.
3. A Black Brother or Sister must obey the decisions and commands of the high council, accept and respect the laws of the Nation.
4. A Black Brother or Sister must accept his or her people's supreme and just protection and punishment as their official discipline and respected law, therefore, under no circumstances, should he or she appeal to the police, the courts or any authorities of the oppressor to get redress from the just will of the people.
5. A Black Brother or Sister must consider any offense against another Brother or Sister as an offense against himself and the entire Black Nation, however small or large the offense or whoever commits it.
6. A Black Brother or Sister must stand and defend, whenever possible, the lives and property of Black People.
   a. We must defend the rights of a whole Black Nation to choose, govern, protect, punish and pursue their course of action for their people, declare war or peace, decide and determine its enemies or friends.
   b. We must defend the rights of the Black Nation to independence, freedom and justice for all Black People, under the Black Law.

c. We must defend the rights of the Black Man to have as many wives as he can afford, according to his religion, culture and/or his economic condition as long as all parties are in agreement.

d. We must defend the rights of a Black Woman to live as a mother and wife with her need of security provided for her by her child's father, who is also her own mate.

e. We must defend the rights of the Black children to grow in his or her own environment without needs or fears of being classed in such unjust terms as a bastard.

f. We must defend the rights of the Black elders to live and die in peace, going on safely without fear of their needs or frightened in their community.

g. We must defend the rights of leaders to teach or express what he sincerely believes is in the best interest of the Black Masses without intimidation or fear of safety for his body.

h. We must defend the rights of the offender to be punished as quickly as he has offended.

7. We should be anxious and honored when an opportunity presents itself through life to aid, show courtesy to, or save another Brother or Sister from a trap that he or she has accidently or deliberately fallen into with the oppressors or controllers of Black People.

8. The Black People's needs should have priority over all wants.

a. Wants—have personal and selfish roots and therefore can never surely satisfy the person or people.

b. Needs—have natural, relevant, biological and cultural roots. They are direct opposites in their motivations. Needs and Wants should be lived by categorically.

9. A Black Brother or Sister should not force Black Women into disgrace of themselves or their Nation for money.

10. A Black Brother or Sister should not disgrace themselves or their Nation for money.

## INTOLERABLE OFFENSES — CAPITAL CRIMES

1. It is an intolerable offense to rape a Black Woman.

2. It is an intolerable offense to kill a Black People's leader.

3. It is an intolerable offense to betray Black People by spying, knowingly informing on and leading into traps, physically harming, intentionally killing any Black Man, Woman or Child for the oppressors, controllers and enslavers of Black People.

4. It is an intolerable offense to destroy any Black Man, Woman or Child by means of any drug habits through encouragement, sales or force sales.

5. It is an intolerable offense to kill, assault or harmfully torture any Black Man, Woman, or Child for personal gratification, in forms of anger, willfulness, intoxication or bulliness.

6. It is an intolerable offense to take sides with and uphold others against your Black Brother or Sister by non-Black People or non-Black Laws.

7. It is an intolerable offense to knowingly allow yourself to be used as a tool by non-Blacks to plot against your own people for their future downfall, oppression or exploitation.

**THE BOSTON CONSULATE OF THE REPUBLIC OF NEW AFRICA**

## APPENDIX II

1. *We want freedom. We want power to determine the destiny of our Black Community.*

We believe that black people will not be free until we are able to determine our destiny.

2. *We want full employment for our people.*

We believe that the federal government is responsible and obligated to give every man employment or a guaranteed income. We believe that if the white American businessman will not give full employment, then the means of production should be taken from the businessmen and placed in the community so that the people of the community can organize and employ all of its people and give a high standard of living.

3. *We want an end to the robbery by the CAPITALIST of our Black Community.*

We believe that this racist government has robbed us and now we are demanding the overdue debt of forty acres and two mules. Forty acres and two mules was promised 100 years ago as restitution for slave labor and mass murder of black people. We will accept the payment in currency which will be distributed to our many communities. The Germans are now aiding the Jews in Israel for the genocide of the Jewish people. The Germans murdered six million Jews. The American racist has taken part in the slaughter of over fifty million black people; therefore, we feel that this is a modest demand that we make.

4. *We want decent housing, fit for shelter of human beings.*

We believe that if the white landlords will not give decent housing to our black community, then the housing and the land should be made into cooperatives so that our community, with government aid, can build and make decent housing for its people.

5. *We want education for our people that exposes the true nature of this decadent American society. We want education that teaches us our true history and our role in the present-day society.*

We believe in an educational system that will give to our people a knowledge of self. If a man does not have knowledge of himself and his position in society and the world, then he has little chance to relate to anything else.

6. *We want all black men to be exempt from military service.*

We believe that Black people should not be forced to fight in the military service to defend a racist government that does not protect us. We will not fight and kill other people of color in the world who, like black people, are being victimized by the white racist government of America. We will protect ourselves from the force and violence of the racist police and the racist military, by whatever means necessary.

7. *We want an immediate end to POLICE BRUTALITY and MURDER of black people.*

We believe we can end police brutality in our black community by organizing black self-defense groups that are dedicated to defending our black community from racist police oppression and brutality. The Second Amendment to the Constitution of the United States gives a right to bear arms. We therefore believe that all black people should arm themselves for self-defense.

8. *We want freedom for all black men held in federal, state, county and city prisons and jails.*

We believe that all black people should be released from the many jails and prisons because they have not received a fair and impartial trial.

9. *We want all black people when brought to trial to be tried in court by a jury of their peer group or people from their black community, as defined by the Constitution of the United States.*

We believe that the courts should follow the United States Constitution so that black people will receive fair trials. The 14th Amendment of the U. S. Constitution gives a man a right to be tried by his peer group. A peer is a person from a similar economic, social, religious, geographical, environmental, historical and racial background. To do this the court will be forced to select a jury from the black community from which the black defendant came. We have been, and are being tried by all-white juries that have no understanding of the "average reasoning man" of the black community.

10. *We want land, bread, housing, education, clothing, justice and peace. And as our major political objective, a United Nations-supervised plebiscite to be held throughout the black colony in which only black colonial subjects will be allowed to participate, for the purpose of determining the will of black people as to their national destiny.*

When, in the course of human events, it becomes necessary for one people to dissolve the political bands which have connected them with another, and to assume, among the powers of the earth, the separate and equal station to which the laws of nature and nature's God entitle them, a decent respect to the opinions of mankind requires that they should declare the causes which impel them to the separation.

We hold these truths to be self-evident, that all men are created equal; that they are endowed by their creator with certain unalienable rights; that among these are life, liberty, and the pursuit of happiness. *That, to secure these rights, governments are instituted among men, deriving their just powers from the consent of the governed; that, whenever any form of government becomes destructive to these ends, it is the right of the people to alter or to abolish it, and to institute a new government, laying its foundation on such principles, and organizing its powers in such form, as to them shall seem most likely to affect their safety and happiness.* Prudence, indeed, will dictate that governments long established should not be changed for light and transient causes; and, accordingly, all experience hath shown, that mankind are more disposed to suffer, while evils are sufferable, than to right themselves by abolishing the forms to which they are accustomed. *But, when a long train of abuses and usurpations, pursuing invariably the same object, evinces a design to reduce them under despotism, it is their right, it is their duty, to throw off such government, and to provide new guards for their future security.*

## APPENDIX III

### WHAT THE MUSLIMS WANT

This is the question asked most frequently by both the whites and the blacks. The answers to this question I shall state as simply as possible.

1. We want freedom. We want a full and complete freedom.

2. We want justice. Equal justice under the law. We want justice applied equally to all, regardless of creed or class or color.

3. We want equality of opportunity. We want equal membership in society with the best in civilized society.

4. We want our people in America whose parents or grandparents were descendants from slaves, to be allowed to establish a separate state or territory of their own—either on this continent or elsewhere. We believe that our former slave masters are obligated to provide such land and that the area must be fertile and minerally rich. We believe that our former slave masters are obligated to maintain and supply our needs in this separate territory for the next 20 to 25 years—until we are able to produce and supply our own needs.

Since we cannot get along with them in peace and equality after giving them 400 years of our sweat and blood and receiving in return some of the worst treatment human beings have ever experienced, we believe our contributions to this land and the suffering forced upon us by white America justifies our demand for complete separation in a state or territory of our own.

5. We want freedom for all Believers of Islam now held in federal prisons. We want freedom for all black men and women now under death sentence in innumerable prisons in the North as well as the South.

We want every black man and woman to have the freedom to accept or reject being separated from the slave master's children and establish a land of their own.

We know that the above plan for the solution of the black and white conflict is the best and only answer to the problem between two people.

6. We want an immediate end to the police brutality and mob attacks against the so-called Negro throughout the United States.

We believe that the Federal government should intercede to see that black men and women tried in white courts receive justice in accordance with the laws of the land—or allow us to build a new nation for ourselves, dedicated to justice, freedom and liberty.

7. As long as we are not allowed to establish a state or territory of our own, we demand not only equal justice under the laws of the United States, but equal employment opportunities—NOW!

We do not believe that after 400 years of free or nearly free labor, sweat and blood, which has helped America become rich and powerful, that so many thousands of black people should have to subsist on relief, charity or live in poor houses.

8. We want the government of the Unitel States to exempt our people from ALL taxation as long as we are deprived of equal justice under the laws of the land.

9. We want equal education—but separate schools up to 16 for boys and 18 for girls on the condition that the girls be sent to women's colleges and universities. We want all black children educated, taught and trained by their own teachers

Under such schooling system we believe we will make a better nation of people. The United States government should provide, free, all necessary textbooks and equipment, schools and college buildings; the Muslim teachers shall be left free to teach and train their people in the way of righteousness, decency and self-respect.

10. We believe that intermarriage or race mixing should be prohibited. We want the religion of Islam taught without hindrance or suppression.

These are some of the things that we, the Muslims, want for our people in North America.

# 8

# THE LINGUISTIC CONTINUITY OF AFRICA
# IN THE CARIBBEAN

*By*

DR. MERVYN C. ALLEYNE

The problem of the culture of African derived peoples in the New World has recently become an issue not only in the academic world, but also on the political front. While Herskovits may be given credit for having initiated a scholarly discussion of the subject and for having separated it from folklore studies, the problem has, since Herskovits, grown to outstanding proportions and has become a major issue in politics at national and international levels.

One of the problems of Afro-American studies is precisely that of determining what the cultural relationships between Blacks and Whites are in this Hemisphere. Where do cultural differences begin and end; and where do non-cultural, or perhaps sub-cultural differences, i.e. differences resulting from social class conditioning, begin and end. Is the life style of the Black community in the United States indicative of cultural distinctiveness historically and ethnically determined, or is it only a variant of a single cultural unit, this variant determined by such factors as the minority status of the Black community, its economic and ecological circumstances, etc.?

The problem is hemispheric and involves not only the interaction between Black and White communities in the United States, but also in the Caribbean and other parts of Latin America; and involves as well the interaction between White or Mulatto communities and some ethnic Indian communities in Latin America. Distinctive ethnic peoples who formerly were seen as distinct

autonomous cultures exist today as marginal appendages to
national complexes. These marginal groups are everywhere defined
sociologically as underprivileged and culturally as disadvantaged
or deprived. Their culture has lost, in the minds of the people, its
automony and separateness, and is generally considered to be
a pathological and deficient expression of the culture of the leading classes. Linguistically, these groups are defined in the same
way. They lose control of their mother tongue and adopt a form
of speech related in some way to that of the leading classes,
but showing other characteristic features which identify them
rather rigidly. Their dialect is considered sub-standard, deficient
and pathological, and becomes the most widely used adscriptive
factor in assigning its users to categories of backwardness and inferiority.

We have of course to distinguish between ideology and reality
in discussing cultural distinctiveness, although the former often
strengthens and helps to preserve the latter. *Negritude* as a system
of ideas was engendered and developed by Black people whose
acculturation to an European-type culture was almost complete.
But *Negritude* and the whole Black awareness movement which
has followed it have led to a new evaluation of the culture
of the Black people of the New World, by which not only are
continuities from Africa strengthened and made overt, but also
cultural links with Africa are created anew although these are
in some cases purely formal without the corresponding African
content. There may even be cases where ideology has created
the conditions which have made possible an apparent reawakening,
not of a material artifact, but of a function for which there is
no evidence of continuity. I am referring to the creative function
of language among the Rastafarians of Jamaica among whom, for
example, there is a constant creation and reshaping of words
to bring about a closer relation of form and thing meant.
Rastafarianism emerged in the early years of this century. The
speech of this group is generally not illustrative of the basic
Creole dialect of the language continuum of Jamaica, but rather
lies somewhere between basic Creole and Standard English.
Otherwise stated, there is a variety of language (basic Creole) used
in Jamaica (chiefly in rural areas) which shows a higher degree
of African formal elements than the speech of Rastafarians. Yet
nowhere else in Jamaica does language serve the function it does
among the Rastafarians.

The study of the speech of Afro-Americans has been, like the other aspects of Afro-American behavior, influenced by the different ideologies of different periods and of different scholars. It has passed through a period when it was considered that there were organic differences, both in terms of physiological characteristics and of intellectual capacity, between Africans and Europeans, and that these differences accounted for the fact that the African or Afro-American was able to grasp but a smattering of the European language with which he was confronted. Opinions about "Negro" speech ranged from statements that "slaves were too stupid, lazy, or ignorant to grasp the fine shades and subtleties of European languages" to statements that "in order to understand the absence in French Creole dialects of the front rounded vowels of French, one merely had to look at the lips of the Negro."[1] A variant of this was the romantic ideology which considered that the African was a simple unsophisticated person and that the benign master spoke to the African slave in much the same way as he would speak to a baby: he simplified his language, and it is this simplified form that the slave learned and made his own. The study of "Negro" speech then passed through a period dominated by the environmentalists who considered that plantation systems were not normal societies and that their harshness prevented normal societal communication needs from developing and therefore prevented a normal language from emerging among the slaves. The egalitarian ideologies looked for and actually believed they found historical models in earlier forms of English (or French in the case of Afro-Gallic dialects) for the deviations from the norm of modern Standard English (or French) in "Negro" speech since they had to show that Blacks were culturally the same as Whites after surface differences related to sociological conditioning were accounted for. E. Fraizier,[2] T. Pettigrew[3] and S. Elkins,[4] among others, have attempted to provide scholarly support for the "melting pot" idea, by stressing that the particular history of Afro-Americans in the United States made it impossible for any aspects of West African culture to persist. They postulate the existence of a generalized value system in American society and a generalized, idealized norm of American behavior. Blacks who fall short of this norm are considered to be victims of a social pathology expressing itself in lack of educational opportunities, poverty etc. Language is seen as one of the major areas in which Blacks fall short of the norm.

Among White social scientists and linguists, work done primarily on the language of Blacks has led to a new position of

cultural relativism which sees distinctiveness and autonomy in the
language and culture of Afro-Americans.[5] It is very curious that
Africanist or Negritude ideologies which have also stressed the
cultural distinctiveness of Blacks, have not been very active in the
domain of language. While it is true that movements for the
reevaluation of Afro-American culture and movements for the
political emancipation of Black peoples have pointed out the
distinctive modes of expression of Afro-American peoples, these
movements have never sought to demonstrate the linguistic
affinity of Afro-Americans with Africans (except in the case of
conspicuous lexical items). The distinctive modes of expression
have served to create and underline ethnic identity and ethnic
empathy; but there have been very few movements seeking to
elevate Afro-American modes of expression to the position of
national languages, even in places where Black peoples have
majority status. Among Black ideologists, the works of Lorenzo
Turner,[6] and Suzanne Sylvain[7] have gone unknown or unnoticed.

It is now a commonplace to say that language plays an important part in the study of culture. Even if we overlook some
of the extreme claims made about the importance of language in
this respect, we must admit that language often provides illuminating examples of how cultures work and how they change. Ethnolinguistics, the science that deals with the relationship between
language and culture, has traditionally dealt with clearly autonomous languages and autonomous cultures; on the other hand,
what we are confronted with in Afro-American language studies
are not forms of speech always of incontrovertible autonomy, but
most often forms which appear to be, in some way, variants of the
speech of Whites. Sociolinguistics, which deals with speech variation within a single speech community, used to be considered
to have nothing to do with culture and was content to relate
language variation in a speech community to social stratification;
and the study of the speech of Afro-Americans has usually been
subsumed under sociolinguistics. Recently, however, there have been
suggestions in sociolinguistic studies that there may be a relationship within social strata between language and what is termed
cognitive orientation, using this term to cover such matters as
world view, value systems, etc., i.e. culture. The question is being
posed as to whether the notion of linguistic relativity (the
Whorfian hypothesis) may apply to differences in linguistic structure between what may be viewed as class dialects.

The question becomes even more interesting when we suspect that what we may be calling variant class dialects are in fact at least sociocultural distinctions which, certainly in so far as the historical process is concerned, have originated from widely differing cultural contexts. Even where we seem to be faced with invariance, this invariance may be the result of convergence of historically dissimilar cultural entities. Both ethnolinguistics and sociolinguistics then become very relevant, since we should want to examine historical processes to see whether they can account for language structure and then infer some connection between language and culture as historical products. For example, if it can be shown that the emphasis on aspect rather than tense in the verbal systems of some forms of Afro-American speech[8] is not properly speaking a deviation from a norm of English, but rather the result of a historical process in which a language or set of languages distinct from English, and in which aspect was more important than tense, developed in such a way as to leave traces at the contemporary period; and if it can be shown that this language change followed developments parallel with developments of other aspects of culture, we may reasonably conclude that there may be some cultural content, or at least cultural parallels, in the verbal systems of these dialects.

If, in considering diversity in form within English, we discover that those variants, which, in the invariance oriented view of structural linguistics and ethnolinguistics, would be considered as free deviations from a norm of English, can be shown to be derived by historical process from a distinct language entity, we might reasonably look for correlations between these variants and other aspects of culture. It must be emphasized that what we are discovering are parallels falling within a pattern; we are discovering correlations. But the patterns and parallels certainly have historical significance as products of a sustained common development of a language and the rest of a culture together.

These linguistic features may say nothing about the present day speakers of the language; there is no claim that they influence present day speakers in any particular way. What influences could the absence of the copula have on users of a dialect without copula is rather difficult to say, at least without some device to determine this in an experimental or inductive way. Isolated features also would not help very much. But when these features accumulate and become systemic, or when they can be shown to be related historically to similar forms in other dialects where they are systemic, we might suspect that we are on to something that has broader cultural implications.

One can observe a growing awareness of the historical processes that account for "Negro" speech in the United States. "Negro" speech is coming to be recognized as a linguistically "normal" dialect which may carry a negative evaluation sociologically because of the social status of its users. The fact that "Negro" speech of a given area and of a given social class may differ from "White" speech of the same area and of comparable social class is coming to be understood to be the result not of biological differences or not solely the result of more intense social conditioning, but to be partly the result of historical processes involving certain kinds of language development and cultural development; and it is coming to be understood that at least some of the unique characteristics of contemporary 'Negro' dialects derive from earlier so-called creolization processes.[9] This would link historically the speech of the Black community of the United States firmly with that of Afro-Caribbean communities.

Linguistic forms, such as the absence of copula (*he sick*), uninflected verb stems indicating perfective aspect (*I see*), exist side by side with *he is sick, I have seen*, and *I saw*, in the speech of some North American Blacks, and are viewed by many as the result of sociological deprivation leading to incomplete mastery of the Standard forms. But these forms of the "Negro" dialect can be related to analogous forms in, say, Sranan and Saramaccan (Creole languages in Surinam) where they belong to stable internally coherent language systems.

These so-called Creole languages pose certain problems, in terms of their genesis and development, which have not been altogether solved, although there may be wide agreement among linguists as far as their opinions go. There seems to be some internal inconsistency in these opinions. Consider the view held about the language history of Afro-Americans of the United States. On the one hand there is growing awareness that there has been continuity and transmission from Gullah—the most deviant of the dialect varities, the one containing the highest degree of Africanisms[10] and generally considered to be a Creole language—through Southern "Negro" speech to the non-standard English of the Black communities of Northern cities. This is then used to demonstrate distinctiveness of the urban non-standard dialect, which in turn is used to support the thesis of a distinctive culture, which presumably therefore has some African basis, the product of historical continuity. On the other hand, there is an adherence to the notion of Gullah and Caribbean Creoles being derived from a pidgin language, itself derived, at least lexically, from Portuguese.

This postulation of a single proto-Creole, identified as a pidgin language, is itself a response to a recognition of similarities or systematic correspondences between all Creole languages, regardless of their lexical base. By the application of the Comparative Method, these systematic correspondences and structural similarities are considered to be explicable only by these Creole languages being historical bifurcations from one source. The assignment of a Portuguese base to this pidgin language is in response to a recognition that the Portuguese were the first Europeans in Africa (Sub-Saharan) and in the slave trade, and to a recognition that some Creole languages show a fair percentage of Portuguese words in their lexicons.[11] There has been a more recent attempt to explain the Portuguese pidgin as being influenced by *sabir,* the Romance based lingua franca of the Mediterranean, this influence being either direct or else by what Kroeber calls stimulus diffusion.[12]

There are some important difficulties which can be observed in these viewpoints. The "pidgin" notion seems to beg the question of genesis. Or if it deals with the question, it implies that there was linguistic discontinuity as far as the transmission of African linguistic forms is concerned. African forms have sometimes, but not always, been recognized as existing in Afro-American dialects, but their presence has been simply affirmed without serious attempts to determine the processes by which they might have entered these dialects. In one case, African elements have been referred to as "borrowings."[13]

The process by which African elements have entered Afro-American dialects and by which they were transmitted seems to be a crucial question. A look at Indo-European linguistics may be of some interest. The most prevalent view concerning the basis for genetic classification in Indo-European linguistics is that continuity of morphology constitutes the relevant evidence for positing genetic relationship.[14] For example, there has been linguistic continuity in Western Europe in terms of the transmission of Latin morphology (in somewhat altered form) or by the transmission of Old Germanic morphology. This makes languages like French, Spanish, etc., genetically related to Latin, and German, Dutch, etc., genetically related to Old Germanic. It is generally accepted that there has been no rupture in the development or transmission process, although obviously there has been change. English itself is considered to be a continuation of Anglo-Saxon and in turn of Old Germanic, although in fact the vocabulary is predominantly Romance or Latin. This is presumably because of two factors. Firstly, from the point of historical process, Anglo-Saxon is considered the base from which English develops, under the influence of French (and Scandinavian). This applies to language as well as to other aspects of culture. Historically, British culture has an Anglo-Saxon base with the superimposition of a number of French (and Scandinavian) forms. Secondly, the morphology of English is presumed to be a continuation of the morphology of Anglo-Saxon, this in spite of the fact that there are a number of French elements in the derivational morphology (cf. the suffixes -ity, -tion, etc.), and perhaps one Gallicism in the inflectional morphology (cf. plural -s).

If we find African elements in Afro-American dialects, the conclusion is inescapable that they belong to the base of the historical process. If we find an almost total absence of Indo-European morphology in Afro-American dialects, but instead find that the morphosyntax can in many respects be shown to be derived from the morphosyntax of West African languages, we can reasonably conclude that there is morphosyntactical continuity from West African languages to Afro-American dialects.

But, as I have said, the way in which the genesis of Creole languages has been presented in much of the current work implies a break in any linguistic continuity with Africa. The implication is that Africans and African slaves gave up African languages, that is, broke with the African linguistic tradition and accepted a pidgin i.e. primarily a European invention, a simplified version of a European language. To relate non-Standard dialects of Black American urban communities to a pidgin would lead to the inference that there has been discontinuity, as far as the transmission of an African cultural item is concerned, and would in fact support the deficiency hypothesis.

I can find no convincing linguistic evidence that Creole languages are deficient or pathological or simplified, or that they ever were. They appear to be reduced or simplified only when juxtaposed to European languages of the same lexical base—as in Jamaica, Antigua, Guyana, Martinique—and when these European languages are viewed as the norm. They are considered deficient because it is impossible to participate in, and manipulate the norm culture by using Creole languages. And therefore Creole languages are deficient only to the extent that their speakers wish to or are expected to participate in and manipulate this norm culture. One would then have to show that the culture expectations, the self images of Creole speakers are in some way frustrated because their language—Creole—prevents them from participating successfully in this norm culture. There is of course some evidence that this is so, and this perhaps constitutes the cultural dilemma of some Afro-American communities like Jamaica, Antigua, Guyana.

In the case of Creole languages such as Saramaccan and Sranan of Surinam, and Papiamentu of the Netherlands Antilles, it is impossible to speak of deficiency or pathology of language or of culture. It is perhaps not an accident that one of the above languages—Saramaccan— is the most African of all New World languages; and similarly for the culture of the people. These languages fulfill a wide variety of functions and are generally assumed to be quite adequate to the tasks.

Another difficulty with the pidgin hypothesis is that whereas it stems in part from the recognition of similarities among Creole languages, these similarities, cutting across differences in the origin of the lexicon, come very conspicuously, as I have said, from African languages. These similarities make Creole languages, as a group, very African creations, and make the whole notion of deficiency untenable in historical or structural terms. For example, Creole languages share a very characteristic verbal system built up of an invariable verbal theme and preposed particles expressing aspect and tense. Creole languages also characteristically have a higher order morpheme class (which we might call predicators) which contains sub-classes of what are called verbs or adjectives in English or French. For example:

| | |
|---|---|
| *mi (d)a waka* | "I am walking" |
| *mi (d)a redi* | "I am getting ready" |
| *mi d(a) fat* | "I am putting on weight" |

This structure has no historical models in Indo-European languages, whereas it is quite characteristic of West African languages. Another very typical West African structural characteristic which occurs in Creole languages is the recognition of identity, attribution, and location, as separate relations. Where English or French structure recognizes only one relation, Creole languages recognize three. Thus in Krio of Sierra Leone: *Ayo na mi sista* "Ayo is my sister;" *Ayo langa* "Ayo is tall;" *Ayo de na os* "Ayo is in the house."

There are other difficulties for the acceptance of the pidgin hypothesis. When an attempt is made to reconstruct the socio-cultural structure of the contact situation between Africans and Europeans, there are many features which appear to be in conflict with the idea of pidgin. A lot of research is now leading to the realization that certain basic cultural institutions such as family, religion, social institutions such as brotherhoods, etc., never collapsed during slavery. These seem to suggest that there were very normal communicative needs within the slave community, and only secondarily between master and slave; and that these communicative needs could not be fulfilled by a reduced language such as a pidgin. It must be emphasized that Africans had their own communicative needs quite above those of their interaction with Europeans. Thus it becomes really irrelevant whether Europeans did pidginize their language. In fact, it may be quite plausible to suppose that some process that might be called pidginization went on, since the European culture and the African culture were both transferred to a completely new locus. Both cultures underwent modifica'ion, sometimes in the form of different types of innovation, sometimes in the form of convergent innovation. What we have to consider are the communicative needs which arose in the new situation and how linguistic resources came to be used to fulfill them. We will then see situations where African languages were preserved in a pure and intact form in situations where the communication needs demanded it, and we will also see cases where other types of linguistic phenomena arose where there were other demands. Afro-American research could fruitfully direct its attention to those areas like Cuba, Brazil, Trinidad, where African languages are preserved or were preserved up to recently, and examine the whole sociocultural matrix of their preservation, and see what communication functions they fulfilled. It would then look at other areas like Surinam and Colombia and again Brazil where maroon communities have developed languages which, as I have said, can in no real linguistic sense be seen genetically as Indo-European and for which the deficiency model cannot be considered relevant. We would find that separateness from the European type culture correlates with preservation of African linguistic features, with internal linguistic consistency, with the irrelevancy of the deficiency model. One can go even further to say that separateness can be defined not only geographically as in the case of the maroon communities, but also institutionally, in so far as Africans were able to keep cultural items separate. We would find that the religious function was kept relatively well separate and this was the most effective of all functions in preserving African languages.[15] Separateness can also be defined linguistically. That is, we find that it is in those areas—Surinam, Curacao, Aruba—where the Creole language is quite distinct, linguistically, from the European language there, in the sense that they do not even share a common lexical base, it is there that we find well-preserved, stable, internally consistent languages.

The question of the sociology of European/African contact and the question of the communicative needs which emerged are very relevant to the understanding of 'Negro' speech and African continuities in language. From the inception of contact and throughout the history of this contact, a dialectic of societal and cultural relations operated to produce social and cultural complexes in the New World. In so far as the African was involved in societal relationships with Europeans, he developed a number of new modes of behavior which reflected these relationships; in so far as he operated within his own ethnic group, he was involved in relations which would tend to preserve the cultural traditions of Africa.

Africans were involved therefore in a two way communication system. In one way, they were in communication with Europeans and in another way in communication among themselves. The picture of this communicative network was indeed quite complex, and it is by accounting for this complexity that we can account for the differentials in cultural continuities. Contact with European culture meant acculturation and some rupture of the African tradition. Inter-African contact was the necessary condition for continuity.

One aspect of the communicative network was that in the initial stages the locus of contact was Africa; it was then later transferred to the Iberian peninsular, and finally to the New World. In Africa during the century or so before slavery began as a capitalist enterprise, it seems that a Portuguese trade jargon emerged to fill the limited communication needs. The precise structure of this medium is unknown and it is a matter of conjecture whether it served as the basis for later Creole dialects. It is reasonable to suppose that it was a medium of limited resources since it was used apparently only in the restricted context of trade. Inter-African communication was carried on in African languages. The cultural correlate of this was that there was no acculturation.

Africans taken to Spain and Portugal in the 15th century were the first to become involved in societal interaction with Europeans and therefore the first to become involved in acculturation processes. Evidence of the linguistic acculturation and of the degree it had attained exists in the Spanish and Portuguese theatre of the period.[16] Many of the features of the pronunciation of Spanish by Africans involved in this acculturation process reappear in the Spanish of Afro-Americans in Cuba, Santo Domingo, Puerto Rico, Colombia, and can be explained as transfers from African type phonological systems. What direct influence these Africans might have had on the language of later New World Africans is hard to say. It is alleged that a Black man was a member of Columbus's crew, but there is no substantial evidence that large numbers of Africans resident in the peninsular joined the Conquistadors.

The slave trade introduced a new aspect into the contact situation. Slaves were uprooted physically from their culture, and often Africans of different origins were thrown together because the area covered by slave traders was quite wide over West Africa. There are also reports of a policy of mixing Africans of different origins to minimize the possibility of revolt. On the other hand, the trade was not organized so efficiently that traders and buyers could carry out the policy of mixing. Often they took whomever they could get. And even when it was possible to pick and choose, it seems that the traders and buyers selected Africans of particular origins because of skills or temperament for which they had become reputed. There was also some bilingualism in West Africa as the result of the spread of some African languages backed by military power.

The picture of the communicative needs of this period and in these conditions is one of complexity. Africans sharing the same language communicated with each other in that particular language, and there are copious accounts of many African languages in use in the New World from the inception of the slavery period. One early historian, Father R. F. Pelleprat noted 13 different languages in use in the French Lesser Antilles: "On compte dans les iles jusqu'a treize nations de ces infideles qui parlent toutes de langues differentes" (*Relation des Missions des Peres de la Compagnie de Jesus* Paris, 1655). But the need for cross-tribal communication among Africans created new pressures on the population. Interaction between Europeans and Africans created further communication needs, and given the power situation existing, it fell to the African to make certain accommodations. What we have then is a picture of the communication channels which can be represented as follows:

Africans ⟷ Africans ⟷ Europeans

Only a fraction of the Africans had any meaningful societal contact with Europeans. The bulk of the African population, both in African towns that sprung up outside European fortresses and later in the New World, were in effective communication only within their own group. That fraction became involved in acculturation processes that erased most of their African culture; whereas for the majority, intra-group relations were the necessary conditions for the preservation and transmission of an African tradition, often however overlain with European forms.

The continuum structure of the language situation in most Caribbean territories is probably not a recent feature, but dates from the very establishment of plantation communities there. From the very inception, Africans were placed in different degrees of contact with Europeans. While it is true that all Africans were in some contact with Europeans and European culture, the degree of contact differed in terms of the occupational differentiation in plantation systems. Degree of contact was obviously an important factor in different degrees of acculturation that Africans underwent. The inverse of low degree of contact with European culture was a high degree of intra-group interaction; it was among field slaves as an occupational group that this was typical. They become the preservers and carriers of the African tradition. On the other hand, cultural ambiguities developed among Africans, chiefly among domestic slaves and among the new ethnic group—mulattoes—who were not merely involved in the production system of the plantation but become relatively well integrated into the social organization of the European community.

The different ways of representing the picture of the communicative channels at different periods in the Caribbean are as follows:

Africans ⟷ Africans ⟷ Europeans
Africans ⟷ Africans ⟷ Mulattoes ⟷ Europeans
Field slaves ⟷ artisans ⟷ domestics ⟷ Europeans
rural ⟷ urban proletariat ⟷ middle class ⟷ (white)

In cases such as the Bush Negroes of Surinam and the community in Colombia called Palenque de san Basilio, the dynamic picture given above became disrupted very early. Africans ceased to be involved in any total production system and were cut off from acculturation processes. These were clearly the most advantageous conditions for the preservation of African culture. And today, more Africanisms exist in the Saramaccan language of the Bush Negroes than anywhere else in the New World. Saramaccan is a tone language (cf. *fii* "to feel," *fii* "free"; *pai* "father in law," *pai* "to produce"). It has coarticulated stops (*gboto* "boat", *kpoto-kpoto* "mud"); prenasalised stops (*mbooko* "fish," *ndika* "fish trap," *ngaku* "to stutter"); and vowel final syllables (to mention nothing but phonological features).

Caribbean territories such as Jamaica, Guyana, Antigua, are characterized by a sociolinguistic situation in which different speech types form a continuum; differentiation being expressable in terms of certain features which appear in the speech type at one end of the continuum undergoing extinction and being replaced by forms showing closer approximation to Standard English. The speech type showing greatest distance from Standard English also shows the greatest proportion of Africanisms (though generally less than in Saramaccan) and it is these African forms that undergo extinction. It may be said that the African forms belong to an older historical layer over which are being superimposed forms showing closer relation with Standard English. For example, *i a nyam i dina* "he/she/it is eating his/her/its dinner" contains pronouns which are Africanisms by the absence of sex discrimination; a verb form which has an invariable main theme and expresses aspect by a particle: grammatical device widespread over West Africa; a lexical item *nyam* which is also widespread in Africa. At other areas in the continuum, we find:

> *im a nyam im dina*
> *si a nyam ar dina* (sex discrimination in pronouns)
> *im a iit im dina*
> *him iitin him dina*
> *him iz iitin hiz dina*

and finally "he is eating his dinner."

A basic factor in the communication system from the very inception of European/African contact was the need among Africans to mediate two cultural systems. This need was experienced in varying degrees among different Africans or groups of Africans. Creole languages were very effective tools in this mediation, since they allowed a minimum of communication with Europeans on the one hand and on the other hand remained ethnic languages from which Europeans were barred. Creole speakers developed a linguistic capacity which allowed them to shift from an ethnic language comprehensible only to the group to another speech level which allowed some degree of communication with the other ethnic group involved in the total system. Karl Reisman, in his research in Antigua[17] notes that, associated with the shaping of linguistic symbols in Antigua is their ambiguation so that they can mediate at least two sets of cultural meanings. Thus the form *kogo hom* is seen by Reisman to be translatable either as "come go home" or as "Congo home". The term is capable of either gloss and the full meaning depends on the association of both glosses. Ambiguation is seen to be intimately connected with the maintenance of a dual cultural system. In more recent times, we have the phenomenon, noted above all in the United States, of a number of 'high affect' words with double meaning: cool, tough, bad, funky, etc. The parallelism suggests that here too we are in the face of a cultural system seeking at times to communicate with and at times to separate itself from another system.

## NOTES

1. See, for example, Rene Payen-Bellisle, *Sons et Formes du Creole dans les Antilles* (Baltimore: Murphy, 1894) p. 22.

2. E. F. Frazier, *The Negro Family in the United States* (Chicago: University of Chicago Press, 1966).

3. T. Pettigrew, *A Profile of the Negro American* (Princeton: van Nostrand, 1964).

4. S. Elkins, *Slavery* (Chicago: University of Chicago Press, 1959).

5. Cf. for example, S. Baratz, "Social science's conceptualization of the Afro Americans" in *Black America* ed. John Szwed (Basic Books, New York, 1970) 56-66.

6. Lorenzo Turner, *Africanisms in the Gullah Dialect* (Chicago: University of Chicago Press, 1949).

7. Suzanne Sylvain, *Le Creole Haitien* (Port-Au-Prince, 1936).

8. That is to say that aspect is always overtly marked within the basic structure of the verb phrase, while tense is often to be inferred from the general context.

9. See, William Stewart "On the Use of Negro Dialect in the Teaching of Reading," in Joan Baratz and Roger Shuy, eds. *Teaching Black Children to Read*, Washington, D.C., C.A.L., 1969.

10. L. Turner, *op. cit.*

11. The Portuguese words in Sranan and Saramaccan (Surinam) and Papiamentu (Curacao) have also been explained by the influence of the Portuguese speaking Sephardic Jews and their slaves.

12. A. Kroeber, *Anthropology* (New York, 1948).

13. Cf. Robert Hall Jr. "Pidgin English and Linguistic Change", *Lingua III* (1935) p. 144.

14. Cf. A. Meillet, *Linguistique Historique et Linguistique Generale*, 11 (Paris, 1938)

15. Thus in Haiti the nasalised high vowels—*i, u,* which mark the phonological system of Haitian Creole off from that of French, are found almost exclusively in words of African origin: *vodu, uga,* which are used in the African derived religion of Haiti.

16. Cf. E. de Chasca, "The Phonology of the Speech of the Negroes in Early Spanish Drama", *Hispanic Review* 14 (1946)

17. "Cultural and linguistic ambiguity in a West Indian village," in *Afro-American Anthropology,* ed. J. Szwed and N. Whitten (New York: Free Press, 1970) 129-144.

# 9

# THE LANGUAGE OF BLACK MESSIANISM: THE CASE OF NAT TURNER

*By*

Arthur L. Smith

As far as most black people are concerned religion has played the dual role of catalyst and dissuader of black liberation protest. Steeped in the traditions of Israel and the Christian ethic black deliverers have often been torn by two masters. Those who saw the possibilities inherent in the gospel of liberation were among the first to be denied freedom of worship, as whites were reluctant to allow slaves to worship a God who urged them to fight for their inalienable liberties. What aroused the whites was the political consequences of free worship. They reasoned that the slaves would sense a spirit of liberation in the principles of Christianity and would be led astray by black preachers, thus forgetting their political and social places within Southern society. They had a lot to fear. They had nurtured a monster within their bosom who grew on the heroic exploits of Moses and who drank the heady wine of rebellion from reading the Christian scriptures.

In 1831 the worst fears of the white Christians came to fruition in the daring bursts of violence perpetrated by Nat Turner and his cohorts. He arose, organized a disciplined cadre of blacks seeking to be free of subhuman and oppressive conditions, and slew nearly sixty whites, leaving behind a legacy of terror and a countryside of fear before he was captured. Such action fulfilled the prophecies of those whites frightened by the violent possibilities inherent in slaves hearing the gospel. Put simply, they would consider themselves to be men. But one can argue that if the slaves did not have the Christian message as a basis they would certainly have found some other foundation for their attempts at liberation. Men cannot live long in oppressive situations without trying to adjust the clasps and hooks of their oppressors; adjustment often comes after attempts to overthrow the system. While the hooks are placed a little deeper here, and there, they often fail to cover the oppressed in total subjugation.

My position, openly taken, is that what Nat Turner believed was not merely the principles and doctrines of fundamental religion, but something much more consequential. Few black men in history have ever been moved with such deep conviction regarding their missions as Nat Turner. In this sense, he is the personification of Black Will; in other words, what he felt and believed was activated toward his concept of black liberation. Indeed his rhetoric speaks of his thoughts and interprets his actions to anyone reading the *Confessions*. Not all of the William Styrons in the world can strip Turner of his burning commitment to see his people free.

Nat Turner, like many black spokesmen, was wedded to black deliverance. In fact, his life was entwined with the black lives around him. As he indicates in the *Confessions,* he is the embodiment of God's justice and, in a sense, vengeance, sent to punish the wayward and to warn the sinful. In this belief, as expressed in his confession to Thomas Gray, Turner exemplified the complexities of black psychology, religion and rhetoric. Therefore when he led the group of fellow blacks to kill whites in the Southampton region of Virginia in 1831 he could believe that he was participating in, and actually materializing the fulfillment of his God granted and encouraged mission to cleanse the earth. His *Confessions* given vocally to Thomas Gray, a white attorney, demonstrates belief that he was appointed to alleviate the sufferings of the oppressed masses.

This present study of Nat Turner is of relevance and moment primarily because by understanding his confessions, that is, by seeing what he was actually into, we might be able to throw some light on the attitude possessed by hundreds of committed blacks who are willing to make an effort at total liberation whatever the price. There are suggestions, also, in Turner's life that could add insights into why W. E. B. DuBois wrote in his diary when he was yet in his twenties that his life would be devoted to the upbuilding of his race; and why Martin Luther King chose to speak in mission-oriented terms. The list of powerful black speakers and leaders could be checked for Turneristic tendencies. One could ask, Did Marcus Garvey see himself as savior of the black race?

Did Adam Clayton Powell? While it would be impossible to argue that all black leaders see themselves as saviors, Nat Turner provides us with an excellent portrait of a revolutionary who viewed himself in such fashion.

Captured by a keen messianism which served as the most instrumental motive in his violent uprisings he became, during his brief war against sin and evil, God's vice-regent to cleanse the earth of anti-Christ. In his mind it was clear that this was to be a classic battle, right against wrong, good against evil, whether he won or lost. Because of his reliance upon the book of *Revelation* it is important to see the primary theme of that book. Conflict dominates the narrative culminating in the ultimate conflict between good and evil. The struggle is not peaceful, but carried out through war and revenge. The urgency of its message is extremely critical making instant identification with any period in human history but having a special significance for slaves under the rule of slave owners. "Fear God, and give glory to him; for the hour of his judgment is come" may have been the urgent language which moved Turner and caused him to work out the drama of death. *Revelation* is a spectacular book. The actors are varied; angels, spirits, the Lamb symbolizing Christ, the beast and Babylon symbolizing Satan and evil. Treading the boards at center stage in the conflict Turner sees himself as a key agent in the final victory of God over Satan.

In his *Confessions* he alludes to, draws parallels with and assigns his primary motivation for killing whites to the fulfillment of prophecies. He mentions that when he was three or four years old, he told something to his peers which his mother overhearing said "had happened before I was born." As a prophet deriving responsibility and authority from God as had John on the Isle of Patmos 1800 years before, Turner proclaims his predestination and outlines his duty. Thus he introduces his narrative by remarking, "I must go back to the days of my infancy and even before I was born."[1] From indications given by Turner in his address to Gray it seems that, as a child, he was not discouraged from claiming supernatural powers. In fact his parents and others exclaimed he would surely be a prophet for the "Lord had shewn him things that had happened before his birth."

According to his testimony he was twenty-two or so before the Spirit spoke directly to him. Three times he received the message "Seek ye the kingdom of Heaven and all things shall be added unto you." Of course, if he could read as he says he could then this statement may well have been one that he read in the Bible at various times. There is little reason to believe that this statement was more than a part of his regular Bible readings. On the basis of this "revelation", he claims that he was "ordained" for some great purpose in the hands of the Almighty. Once again in his *Confessions* he allows us to see the messianistic trait emerging from his character. Knowing his mission, and believing himself to be the leader of the mission, he began preparing his fellow slaves for the insurrection, "I now began to prepare them for my purpose, by telling them something was about to happen that would terminate in fulfilling the great promise that had been made to me . . . ." It is not too much to ask of the slaves that they believe him. Many slaves were extremely superstitious and Turner came prepared with more "hard evidence" than most that he was somehow ordained of God to carry out this task. In addition there were always more people ready to be believers than there were people prepared to be "messiahs" with the almost certain possibility of martyrdom.

During the time of the Spirit's revelations to him, Turner escaped from an overseer and hid in the woods and likely would have made it to freedom had he not reconsidered his duty. He had to fulfill the purpose which had been laid out for him. Subsequently he returned to his overseer with the internal conflict for freedom and obedience, not so much to the overseer but to God, raging within him. Further revelations delineating his purpose were made known to him through an additional vision. He saw ". . . white spirits and black spirits engaged in battle, and the sun was darkened—the thunder rolled in the Heavens, and blood flowed in the streams." What Turner apparently saw on the fields of Heaven was the prelude to the ultimate conflict God was to have with the Prince of the World, Satan. Black and white spirits in their most elemental dimensions probably represented the forces of good and evil. Whether Turner intended to change the commonly accepted functions of those words in American society where white represents good and black represents evil is not clear. Another explanation might reduce the complexity by suggesting that Turner was simply speaking about black and white humans in earthly warfare. This explanation dispenses with the one functional concept of the words "black" and "white" in a moral context while not totally evading the question of slavery's victims and victimizers as representatives of good and evil. Conceivably, Turner's familiarization with *Revelation* may have caused him to report a close facsimile of the fifth chapter where seven white angels poured out the wrath of God against the evils of the earth and the rivers became blood. Whether this is true or not, Turner perceived himself as God's judgment upon the whites who held blacks in servitude.

Immediately following the vision, a voice cried out saying, "Such is your luck, such you are called to see, and let it come rough or smooth, you must surely bare it" Once again the "messianic call" comes to Turner; he cannot reject it and reports "I now withdrew myself as much as my situation would permit, from the intercourse of my fellow servants, for the avowed purpose of serving the Spirit more fully." Leading the life of a prophet, thinking, meditating, and plotting, Nat Turner became obsessed with his mission. The language is that of a man possessed; a man completely controlled and convinced by visions and self-persuasion. During this period of withdrawal, like John the Baptist in the wilderness, the Spirit revealed to him the "knowledge of the elements, the revolution of the planets, the operation of tides, and changes of the seasons."

In order to perform the work of God he had to be made perfect. And from the beginning of his life that had been God's plan for him, thus he was finally made perfect in preparation for the mission. Convinced of his perfection he could conceive no wrong nor commit any crime, therefore the handiwork of death which was to be manifest at his hands was God ordained. And like "messianic spirits" before and after him he moved in an artificial environment created by his own deception and maintained by that of his followers. More pressing than ever now, the cataclysm stood in the wings awaiting the signal from Heaven. Turner details the signs that led to his eventual revolt:

> . . . while laboring in the field, I discovered drops of blood on the corn as though it were dew from heaven—and I communicated it to many, both white and black, in the neighborhood—and I then found on the leaves in the woods hieroglyphic characters, and numbers, with the forms of men in different attitudes, portrayed in blood, and representing the figures I had seen before in the heavens. And now the Holy Ghost had revealed itself to me, and made plain the miracles it had shown me—For as the blood of Christ had been shed on this earth, and had ascended to heaven for the salvation of sinners, and was now returning to earth again in the form of dew—and as the leaves on the trees bore the impression of the figures I had seen in the heavens, it was plain to me that the Saviour was about to lay down the yoke he had borne for the sins of men, and the great day of judgment was at hand.

Blood like dew from heaven, hieroglyphics portrayed in blood, and men in different attitudes indicate an interrelationship between violence and perhaps various degrees of sinfulness. Later in the narrative Turner says that he saw human forms in blood on trees in the forest. The terrible battle between good and evil was now being carried to earth to be waged by Turner against sinful men. His statement that Christ was returning to earth in the form of dew seems to suggest the constancy and pervasiveness of God's will. Continuing to prepare himself for the mission he was baptized by the Spirit.

On the 12th of May, 1828 Turner heard "a loud noise in the heavens, and the Spirit instantly appeared . . ." saying to him that the "Serpent was loosened, and Christ had laid down the yoke he had borne for the sins of men," and that he "should take it on and fight against the Serpent for the time was fast approaching when the first should be last and the last should be first." While the meaning of these statements is exceptionally complex, it would seem that if in fact the day of judgment was at hand, God himself would deal out punishment for the sinners. However, it is possible that in Turner's theological system, only men, as God's agents, could carry out providential decrees on earth. Therefore when the Serpent was loosened Turner as God's viceroy had to rise up and slay him regardless of the consequences. Such was the divine mission that obsessed Nat Turner from early childhood to maturity and blossomed into the revolt he led in 1831.

Turner was an astute man with keen intelligence. He had learned to read and write when it was illegal for slaves to have books or for whites to teach them the alphabet. Native intelligence had early marked him as a leader of his peers. What made him believe that he could carry out the mission? Certainly the odds were against any overthrow of the organized slave system and its sympathizers. But Turner had the precedents of *Revelation* on his side. If God had laid Babylon to waste "in one hour," then surely he could oversee the triumph of Turner's forces. God was clearly on his side. And there was also an implied promise of support, "And all the trees of the field shall know that I the Lord have brought down the high tree, have exalted the low tree, have dried up the green tree, and have made the dry tree to flourish." Furthermore, success was relative and after all Turner asked, "Was not Christ crucified?" In his mind martyrdom contained the very seeds of victory, he had only to plant his message deeply.

Although the indomitable messianism moved in his mind and stirred his emotions, Turner seemed to sense the impossibility of total liberation of the slaves. The language of finality betrays his bloody heroics; and a ritualized farewell supper, like Christ's before the cleansing campaign may well have suggested his reservations. Actually he did not see his battle merely in the secular sense of a slave insurrection. When asked by Thomas Gray to give an account of his activities he replied, "Sir, you have asked me to give a history of the motives which induced me to undertake the late insurrection, as you call it." He continued to present his narrative in the metaphysics of a holy war.

Nat Turner's messianism was expressed with unflinching candor. He was God's warrior and there could be no other mission for him than the one outlined by Heaven. Diversions came often but not successfully. Belief in his own righteousness and perfection went with him to the gallows. Regardless of what men did to his body, his spirit would reside in peace and glory with God. Even Thomas Gray had to notice with awe Turner "clothed with rags and covered with chains; yet daring to raise his manacled hands to heaven, with a spirit soaring above the attributes of man."

Reliance upon sacred and traditional authority as collaborators of his predestination more firmly established for him his call to battle. In careful examination of Turner's own words and their parallels in biblical literature, one finds that his motivations had strong roots in Christian theology. In his description of his child-hood, the solidarity he felt with the environs, the approval and support received from his parents, grandmother, owner and peers engineered a solid foundation for a powerful ego and an unbreak-able spirit. As an infant he was a person of unusual and gifted talents. Telling his peers about an event which had occurred before his birth brought astonishment and praise of his seemingly inherent ability to see into the past. His parents strengthened his belief that he had supernatural powers by saying that he "was intended for some great purpose, which they had always thought from certain marks on (his) head and breast." Hence the emer-gence of a messianic self-concept which flowered with each an-nouncement of support and approval and became crucial in the latter, more cognitive phase of planning.

While the mission-oriented spokesman, such as Woodrow Wilson became during his League of Nations Campaign, is com-mon, the spokesman possessed from youth with the idea of mission is rare. Such a man was Nat Turner. Obviously proud of his youth and seeing in it clues to his mission, he devoted much time to describing his formative years. Of his precociousness, he stated:

> My grandmother, who was very religious, and to whom I was much attached—my master, who belonged to the church, and other religious persons who visited the house, and whom I often saw at prayers, noticing the singularity of my manners, I suppose and my uncommon intelligence for a child, remarked I had too much sense to be raised, and if I was, I would never be of any service to anyone as a slave—To a mind like mine, restless, inquisitive and observant of everything that was passing, it is easy to suppose that religion was the subject to which it would be directed, and although this subject principally occupied my thoughts—there was nothing that I saw or heard of to which my attention was not directed. The manner in which I learned to read and write, not only had great influence on my own mind, as I acquired it with the most perfect ease, so much so, that I have no recollection whatever of learning the alphabet—but to the astonishment of the family, one day, when a book was shewn to me to keep me from crying, I began spelling the names of different objects—this was a source of wonder to all in the neighborhood, particularly the blacks—and this learning was constantly improved at all opportunities.

Religion figures heavily in this statement and must be explored in view of the intellectual poverty of plantation life. As an important cultural component of southern society, both black and white, religion provided the primary diversion from constant work and boredom. Furthermore, for the slave the biblical lessons and stories, even in the restricted context imposed by white censors, supplied an idea of human relationships. In addition the Bible gave guidelines from which inferences and judgments could be made about the immediate social milieu. The only book Turner was perhaps ever able to read in depth, because of accessibility, was the Bible which stimulated his imagination and at every turn supported his call to mission. What Turner saw as overwhelming approval from his peer group also confirmed his ideas of mission. He says, "I was not addicted to stealing in my youth, nor have ever been—yet such was the confidence of the Negroes in the neighborhood, even at this early period of my life, in my superior judgement, that they would often carry me with them . . . to plan for them." Thus as a child he exercised leadership skills which were approved and applauded by his peers. This approval by his peers at such an early age was sure to remove any doubts he may have had later about his calling.

What surfaces in Turner's *Confessions* as a belief in his mission to alleviate black suffering marks a black messianism which has occasionally appeared in the rhetoric of black spokesmen. Apparently the images employed and statements made in verbal discourses betray the speakers' awareness of their people's oppression. In this context it is not difficult for one born with acute perception, able to discern the complexities of the black socioeconomic situation, to earnestly desire to remove the shackles from the oppressed. Of such quality were men such as Charles Remond, Frederick Douglass and William E. B. Dubois. Other blacks have gone beyond this earnestness to become obsessed with black salvation. Of this stripe were Nat Turner, Booker T. Washington, Marcus Garvey, Malcolm X and Martin Luther King. It is not too much to say that each of these men became possessed with a certain vision, a possibility, a hope in the midst of abundant despair. Epitomizing black messianism Nat Turner was both person and process and his *Confessions* remains to document the language of men in tune with the desires and needs of a people.

## NOTES

1. Peter I. Rose, ed. *Americans from Africa: Old Memories, New Moods.* New York, Atherton Press, 1970, p. 79. All quotations are from this text.

# 10

## BLACK RENAISSANCE AND NEGRITUDE

*By*

S. OKECHUKWU MEZU

On October 21, 1850, Sainte-Beuve set out to define classicism with a great deal of hesitation. "A delicate question," he said, "and one to which according to the time and age, one could very well propose rather diverse solutions. Someone asked me the question today, and I would like to try if not to solve it, at least to examine it, to explore it in front of the readers, even if only to engage in a search for a solution and if I can, to make clearer your and my conception of the subject." Sainte-Beuve went on to say that classicism meant a different thing for the Romans, and for the modernists during the reign of Louis XIV or even when the word classicism was defined with respect to Romanticism. Sainte-Beuve finally concluded that every epoch, every reader, will very likely maintain his own definition of classicism. This is very true of negritude.

Montaigne in his essay, "De l'Expérience" said also that "no two men have ever judged in the same way the same thing, and it is impossible to see two opinions exactly similar, not only in different people, but in the same man at divers times". Critics are essentially human and are likely to judge issues differently. Negritude means something different to every one and each writer or critic sees in the word what is of interest to him. The marxist looks at it in economic terms, in terms of conflict and class struggle. Thus the marxist equates various aspects of the negritude movement as revolutionary or conservative.

Jean-Paul Sartre in his article "Orphée noir" sees the movement as a struggle to overthrow the oppressive forces of cultural domination, a struggle similar to the proletarian effort to dethrone the

capitalist structure by replacing it with the dictatorship of the
proletariat or a classless society. But whereas the proletarian revolt
is economic and physical, the negritude revolt is intellectual and
humanistic since the values at stake are not economic and material
but cultural and aesthetic. The negritude effort therefore is to
implant a "dictatorship" of black cultural values that will naturally
lead to a non-race-conscious society.

The anthropologists, on the other hand, especially the essen-
tialists amongst them, see the negritude movement basically as a
cultural assertion and manifestation of the old Africa in the
modern world. An attempt is made to find, and often when they
do not quite exist, to create a sort of life force that supposedly
governs the actions and reactions of the black man. The anthro-
pologist sharing this view then equates negritude as the black or
the African way of writing, the African or black world view,
*Weltanschauung, vision du monde.* Any black writer that does not
quite fit into the general pattern established by the essentialist is
considered one who has abandoned the basic and all-embracing
philosophy of his people.

For some sociologists, negritude is basically the result of the
intermingling of the social forces of the century. It is a result of
the conflict between the old and the new, the effort to conserve
and modernize, the struggle between races, the color problem which
William Du Bois at the beginning of the century said would be
the major problem facing the generations to come.

Negritude is thus seen as the sudden sometimes shocking realization by the black man that he is black and that his color is no
longer accidental but substantial and consequential, and perhaps
fatal. Negritude thus becomes a type of literary ghetto in the
Western world, as revealing, depriving and exploited as the urban
ghettoes of contemporary cities. Some psychologists see negritude
as some kind of sublimation, an outpouring of centuries of repressed
feelings simmering in the collective unconscious, feelings that have
finally found expression in a unique kind of way in literary creation. Persecution complex, transference, the other, usually the
white man, form the solid or rather shaky basis for this literature.
Such a view would make the literature of negritude a therapeutic
process favouring greatly the creation of poetry and the writing
of autobiographical novels. The individual psychoanalyses himself
in order to save himself from madness. The writer lays the blame
on the other, the oppressor, the white man, in order to justify the
status of his people if not his own.

But there is also the traditional critic who sees negritude as a literary phenomenon, a humanism that symbolizes an epoch, that describes an era and characterizes a certain generation. Negritude, the traditional critic contends, should rightfully take its place at least in African, if not in black and world literary history, just like its great antecedents in the western culture, movements like the Renaissance, Classicism, Romanticism, Symbolism and Surrealism.

There is certainly an element of truth in these various definitions of the idea, the notion, the concept, the movement of negritude, for it is all of these things.

But each definition, each view, each approach, in wishing to be exclusive does injustice to the whole idea and tells only a partial truth. It was Aristotle who wrote in Tome I, Book II of his *Metaphysics* that no one can grasp adequately the truth, or even miss it completely. Each philosopher, he continued, finds something to say about nature. In itself, this contribution is nothing without doubt, or of little importance, but the totality of the ideas and reflections produces fruitful results. To add to this, from a purely structural point of view, man is indivisible and cannot realistically be divorced from his society, the collective unconscious, traditions and progress, aspirations and realizations. The African or black writer of the negritude period is therefore both an individual and a product of his society, a cousin of the modern world of technological superinventions and a child of the traditional world of cosmic animis. He is both a product of colonialism and slavery as well as the independence movement and the struggle for equal rights; a victim of western prejudice and an heir of western enlightenment. He is in short the product of opposing forces, the unism of traditional African life and the dualism of centuries of western civilization. A fair examination of the meaning of negritude therefore should take into consideration all these varied and sometimes opposing forces and feelings—historical, sociological, economic, political and even psycho-somatic forces that try to shape and unshape individuals and nations. A brief literary history would perhaps best situate negritude in a structural world.

For centuries, for more than three thousand years, the white writer, writing for a white audience has written from a white point of view. Dante, Petrarch, Ronsard, Schiller, Lamartine, Eluard, Hugo, Spencer, Yeats, have been singing the beauty of the white world, in particular the white woman, her blond hair, her blue eyes, her white fingers, red lips and rosy cheeks that blush at the

sight of the loved one. The white writer has praised and glorified
this beauty because it is an integral part of his experience, his
white experience. The black woman rarely appeared in this
literature. When as in the case of Jeanne Duval, she plays an important role in the life of a poet Baudelaire, she is a prostitute and
her beauty is always considered satanic, her inspiration devlish, her
affection, the antipode of real love. A white angelic beauty like
Madame Sabatier, lofty, inaccessible, "pure", is set up in contrast
to her. And even with Jeanne Duval, Baudelaire's attention is not
on the woman as an individual. The prostitute is merely utilized
as an instrument of escape to the tropics. What counts is not the
beauty of her long hair but the associations it conjours and the
evocations it recalls. Sometimes also in the letters of Le Chevalier
de Boufflers to Madame la Comtesse de Sabran between 1778-1788,
mostly written from Senegal, a young black girl appears on the
European scene in a Parisian home but always as an ethnic
curiosity. Generally, the treatment of blacks in Western Literature has left much to be desired. Sometimes it is in the form
of biting irony, at other times caustic sarcasm and elsewhere bare-
faced racism. These are everywhere and are often found in the
most unlikely places, including Cervantes' *Don Quixote*, Mon-
tesquieu's *Esprit des Lois,* in Benjamin Franklin, Hegel, Rimbaud's
"Mauvais Sang" in *Une saison en enfer* and in William Blake's
"The Little Black Boy", in *Songs of Innocence* in which the poet
writes:

My mother bore me in the southern wild,
And I am black, but O! my soul is white;
White as an angel is the English child,
But I am black, as if bereav'd of light.

Later the prejudice against the black man would become more
pronounced and articulate with writers like Arthur de Gobineau
in his *Essai sur l'inégalité des races humaines* (1854) and with
Gustave Le Bon in his *Lois psychologiques de l'évolution des
peuples.*

Whites for a long time did all the writing that was done and
most of the reading too. Coupled with all these, whites created
quite a few things and discovered many more including the dark
continent of Africa, "dark" in color and intelligence. Whites set up
various scales based upon their own experiences. One of these
scales is the solar hierarchy within which, arbitrarily, white was
a symbol of glory and joy while black became synonymous with
sorrow and mourning. Whiteness became associated with the
beauty of the day and darkness with sorrows and hallucinations of

the night. The useless member of a group became also the *black-sheep of the family*. Even Arthur Rimbaud in his colored audition unconsciously underscored this phenomenon in his assignment of properties to white and black:

(A: Noir)
A, Noir corset velu des mouches éclatantes
Qui bombinent autour des puanteurs cruelles,
Golfes d'ombres

(E: Blanc)
E, candeurs des vapeurs et des tentes
Lances des glaciers fiers, rois blancs, frissons d'ombelles.

In addition to all the other disadvantages, there was also the slave trade which snatched from Africa over four hundred million blacks and put them in plantations in the Americas and the West Indies. Not satisfied perhaps with these indignities, the whites came also to Africa to colonize and exploit the area and fourteen small European "nations" divided amongst themselves in Berlin in 1886 the gigantic continent, the "tribes" of Africa that had escaped the mass enslavement of their people. Just as in America, the slave owners made no effort to understand the feelings of their slaves, their customs and their attitude to life and used them just as animals of burden, the men for their economic welfare, the women for their sexual gratification, so too in Africa, the French amongst other people around 1906 introduced the policy of assimilation which sought to make every black African within their sphere of influence a little white Frenchman, beginning with courses on the history of their "ancestors, the Gauls of Roman times". The British for their part, generally left the people alone as long as they did not revolt against their rule. But sometimes they created chiefs where there were none, amongst the Igbos for instance; and deposed them where they had centuries of customs, history and royalty behind them, the Obas of Lagos for instance. The course of history and literature was fine as long as there was no challenge to this white view of the world. *Blanchitude* reigned supreme because there was no *negritude* to challenge it. The white audience was not aware of this or purposely closed its eyes to it because light becomes light only in the presence of darkness. A crisis, an existentialist crisis was necessary to shock the world into the conscious realization of the black presence.

## THE BLACK RENAISSANCE

This black presence became felt at the middle of the nineteenth century. One can really speak of a *Black Renaissance* in literature and the arts. The 1848 abolition of the slave trade gave moment to this movement and that date can be considered a landmark in the black Renaissance movement as 1453 was to the European Renaissance of the 16th century. Before then, the Negro's conception of self was always based on comparison with the white man. In the words of William Du Bois in *Souls of Black Folk*

> After the Egyptian and Indian, the Greek and Roman, the Teuton and Mongolian, the Negro is a sort of seventh son, born with a veil, and gifted with second-sight in this American world—a world which yields him no true self-consciousness but only lets him see himself through the revelation of the other world. It is a peculiar sensation, this double-consciousness, this sense of always looking at one's self through the eyes of others, of measuring one's soul by the tape of a world that looks on in amused contempt and pity."
>
> (Souls of Black Folk, *Three Negro Classics*, pp. 214-215)

Booker T. Washington, writing about the Reconstruction period in America, emphasized the importance of Latin at the beginning of the period. Two ideas were constantly agitating the minds of the colored people, or at least the minds of a large part of the race. One of them, he says was the craze for Greek and Latin learning, and the other was a desire to hold office. Then, he continues, there was a feeling that a knowledge, however little, of the Greek and Latin languages would make one a very superior human being, something bordering almost on the supernatural. This search for Greek antiquity will sooner or later give rise to another search equally vital and more pertinent and relevant, the quest for their own historical sources, the quest for Africa and black values, the height of which will come at the turn of the century.

In 1897, for example, Alexander Crummel organized the Washington Negro-American Academy, a movement of defense to rally black intellectuals of America for the sake of promoting research on problems affecting the black man. In 1900, a lawyer from Trinidad, H. Sylvester Williams, with the support of Bishop Alexander Walters of the African Methodist Episcopal Zion Church, a black separatist church, organized the first Pan-African Congress. In the United States of America, following a manifesto launched in 1905 by William Du Bois, the Niagara Falls conference was called and after further reunions gave rise to the National Association for the Advancement of Colored People (N.A.A.C.P.) in 1910. Through its Journal, *The Crisis* (1909), this organization was able to influence and spur on cultural awakening of the black man in United States. The black man was awakening from a prolonged sleep. He was looking for a way of coming out of his shell, of getting rid of his lethargy. More conscious of his individuality, he wanted to liberate himself and once free to liberate his brethren. The black man was no longer ready to accept as a dogma all that is brought to him by religion or history. He was no longer satisfied with being a *slave* or even an *emancipated slave* in America and a *native* or even an *educated native* in Africa. He was no longer ready to submit himself to western values abroad and suffer colonial domination on the motherland. And colonial domination there was for by 1902, the map of the black continent showed an Africa divided among the so-called European powers: England, France, Germany, Portugal, Belgium, Italy, Turkey, Spain. Only Morocco, Ethiopia and Liberia were independent. As if to emphasize its decision to stay forever in Africa, for administrative and economic reasons, France was creating federations in Africa. The French West African Federation in 1904 and the French Equatorial African Federation in 1910. England followed in 1914 with the creation of the Federation of Nigeria, the *Amalgamation* of the Northern, and Southern Protectorates and the Colony of Lagos.

On the other hand, the black man, the African in Africa, his descendants in the new world, were in direct contact with the white man. Africans undertook voyages of discovery and at the turn of the century, the black intellectual will discover unexplored lands, the unexplored new lands of Europe and America, the slave jungles of America that brutalized and cannibalized millions of their relations, the native belligerence and barbarism of the white European that would be reconfirmed in 1914. Having discovered these new worlds, the African will never cease to explore these territories, to study them, analyze them, and unmask them. A new horizon was spreading before the world. It is in this context that one should examine the writings of Wilmot Blyden, William Du Bois, some aspects of the teachings of Booker T. Washington and the politics of Marcus Garvey with his "Back to Africa" movement, which sought to repatriate blacks to the African continent. Blacks intensified their formation, at this period, of black separatist churches as a protest against segregation in the white dominated protestant churches. These cultural, political and religious agitations of various kinds manifested a new sentiment.

Though separated from it by four centuries, this movement can be compared to the European Renaissance, especially the French one, of the sixteenth century, the *white Renaissance*. That renaissance marked a break with the Middle Ages, the *Dark Ages*, the mode of thinking, accepted ideas. It marked a new consciousness on the part of the white humanist who discovered that his white patrimony went back to Greco-Roman times. This discovery of the self on the part of the European did not come suddenly but due to a long transition and as a result of disparate movements and more particularly to the flight of artists towards the West following the capture in 1453 by the Turks of Constantinople. The idea here is not to set up in this twentieth century an analogy of events in Europe in the 16th century but the similarity is nevertheless real. For the black man of the twentieth century, the 1848 abolition of slavery can be considered as the major incident that unleashed the movement.

Though emancipation in the United States came later, it is recognized that 1848 signalled a new age of greater militancy and radicalism in the abolitionist movement with Frederick Douglas, up till then basically a moderate and an advocate of moral suasion, increasingly adopting the philosophies of the militant John Brown and the fiery Henry Garnet who exhorted his people in these terms:

> Brethren, arise, arise! Strike for your lives and liberties. Now is the day and the hour. Let every slave throughout the land do this, and the days of slavery are numbered. You cannot be more oppressed than you have been; you cannot suffer greater cruelties than you have already. *Rather die freemen than live to be slaves.*

Just as the geographical discoveries of the European Renaissance enlarged the horizons and supposedly the minds of the Europeans, the voyages for study and research, for campaigns and diplomacy of Africans and black Americans in Europe, of black West Indians in America, Europe and Africa, revealed a new world to them. These future humanists will illuminate the way for future black scholars, writers and artists. What Benjamin Banneker tried to do with science, Wilmot Blyden battled to demonstrate with his humanism. Wilmot Blyden, of *pure Negro descent from the Igbo tribe* (like Olauda Ekweano, better known as Gustavus Vassa, author of *The Interesting Narrative of the Life of Olaudah Equiano or Gustavus Vassa the African, Written by Himself—1789*), wrote *A Vindication of the African Race: being a brief examination of the argument in favour of African Inferiority* (1857) and *The Negro in Ancient History* (1869).

The two Renaissance movements encouraged a critical approach to life and brought about a certain kind of rupture with the past. New modes of worship were opened as man sought to free himself from the strong arms of decadent tradition. As the

African Methodist and Episcopal churches multiplied in America, and as the English in Africa continued to use christianity to destroy cherished African traditions, Wilmot Blyden advocated the establishment of Africa-based churches.

In fact the United Native African Church was formed in 1891. A new liberal humanism was bringing down the rigid walls of traditional erudition. In the European Renaissance, more important than the awakening consciousness on the part of the individual, the race and the nation; more important than the rupture with the ancient political and religious order was a new humanism, a new quest for pagan antiquity. This quest in Europe of the sixteenth century gave rise to new scholarship and in turn influenced the literary style as well as styles in painting and sculpture. At the turn of the century, the black man also wanted, during his Renaissance, to glorify his past, his "pagan" antiquity, the past for long lost and only recently rediscovered due to the tireless efforts of black humanists. There was a new sense of being, a new optimism developing. The black man at the beginning of the century recognized that Africa was not a continent without culture and civilization but on the contrary, the source of cultures, the living museum of ancient civilizations. Africa was not a *tabula rasa*. Black humanists had spoken and spoke about the contributions of Africa to civilization: Tertulian, Augustine of Hippo, J. Africanus Horton and Wilmot Blyden spoke about Africa's contributions to Egyptian and Greek civilizations. The kingdoms of Ghana, Songhai, Biafra, Bini, Mali as well as the universities of Timbucktu and the art centers of Ife and Ugbo-Ukwu would be resurrected.

As the European Renaissance gave rise to new forms of art and music, the Black Renaissance and the discovery of African art would give rise to the Cubist Movement in painting. As early as 1907 Pablo Picasso in his *Femme* (sketch for *Les Demoiselles d'Avignon*) and in the same year the masterpiece itself, *Les Demoiselles d'Avignon,* was opening a new era in modern painting. African influence is evident in his *Figure* (Paris 1907) and *Figurine* (Paris 1908) the latter in bronze. In his painting and in his sculpture, just as in traditional African art, Picasso tried to destroy the physical form in order to capture and suggest the essential quality of the subject, which exists not in time and space but in the immateriality of life. In music also, the beginning of the century marked the ascendency of jazz and blues and in Paris of *la béguine* a West Indian dance popularized by Josephine Baker.

European white scholars stepped into the show also as Leo
Frobenius, Maurice Delafosse, Henri Labouret, (in Africa) Ferdi-
nand Ortiz in Cuba began their ethnological or anthropological
studies of the black races, sympathetic, though still from the
European optique. William Du Bois contributed also his history
book *The Negro* (1915) as *The Association for the Study of Negro
Life and History* was formed in Washington, D.C. African civilization became an interesting field of study and political and
missionary volunteers were everywhere. Even Albert Schweitzer,
representing *Dives* (Luke 16: 19-31), the white man endowed
with all the benefits of "culture and science", left in 1913 for
Gabon in Africa to help *Lazarus*, representing the Negro, exploited
and oppressed and lacking even "European" medicine for his
disease and pain, the consequences of his oppression. African
artifacts graced Parisian and London living rooms and several
special editions of magazines were consecrated to Africa. Journal-
ists vulgarized the discoveries or the writings of the anthropologists.
In America, *The Crisis* played a leading role in the cultural awakening of the new world. On its staff then were Dr. Du Bois, James
Weldon Johnson, Walter White and Jessie Fauset.

The culmination of these movements, in literature at least, was
the Harlem Renaissance in New York and over in Europe the
Negritude Movement in Paris. The Harlem Renaissance, a period
in the greater movement of Black Renaissance, unleashed a black,
vibrant and creative energy. Inspired by black humanists, black
writers emerged and successfully challenged the system imposed
by white writers on the literary world. The year 1925 can be
considered the summit of the movement in Harlem. Alain Locke
was certainly one of its most articulate exponents, at least from
the theoretical point of view. Describing this phenomenon, in "The
New Negro", in *The New Negro: An Interpretation* (1925), he
writes:

> In the last decade something beyond the watch and guard of
> statistics has happened in the life of the American Negro and the
> three norms who have traditionally presided over the Negro problem
> have a changeling in their laps. The Sociologist, the Philanthropist,
> the Race-leader are not unaware of the New Negro, but they are
> at a loss to account for him. He simply cannot be swathed in their
> formulae. For the younger generation is vibrant with a new psy-
> chology; the new spirit is awake in the masses, and in the very
> eyes of the professional observers is transforming what has been
> a perennial problem into the progressive phases of contemporary
> Negro life.

Alain Locke spoke of the migrant masses shifting from the countryside to the city, hurdling several generations of experience at a

leap. He spoke about the changing life-attitudes and self-expression of the young Negro, in his poetry, his art, his education and his new outlook, full of poise and greater knowledge of what it is all about. What Alain Locke articulated philosophically, Claude McKay described in his novel, *Banjo,* a marvellous apologetics of black culture.

A whole new vocabulary was introduced into the field of literature. Certainly, had Phyllis Wheatley lived during the period of the Black Renaissance, her poetry would have been radically different. James Weldon Johnson in "O Black and Unknown Bards" wrote:

> O black and unknown bards of long ago,
>     How came your lips to touch the sacred fire?
> How, in your darkness, did you come to know
>     The power and beauty of the minstrel's lyre?
> Who first from midst his bonds lifted his eyes?
>     Who first from out the still watch, lone and long,
> Feeling the ancient faith of prophets rise
>     Within his dark-kept soul, burst into song?

There is no revolution, as of yet, from the point of view of syntax and versification but in that poem already a new set of vocabulary is introduced into the literary world. *Black, Darkness,* and similar words suddenly lose their traditional connotation in white literature.

In *God's Trombones: some Negro sermons in verse,* James Weldon Johnson will also introduce the Negro rhythm into literature. Describing a Negro preacher, James Johnson said:

> An electric current ran through the crowd. It was in a moment alive and quivering; and all the while the preacher held it in the palm of his hand. He was wonderful in the way he employed his conscious and unconscious art. He strode the pulpit up and down in what was actually a very rhythmic dance, and he brought into play the full gamut of his wonderful voice, a voice—what shall I say —not of an organ or a trumpet, but rather of a trombone; the instrument possessing above all others the power to express the wide and varied range of emotions encompassed by the human voice—and with greater amplitude. He intoned, he moaned, he pleaded—he blared, he crashed, he thundered. I sat fascinated; any more, I was, perhaps against my will, deeply moved; the emotional effect upon me was irresistible.

This is a combination of poetry, prose, song and music in the typical African fashion. The music is not only external but internal, conscious and subconscious. The sufferings of the race are depicted, the aspirations of the people are suggested. In a poetic trance, the preacher, like the *griot* of Senegal, the *onye-ntu* of Igboland, abandons himself, his whole being as a medium to the inspiration from within, from above, as he sings, chants, forecasts, foretells, admonishes, praises and castigates to prick the conscience of the wicked, encourage the suffering and the dying— and also to the fright of children awakened by his or her voice (pleading, intoning, crashing, shrilling, thundering, blaring, supplicating, moaning, fascinating, emotional, firm, irresistible, fading, dying . . . .) in the middle of the night.

Writers, then in America, who hesitated about the new movement were greatly encouraged by *The Souls of Black Folk* (1903) of William Du Bois, printed and reprinted over and over. William S. Braithewaite spoke for quite a few members of the race when in Locke's anthology, *The New Negro*, he wrote that *The Souls of Black Folk* "has more profoundly influenced the spiritual temper of the race than any other written in its generation."

The revolution in vocabulary continued. Countée Cullen in his "Tableau" would refer to the color black as "the sable pride of night" and Claude McKay would in "The Tropics in New York" tantalize the temperate and white world with the luscious freshness of tropical fruits:

Bananas ripe and green, and ginger root,
   Cocoa in pods and alligator pears,
And tangerines and mangoes and grape fruit,
   Fit for the highest prize at parish fairs.

In Jean Toomer's *Cane*, the color black loses also its derogatory connotations for Negro slaves are referred to as "dark purple ripened plums, squeezed, and bursting in the pine-wood air . . ." The River Seine, The Rhine and the Rhone will no longer dominate the literature of the future for there is a Langston Hughes to Speak of Rivers, the Nile, the Congo "ancient as the world and older than the flow of human blood in human veins". The Negro was no longer ashamed of his color. He was even ready to exhibit its beauty as Langston Hughes in "Jazzonia" published in *The Crisis*:

What jungle tree have you slept under,
   Midnight dancer of the jazzy hour?
What great forest has hung its perfume
   Like a sweet veil about your bower?

What jungle tree have you slept under,
   Dark-brown girl of the swaying hips?
What star-white moon has been your lover?
   To what mad faun have you offered your lips?

With Countée Cullen's "Heritage," the Negro will learn to speak with pride. The Sun will have the color of copper and black will become the symbol of royalty. The real revolution had been achieved in American literature, it would be up to the future generation to push this revolt to the point of anarchy, the total destruction of the white man's language, syntax and idioms, a total negation of white values and structures, a point achieved some thirty years later in the sixties, a polarization that will no doubt give rise to a synthesis of ideas, structures and styles.

Hopefully, words would recover their denotations or syntactical representations as blacks continue to push their racial pride to its logical conclusion and as whites begin to realize that there are other than white perspectives on life.

The wind of the American revolt, the Harlem Renaissance in Literature, was blowing all around Europe where a gradual re-examination of African civilization had already begun with the help of French and European writers, scholars and artists. Langston Hughes, William Du Bois and Claude McKay made several trips to Europe where they met blacks from Africa and the West Indies—Blaise Diagne, Dr. Leo Sajous, Paulette Nardal, Jean Price-Mars. Leo Sajous and Paulette through their review *La Revue du monde noir*, between November 1931 and April 1932, popularized the Harlem Renaissance through articles on black literature and civilization. One of their aims was to "create among the Blacks of the entire world, without distinction of nationality, a moral and an intellectual bond that will allow them to better love and understand one another fraternally, to defend more efficaciously their collective interests and to embellish their Race". The editors of the new publication were well aware of the movement in New York. They even knew about the Harlem review *Fire* (only one issue was ever published) edited by a Pleiade of Harlem writers—Wallace Thurman, Aaron Douglas, John P. Davis, Bruce Nugent, Gwendolyn Bennet, Zora Neale Hurston and Langston Hughes. In their Paris publication, they reproduced the words of Langston Hughes in the introduction:

> We younger Negro artists who create now intend to express our individual darkskinned selves without fear or shame. If white people are pleased, we are glad. If they are not, it doesn't matter . . . If colored people are pleased, we are glad. If they are not, their displeasure doesn't matter either.

At the same time in Paris were three young students, among many others, Leopold Senghor from Senegal, Aimé Césaire from the Martinique and Léon Damas from the Guadeloupe. They could not escape the ferment created by the interest in black civilization. They read every word published in *La Revue du monde noir* and held long discussions with the elder generation at the home of Paulette Nardal. Imbued with a new sense of mission, without a formal decision they set out to accomplish for the French-speaking black world what the Harlem writers had done for the English-speaking world.

Personal experience of racism in Europe reinforced their racial pride. The failure of European science and technology as well as its rationalism confirmed their newly-found belief that black civilization alone held the answer to man's future. These anti-racist feelings were redoubled by the growing racism in Germany, fascism in Italy and Spain and the struggle against the Machado regime in Cuba. In the midst of these developments, disturbed by the failure of white wisdom to prevent the First World War and its consequent disruption of society, the white writers themselves were turning to Surrealism for social and cultural salvation. The young students in Paris, Senghor in particular, saw in the sur-realist technique an imitation of the black African traditional poet. The Surrealist was out to bridge the gap between dreams and reality, science and fiction, the material and the spiritual world. They delved into their unconscious, after Freud had revealed it to them, to discover this world. The Senegalese Senghor could look down on them with scorn because, he argued, in Africa, man had not yet been divorced from his ancestors and his environment. When *La Revue du monde noir* ceased publication, another review came up, *Légitime Défense* edited by Etienne Lero and his group of friends, with a socialist and marxist orientation. Senghor, Cesaire and Damas with their friends organized their own magazine (1934/35) *L'Etudiant noir*. Like the Harlem *Fire* only one issue came to light. There, like their Harlem counter-parts, they sought to articulate their blackness irrespective of the reaction of white people and black people alike.

These and a combination of other forces gave rise to the literature of negritude. Any attempt to define the word *Negritude* must therefore take into consideration its origins and its place within the context of the development of the black civilization during the Black Renaissance.

# 11

## NOTES TO BLACK AMERICANS FROM
## AFRICAN LITERATURE IN ENGLISH

*By*

G. C. M. Mutiso

The black revolution is the universal attempt by Blacks to assert their cultural patterns and to begin to control their socio-political destiny. It is an attempt to mold people into a society with values which differ from those of white people who have been and continue to be the dominant power group. It is also an attempt to absorb technology and tame it.

African literature is literature written by black people, and I refuse to be drawn into an argument to determine whether a white person writing about an African society writes black literature. The fact is that there has been a great deal of literature written in Africa, particularly since World War II. There have even been major literary schools. The first important school was the Negritude School. It can be described as that school of literature primarily concerned with arguing the humanity of all black cultures, the exploiting rapacity of European culture, and finally, the brutalizing effects of technology. Its fathers and perpetuators have been primarily black intellectuals of the Francophone areas. The major ones have been Aime Cesaire, Leopold Senghor, David Diop, Chicaya U'Tamsi, Alioune Diop, Leon Damas and many more. Probably the roots of the Negritude School stem from the nature of the French colonial policy of assimilation of the few intellectuals and the great emphasis on French culture.

This paper was originally read in a slightly different form at Schomburg Library in Harlem, New York as part of the Columbia University Lecture series on Africa and Afro-Americans.

The other major grouping of African literature one can make is that of North Africa, meaning basically literature from Arabic-speaking Africa. This has been closed to most of us because the Arabic language is not as widely used as English or French.

Another major classification is the African literature of South Africa. It has been pointed out that it is protest literature at best. It protests against the inhuman society created by the insane racists of South Africa. Its setting is primarily urban. It catalogs the racism of South African society. Perhaps this literature would be easily understood by Blacks in the United States because of its two major component elements, urbanity and racism. Indeed one gets the feeling in talking with American Blacks that Peter Abrahams, Alex La Guma, Ezekiel Mphahlele, Brother Willie and many more South African wri'ers are well read and known. This is commendable because the black political revolution in a very basic way will not be completed as long as racist South Africa exists.

Finally, another body of African literature is the literature emanating from Anglophone Africa. It is paradoxical that the literature did not clearly espouse negritude as the literature from Francophone Africa. Perhaps the reasons lie in the nature of British colonization. The British did not seek to train intellectuals. They primarily trained bureaucrats and artisans. Indirect rule meant that they were not particularly interested in passing on to Africans English culture. As a matter of fact, from the British point of view, an African could never acquire culture.

Anglophone literature has been my primary research interest. I have sought to tie it to the Black revolution as defined earlier. The rationale for this linkage is the belief that socio-political theory may be derived from the literature. I think we should be aware that this kind of concern is rejected in the general political science tradition. Perhaps it is time we as blacks begin to move away from what is traditionally "academic" and not tied to the social requirements of our preparing ourselves to implement fundamental change in our communities and ultimately in civilization as a whole. The point is, we have to begin to define what is academic in terms of Black peoples' academic interests which to me are not necessarily the same as the interests of the traditional structures. We furthermore should demand that the ideas of black thinkers be taught to all our children at all levels. This is the only way we can insure their socialization to our Black ethic.

## DYSFUNCTIONAL COLONIAL EDUCATION

Colonial education was not supposed to produce thinkers. It was primarily geared to producing robots who were servile and obeyed the instruction of the master race. Amu Djoleto lucidly deals with the problem in his novel, *The Strange Man*.[1] The man is strange because he thinks and questions. The norm is to obey and submit; therefore, creative thinking or logical questioning are seen as deviant characteristics.

Mensa is the protagonist in the novel. He is, from a very early age, articulate. He questions everybody and everything. His parents see this as a good trait and encourage it. However, the local catechist—that despicable convert who did the dirty Christian work of running the bush churches and schools—is highly authoritarian. To save him from this tyrant, the parents decide to send Mensa to Accra, to stay with his father's cousin who is also a catechist and teacher. The parents hope that the relative will be more enlightened than the local catechist. In a letter to his cousin, Lomo, Anang explains Mensa's character:

> "I would rather let you know at once that Mensa is given to having his own way. This quite often gets him into trouble. Recently he castrated a fully-grown he-goat unauthorized and this has disturbed the village a bit. Personally I do not think this is a serious crime since his intention was to make the goat less mischievous. But he erred, I admit, in doing something that shouldn't be done. Such daring too is not expected of a boy his age. His conduct has led our catechist, your colleague, to believe that I am not capable of training my children. He has therefore threatened to see that Mensa reforms as quickly as possible and has urged my wife and myself to let him admit Mensa to his school after Christmas holidays.
>
> While my wife and I don't doubt his good intentions, we feel, however, that from what we've seen in the past, he will subject our son to constant caning. We are unable to accept this method as the best possible way of keeping our son out of mischief.
>
> My wife and I have therefore decided to ask you whether you'll be kind enough to have our son stay with you so that you can train him with kindness and understanding. Naturally, you as a teacher will know better how to train him. I, as a farmer, can only suggest."[2]

What the father does not know is that Lomo, the teacher, has been dehumanized by his training and feels, like the local catechist, that brutalizing the young is part of the educational process. In Lomo's house there live four children of his relatives besides his two, and they have to submit to harsh and rigid rules. The food is inadequate and thought is suppressed. The cathechist argues that, "if free thought was allowed to flourish, it would give a lot of trouble to civilized society. No good educational system should, no doubt, make a boy as docile as possible. It should make a boy a good diplomat, who would say he was not aware of something not because he was not really aware of it, but because he could not be proved to be aware of it; he must be the kind of boy who should specialize in manufacturing white lies as a means of profiting from it."[3]

Mr. Lomo's duty then is to bring this so-called good school system to be by terrorizing the students until they accept his values. It is ironic that on top of all that, the boys are required to go to church and memorize the sermons every Sunday, "rain or shine"!!

The techniques in school are far from relevant. Primarily all teaching involves rote memorization and deviance from this pattern leads to caning sometimes so brutal that the victim is unable to sit down. Most of the time is spent in meaningless marches and inspections of ears and nails.

For six years Mensa endures Mr. Lomo's insanity. By lying Mensa is able to avoid physical abuse. By stealing he manages to get basic necessities.

Mensa's brainwashing continues in high school, after the death of his father, where brutality of teachers and senior students is also an accepted norm. The emphasis here is always on obedience to those who are better than and therefore, above you. You serve them, you never question. In this totalitarian atmosphere Mensa becomes a victim of nervous tension. However, he perseveres and, eventually like most people out of high school, he joins the colonial service where young people who had been broken by the school system hang on like cobwebs to meaningless jobs.

The school training which forces students to develop the habits of lying and avoiding responsibility become relevant in the world of civil servants who intrigue against their honest colleagues in the colonial and post-colonial era.

Mensa, of course, is hardworking and not corrupt. This leads to other civil servants' resenting his deviance and therefore plotting against him. Mr. Roberts is the typical African civil servant. He identifies with the so-called modernity of Europe and not with traditional Africa. As a matter of fact, for thirty years he lives in Accra without going home[4] to the village of his birth. He gets enough money to spend on wine, women and song by intimidating the junior interpreters into giving him kickbacks, a survival technique learned in school.

Mensa, through perserverance and hard work saves money to build a house and educate his children. But he is always damned by the traditionalists and the corrupt and incompetent "moderns". These people are church-oriented in a perverted way, and they absolutely resent his achievements. When he dies they recognize his "weight" as we would say at home. Everyone ultimately recognizes his worth as a person and his integrity.

This rather long synopsis has been given to really illustrate the sigificance of education in the African colonial setting. Other writers like Joseph Wilfred Abruquah in *The Cathechist*,[5] and William Conton in *The African*,[6] make the same points. If we are to understand the social problems existing now, we have to go back and question what values have been taught in our school systems. We have to question the substance of the educational system. Clearly, Mensa and many more never heard of their African heritage in school. Clearly, too much regimentation led to a lack of initiative and thought. It was education for the *status quo*. Hence, we should not be surprised when today the African bureaucrats, politicians, and even intellectuals do not offer any significant statements on social change. It is the duty of the Black revolution to change all educational systems toward social relevance. We can teach this point to our students through black literature. Of course, I have not dealt with all the writers' comments on education, but in general, the observations treated here are common in the literature of the African Anglophone school. Acquainting Africans in America with what African writers have said about the educational system in colonial Africa is one way of giving them an understanding of the kinds of effects the educational system in America has had on them and consequently on the Black revolution.

## THE COMMUNAL ETHIC

Could I, early sequester'd from my tribe
Free a lead-tether'd scribe
I should answer her communal call
Lose myself in her warm caress
Intervolving earth, sky and flesh.[7]

The above quotation is by a modern intellectual who decries his breaking with the communal past. The communal concept dominates all aspects of African life. Dances are communal; worship is communal. Property was communal before the colonial era and there are today attempts to continue this tradition. This inherent bias toward the communal means that individualism has

always been seen as deviant. Obviously this can have a significant
impact on the nature of the institutions and life of a society.

Tradition plays a big part in reinforcing the communal ethic.
A father tells his son:

> With us, son, the word "why?" is not a common word. Our tradi-
> tion never gives an answer because it never asks the question. To
> it there is only one law in life and that is obedience.[8]

> Tradition is sacred. Custom is above all. To question tradition is
> sacrilege. If men do not respect tradition, how can society stand?
> How can we be proud of our forefathers and pass on our pride to
> our children? What would happen if you or I were allowed to
> change our ancient practices as we like? For us tradition is not a
> passing thing. It is the earth on which we breathe.[9]

> Tradition, as you say, is indeed a sword: but it is not a sword that
> destroys. It is the sword which protects us from the inroads of
> foreign and dangerous ideas.[10]

Thus the individual is always pitted against the tradition which
is communal. In individual acts like marriage, he is not free to
choose his partner or the manner of the marriage. To wit:

> We have our pride and must do as our fathers did. You see your
> mother? I did not pick her in the streets. When I wanted a woman
> I went to my father and told him about my need of her and he
> went to her father. Marriage is a family affair. You young people
> of today may think you are clever. But marriage is still a family
> affair.[11]

This overriding concern with tradition underlines the fact that
fear and insecurity accompany thoughts of change, particularly if
the change is pointing towards individualism. Some writers openly
point to this fear of individualism. "By sending his son to school
and college, he had already opened the way to new and startling
ideas."[12]

Austin J. Shelton, after studying Nzekwu's *Wand of the Noble
Wood*, Achebe's *No Longer at Ease*, and Soyinka's *The Lion and
the Jewel*, among others concludes that:—

> the value most clearly approved in these . . . works is traditional
> communal responsibility revealed partly in the condemnation of
> self-seeking individualism. Communal responsibility (to the extended
> family, the clan, the gods) is sanctioned by traditional African
> societies and furnishes the criteria whereby one can make judgments
> which will be correct and perform actions which will be justly
> rewarded. As a value system it is preferred to European individual-
> ism . . . When the African becomes acculturated he either loses a
> number of his communal values and substitutes for them European
> individualism, or adds the individualism on to his communalism.
> But adaptation to the European way can be disappointing, for such
> change often does not carry with it all the rewards anticipated
> by the African.[13]

Consider the predicament of the pharmacist Wilson, In Cyprian Ekwensi's *Beautiful Feathers*. As an individual he knows that the money he makes in his pharmacy must be reinvested if it is going to succeed. This is an illusion since

> the mild success of his enterprise brought the first flood of Yaniy's relatives with 'give me' hands outstretched. Their inlawness had become onesided, an  affair in which they as bride-givers become perpetual recipients of gifts and support from the bride-taker.[14]

One can ask whether a social system making this kind of demand is conducive to accumulation of wealth for development. In America, Black America, where rampant individualism has been the order of the day, maybe some communal concern is in order.

Sometimes strange self-sacrificing acts are performed in the name of communal traditions. Consider the case of the shooting of Benjamin-Benjamin in *One Man, One Machet*. He was a half-illiterate, crooked politician who preyed on the illiteracy of the papulation and swindled a lot of money. The colonial government could not punish him for lack of concrete evidence. However, Chief Olowokere shot him (and then shot himself). He explains,

> I shot and killed him . . . And I do not regret killing Benja-Benja. He was a crook. He ought to have been sent to jail for seven years for the amount of money he stole from the various amounts collected from the people.[15]

Here the Chief is pointing out that the communal code is higher than the concern for any individual or individuals. This is why he killed Benja-Benja and attempted to kill himself. The "higher" value was the society *in toto,* and not the two individuals.

Several points are worth noting. A "modern" African tends to accept the primacy of the communal over the individual, even though he may claim to accept the "European" principle of efficiency. One is not so sure that these are compatible. The communal ethic is not only accepted by the traditionalist but is shared by the moderns. J. P. Clark in lamenting the present state of affairs invokes "the communal gods at the gate."[16]

Those characters who are purely individualistic in African literature, whatever good they are doing, always end in tragedy. The writers in depicting them in this fashion are emphasizing the all pervasive nature of the communal ethic and are stressing the fact that during the process of change some will suffer.

On the tragic end of individualistic characters, consider Simi "of the lazy eyes." Here is an independent individualistic character who picks and chooses her lovers. She is urbanized and urbane. When she, after years of the game, picks Egbo as her favorite, he is taken away "by a simple college girl!"[17]

Another such character is Ochola in Grace Ogot's, *The Promised Land*. He is enterprising and therefore moves away from an area of high population density to richer agricultural land. Because he has left the communal (tribal) lands, after at first becoming wealthy, he becomes very sick and must leave the riches behind. The disease is regarded by the people as clearly linked to his stay on non-communal land.[18]

In Achebe's *Arrow of God*, Ezeulu, the priest of Ulu (a god) is individualistic. When he refuses the chieftainship offered by the colonial government, and also when, in spite of the insistence of the clan, he refuses, while in prison, to perform the symbolic act of eating the yams, an act which would permit the people to begin the harvest, tragedy follows. As the head priest, he is supposed to follow the tradition so as to avert disaster that is brought on by the waste of crops. When he defies tradition, misfortune strikes. Besides his other misfortunes, his son dies. What happens is the result of his rejection of the communal ethic as Achebe aptly sums up:

> So in the end only Umuare (the Village) and its leaders saw the final outcome. To them the issue was simple. Their god had taken sides with them against his headstrong and ambitious priest and thus upheld the wisdom of their ancestors—that no man, however great, was greater than his people. That no man ever won judgment against his clan.[19]

Obi Okonkwo, the hero of *Things Fall Apart* succumbs to a similar fate. Okonkwo has been entrusted with bringing up Ikemefuna, a hostage from another village. Ultimately, Ikemefuna must be sacrificed. Okonkwo is not supposed to have anything to do with the sacrifice but he accompanies them when the clan elders go to kill Ikemefuna. When Ikemefuna is struck and runs toward him he cuts him down because he was "afraid of being thought weak."[20] This is the beginning of tragedy. Later Okonkwo accidentally shoots and kills a clansman. He must be exiled and everything he owns has to be destroyed to appease the tribal gods.[21] This would not have been so bad if Okonkwo had not basically been motivated by the need to achieve wealth and status unlike his lazy father. This individualistic desire not to be a "nothing" like his father, is the explanation for his tragedies.

Concerning the social events surrounding death, Mopeli-Paulus points out that however repulsive ritual murder is, once a chief— in the name of the tribe—appoints one to do it, the communal obligation is higher than any individual's preference, with the corollary that ultimately it is the chief's responsibility— a point which many students of power and politics have missed.[22]

The ongoing fear of failing the communal obligation is found even in such an undertaking as education. A young boy beginning school tells us,

> My father went on to remind me that I have now started to climb a palm tree which was high and difficult to climb; that many were watching my progress, and much ripe fruit was awaiting me on the successful conclusion of my climb. He ended with the warning that if I failed to reach the top, those watching me, both living and the dead, would curse me for failing them. On the other hand, if I reached the top in order simply to gorge myself with fruit, I would surely become sick and fall to the ground and die. But if I returned to my people to share with them the fruits of my labors, then all would sing my praise and honor those who brought me to life.[23]

Note that even if he does well, the honor is not his but his family's, his clan's and his tribe's.

The primacy of the communal ethic sometimes works well in controlling deviants and forcing them into normalcy. Consider the case of the "drunkard" Danda in Nwanko's novel, *Danda*. He is not able to take care of himself or for that matter, his family (relatives). He remains single until well past the age of marriage but pressure builds up until he has to marry. Not only does he marry, but the pressure of his family ultimately channels his affairs into a semblance of stability. He reaches the highest *ozo*\* level, and so an undeserving character rises to the highest level of society because of communal coercion.[24]

On the other hand, the communal ethic definitely can hamper the general welfare by blocking those who want to work for the general good, because it is a

> Tyranny which gathers a whip
> From the timid crowd
> And (with their own dejected fears)
> Molests the weak.[25]

This tyranny can be misused as it is against Mr. Kalaa in Wilson Mativo's *Our True Speaker*, who seeks to oust the corrupt Mr. Malu from Parliament. The latter, at election time, exploits the rural population's desire for such trifles as candy and soda but does not work for the good of his constituents by providing such improvements as roads, schools and hospitals.[26] The same tyranny operates in *When Love Whispers*, to lead to an educated woman's

---

\*An Igbo social rank.

marriage to an illiterate chief just because she is going to have a
baby out of wedlock.[27]  Similarly, in the *Looming Shadow,* a
person is accused of witchcraft and practically the whole village
turns against him[28]

Finally, the individualist is, by definition, schizoid in African
literature. Whenever the individualist manages to break away
from the operational aspects of the communal ethic, he is haunted
by his action. Lombe, a civil servant, sees the city which gives him
the chance to escape the communal ethic as a trap. The experience
in the city turns out to be a costly one for Lombe who in the
exercise of his freedom takes up with a bar girl, impregnates her
and finds out ultimately that she is his step-sister. Lombe is
seriously shaken by these events and takes refuge in the village
where the communal ethic is strongest. He goes there "for a long
search".[29]

Three other major characters in African anglophone literature
demonstrate similar schizoid tendencies. One is Obi Okonkwo in
*No Longer at Ease.* Obi returns from the United Kingdom con-
fident he can withstand the pressure of the communal ethic, but
ultimately he admits that the clan organization has a claim on him.
His education was for them. Therefore he must reward them by
living up to their expectations of him—having a car, a good house,
and placing relatives in government positions. This ultimately
means that he must accept bribes to keep up with the "mukasas"
(Uganda's equivalent of the Joneses). After this we are not surprised
when he is accused of wrongdoing. The clan organization, however,
does not become angry, but rather berates him for being cheap—
not taking big bribes befitting his position![30]

A perfectly schizoid individualist character is Egbo, the fiery
aristocrat-nationalist, who works in the Ministry of Foreign Affairs
in Soyinka's *The Interpreters.* He broke with the communal ethic
when he refused to take title as the next in line for a tribal chieftaincy. Yet, he has kept in touch by saying:

> Perfunctory doles towards the Union of Osa Descendants . . .
> messages between the old man and himself . . . all these had built
> up ties surreptitiously . . . delegates too, to feel him out, sent by
> Egbo Onosa as he knew quite well—destiny they always said, you
> were destined . . . All these and much more . . . his one overwhelm-
> ing need to retain that link with some out-of-the-run existence . . .
> illicit pleasure at the thought that a kingdom awaited him when-
> ever he wanted it . . . And he only plunged again into the ancient
> lie of still sediments. How long will the jealous dead remain among
> us![31]

Reminded by Bandele that he himself made the choice to reject the title, Egbo elaborates for us the nature of choice open to the individualist in the African social milieu. It is unlike the choice in Western social thought. To wit:

> Even that choice is a measure of tyranny. A man's gift of life should be separate, an unrelated thing. All choice must come from within him, not from promptings of his past.[32]

This derives from the nature of his perception of what the past should be.

> "You continue to talk of the past as if it has no place with us."

> "It should be dead. And I don't just mean bodily extinction. No, what I refer to is the existing fossil within society, the dead branches on a living tree, the dead runs on the bole. When people die, in one sense or the other, it should not matter what they were to us. They owe the living a duty to be forgotten quickly, usefully. Believe me, the dead should have no faces . . . Is it impossible to seal off the past and let it alone? Let it stay in its harmless anachronistic unit so we can dip into it at will and leave it without commitment, without impositions! A man needs that especially when the present, equally futile, distinguishes itself only by a particularly objectionable lack of courage . . . I merely say that the dead should be better tucked away. They should not be interfered with because then they emerge to thrust terrifying dilemmas on the living. They have no business to make impositions on us."[33]

If this were all, it might be said that Egbo has rejected the communal ethic which argues that the "dead, the living and the yet to be born" have continuing symbiotic obligations. Egbo would then be individualistic in the Western sense. Yet he draws back from this position. He continues:—

> If the dead are not strong enough to be everpresent in our being, should they not be as they are dead? . . . But what are we then . . . to continue making advances to the dead? . . . Why should the dead on their part fear to speak to light?[34]

He is pulled by the attraction of tradition because he feels it has something to offer—but what? Culture? Opposition to the barbarity of politicians? He travels toward the traditional Kingdom intending to make peace, but on reaching very close,

> The spectre of generations rose now above him and Egbo found he would always shrink, although incessantly drawn to the pattern of the dead. And this waiting near the end of the journey, hesitating on the brink, whining as he admitted it—was it not exhumation of a better past? Belatedly thinking, who am I to meddle? Who? Except—and this counted for much—*that he knew and despised the age which sought to mutilate his beginnings.*
>
> And there was personal threat to his grandfather but then, he did not doubt that the old man understood the political risks and would accept reversals. And Egbo wished, if that could be all! If the fight were only political, nothing more. But Egbo had felt a virile essence, a redeeming grace in the old man and in that existence.

> And this was being destroyed, he knew, and by cozening half-men
> who came bloated on empty wind. There is also pride of race.
> Egbo said, "I am after all, an Egbo" . . . (he) had become different
> at this point, waiting to go on shore and grapple with his failure to
> insulate, different from the distant disillusionment, his fears for the
> dignity of his roots, and the fate of a burnt out fire-eater. He
> acknowledged it finally, this was the place of death. And admitted
> too that he was drawn to it, drawn to it as a dream of isolation,
> smelling its archaic menace, and the violent undertows, unable to
> deny its dark vitality.[35]

This search in the past involves rejecting the values of the
present, but it collides with individualism, as the rather extended
quotation suggests. Later Egbo catalogues the advantages of tribal
chieftaincy as polygamy, "hobby" power, and wealth accrued by
controlling smuggling routes, but in these he is not interested. He
is for abolishing the latter with the help of young people like
himself, but they are not interested since they are

> . . . (t)oo busy, although I've never discovered doing what. And
> that is what I constantly ask—doing what? Beyond propping up the
> herald-men of the future, slaves in their hearts and blubber-
> men in fact, doing what? Don't you ever feel that your whole
> life might be sheer creek-surface bearing the burden of folls, a
> mere passage, a mere reflecting medium of occasional sheer mass-
> controlled ferments beyond you?[36]

The writer most clearly points out in this passage that the
issue is not just the rejection of the traditional communal ethic,
but rather the creation of an atmosphere in society where people
acting as individuals can find a communal ethic, but will not
be dominated by the tyranny of tradition. He infers that the
failure to achieve the latter is tied to the ascendancy of irrelevant
politicians when "the winds of change blew them into power"[37]
and also the failure of the supremely individualistic intellectuals to
come to grips with their duty to the community. The same idea
is expressed by Patrick, a character in *Blade Among the Boys*.[38]

In summary, the primacy of the traditional communal ethic
as opposed to an individualistic ethic dominates literary expression
of the African socio-political milieu. Those characters who follow
the latter ethic are in one way or other eliminated, and the
intellectuals recognize that they have to break away and establish
a milieu where the primacy of the individual is clearly established
but with a collective social conscience which is not tyrannical.

Those in America involved in the Black revolution will
eventually have to anchor their movement on the concept that
community is of some value. This conclusion is reached because
all forms of statements for "Black Power" and "power to the
people" reflect an instinctive groping for unity among black people.

## NOTES

1. London: Heinemann 1967, p. 279.

2. *Ibid.,* p. 63.

3. *Ibid.,* p. 93.

4. *Ibid.,* p. 209.

5. London: Allen and Unwin. 1965

6. New York: New American Library. 1961

7. J. P. Clark, "Agbor Dancer," *Poems* (Ibadan: Mbari, 1962), p. 12.

8. James Ene Henshaw, *Children of the Goddess and Other Plays* (London: University of London Press, 1964), p. 83.

9. *Ibid,* p. 19.

10. *Ibid,* p. 29.

11. Cyprian Ekwenski, *Iska,* London: Hutchinson, 1966, p. 21. See also Francis Selormey, *The Narrow Path,* New York: Praeger, 1966, p. 5 and James Ngugi, *The River Between,* London: Heinemann, 1965, pp. 161-75.

12. Selormey, *The Narrow Path,* New York: Praeger, 1966, p. 6.

13. Austin J. Shelton, "Behavior and Cultural Value in West African Stories," *Literary Sources for the Study of Culture Contract, Africa,* XXXIV (1964), p. 358.

14. Ekwensi, *Beautiful Feathers,* p. 28. See also T. C. Nwosu, "BB," *Ibadan,* No. 24 (June, 1967), p. 40.

15. Aluko, *One Man, One Machet,* London: Heinemann, 1964, p. 185.

16. Clark, *Poems,* Ibadan: Mbari, 1961, p. 48. See also his play *Ozidi,* London: Oxford University Press, 1967, passim.

17. Soyinka, *The Interpreters,* London: Andre Deutsch, 1965, pp. 241-44.

18. Ogot, *The Promised Land,* Nairobi: East African Publishing House, 1967, pp. 184-94.

19. Chinua Achebe, *Arrow of God* (London: Heinemann, 1964), p. 287.

20. Chinua Achebe, *Things Fall Apart,* (New York: Obolensky, 1959), p. 63. See also Soyinka, "The Strong Breed", in *Five plays* (London)

21. Achebe, *Things Fall Apart,* p. 129.

22. Peter Lanham and A. Mopeli-Paulus, *Blanket Boys' Moon* (London: Collings, 1953), pp. 301-304; A. Mopeli-Paulus, *Turn to the Dark* (London: Cape, 1956) passim.

23. Conton, *The African,* p. 25.

24. Nwanko, *Danda.* London: Panther Books, 1967. passim., pp. 170-71, particularly.

25. Latunde Odeku, "Wandering Lines IV". *Twilight Out of the Night* (Ibadan: University of Ibadan Press, 1964), p. 79.

26. Wilson K. Mativo, "Our True Speaker", *East African Journal* (January, 1968), pp. 49-52.

27. Ekwensi, *When Love Whispers* (Onitsha: Tabansi Bookshop, 1947) passim.

28. Kayria, *The Looming Shadow.* (Garden City: Doubleday, 1967), passim.

29. David Rubadiri, *No Bride Price*. (Nairobi: East African Publishing House, 1967.), passim., particularly pp. 125-27.

30. Chinua Achebe, *No Longer at Ease*. (New York: McDowell, Oblenski, 1966), passim., especially pp. 31-32 and 83-98.

31. Soyinka, *The Interpreters*, pp. 119-20.

32. *Ibid.*, p. 120.

33. *Ibid.*, pp. 120-21.

34. *Ibid.*, p. 9.

35. *Ibid.*, pp. 11-12. (Emphasis mine.)

36. *Ibid.*, p. 12.

37. The winds of change refer to the beginning of the nationalist movements which culminated in African independence.

38. Onuora Nzekwu, *Blade Among the Boys* (London: Hutchinson, 1962), passim.

# 12

## PAN-AFRICANISM AFTER 1958:
## THE TRADITIONALIZATION OF A RADICAL MOVEMENT
*By*
### Dr. Uma Oke Eleazu

For an observer who was at the All African Peoples Conference of 1958, breathing the exhilarating air of newly independent Ghana, listening to all the militant talk about how we were going to crush imperialism, mobilize world opinion in support of African liberation, promote understanding and unity among peoples of Africa, develop a feeling of one community among the peoples of Africa and so on—one came away with the feeling that one was at the threshold of momentous events in Africa. Nor did those present and leading delegations think they were merely forming empty words when they were phrasing what must now appear as specious resolutions. Among other things, it was agreed that the conference "endorses Pan-Africanism and the desire for unity among peoples;" (and) "expresses the hope that the day will dawn when the first loyalty of African states will be to an African Commonwealth."[1]

In order to further the aim of unity, it called for the abolition or adjustment of frontiers that divide ethnic groups arbitrarily and left the search for permanent solution to the independent states of Africa. It also called for abolishing passports and certificates in inter-African travel either for tourism or scholarly venture to facilitate the free movement of Africans from one territory to another. It envisaged reciprocal citizenships for Africans from the same regional area "so that ultimately no African shall be considered an alien in any part of Africa."[2] Further, there was to be reciprocal teaching of English and French, and Africans wherever they were in control, were to use radio, the press and other media of mass communication to promote the ideals of Pan-Africanism. On the whole, nothing could be more radical than the proposals of that conference. Like all socio-political movements, Pan-Africanist thought aimed at changing the social order which was imposed on Africa by European imperialism. For historians of Pan-Africanism, the All-African Peoples Conference of 1958 was the high water-mark of the Pan-Africanist idea. At last the peoples of Africa gathered in Africa to talk about how to change the European social order that had been foisted upon them. Again, like other socio-political movements, its ethos was animated by a mixture of romanticism, idealism and a detestable realization of the place of the colonized (whom Frantz Fanon called the *Wretched of the Earth*). A careful reading of the resolutions show that they were alive to the fact that there was no immanent unity which they were going to recapture—but rather they described the unity of African peoples as something to be desired and achieved.

One can contrast this with what must have been an urbane, sedate looking gathering of delegations representing "Independent African States" which also met in Accra earlier in the same year (April 1958) to "assert and proclaim the *unity among ourselves and our solidarity with the dependent peoples of Africa* as well as our friendship with all nations."[3] Where the AAPC spoke of breaking down barriers such as passport controls and adjusting "artificially created boundaries", the CIAS (Conference of Independent African States) spoke of "preserving the unity of purpose and action in international affairs . . . . to safeguard our hard-won independence, sovereignty and territorial integrity . . . ."[4] As a matter of fact, throughout their lengthy Declaration and resolutions, the word "Pan-Africanism" or its derivatives do not appear. Instead, the CIAS spoke of unity of Africa, "African Personality" or simply African peoples. It is instructive and germane to our later argument to note here too, that the AAPC and the Pan-African Congress of 1945 used such terms as Pan-African or Black Africa. Both also did note the artificial divisions and territorial boundaries created by the imperialist powers, and therefore called for deliberate steps to adjust or abolish them. In January 1960, the second AAPC was held in Tunisia. A number of radical resolutions were passed. As in the first, the implementation was recommended to the Independent African States. On African unity, the resolution included the following clause:

"Since the great idea of Pan-Africanism constitutes a new element in the national consciousness of African people; after analysing the idea of unity which uplifts the African peoples, the conference decides to mobilize the African masses around this idea and to make its realization the fundamental objective of their action and their tnought . . . ."[5]

Then followed a long list of action programs which the Independent African States were supposed to undertake to bring about the realization of the goals espoused.

In the second Conference of the Independent African States held in June, 1960, the issue of Pan-Africanism came up in the form of the nature African unity should take. Some states, with Ghana leading, thought a Union of African States was the solution while others led by Nigeria thought the idea of such a union was premature.[6] The issue of the nature of unity and whether it was realizable at the time is not a matter that we are concerned with now. Rather, it should be pointed out that the AAPC, the more broadly based organization, had goals "for the people" which called for leadership. The leadership was sought among the already independent African States who had to translate those ideas into realizable objectives.

Much of the later history of Pan-Africanism has centered around the issues of the nature and form of unity that can be achieved. Several studies of Pan-Africanism tend to see the OAU as the organizational embodiment of the Pan-Africanist idea.[7] These studies have been of the "career type." They trace the origin of Pan-Africanism to the diaspora of the New World and then follow the vicissitudes of the early congresses and conferences which culminate in the 1945 Congress at which supposedly Pan-Africanism was finally Africanized—that is, brought home to mother Africa. From then on, the modern history of the movement moves from thought to action, leading to African methodism and African independence. Some have tended to study the OAU as an international sub-system dealing with the problems of Africa. On the other hand, the contributor who wrote the article on Pan movements for the International Encyclopedia of the Social Sciences dismissed Pan-Africanism simply by saying that:

"Pan-Africanism also fails to qualify as a movement. It is rather an affirmation of a unity that does not exist. Pan-Africanism is used for political purposes by the governments of the various African States, but as yet, it exercises no appreciable influence on their policies."[8]

Speaking at the inauguration ceremony of the University of Zambia, the keynote speaker, President Julius K. Nyerere noted that while the present leaders are dealing with the urgent problems facing their separate States, they have very little time for serious thinking about the way forward to Pan-Africanism. He then asked,

> "Who is to keep us active in the struggle to convert nationalism to Pan-Africanism if it is not the staffs and students of our universities? Who is it who will have the time and ability to think out the practical problems of achieving this goal of unification if it is not those who have an opportunity to think and learn without direct responsibility for day-to-day affairs?"[9]

It is in this spirit therefore, that this paper approaches the study of Pan-Africanism. My main interest derives from a phenomenon which has been observed and recorded by other social scientists in regard to social, political and religious movements and, to some extent, to certain types of organization. Robert Michaels, in his study, *Political Parties*, had noted that: "It is organization which gives birth to the domination of the delegates over the delegators. Who says organization says oligarchy."[10] Some of his critics have suggested that he over-stated his case, yet there is no denying the fact that there is such a tendency as his "Iron Law of Oligarchy", or what Selznick was to describe as "the general re-calcitrance of the human tools of action." This is the tendency for goals to be "subverted" or displaced in the process of giving a movement organizational stability by creating leaders who in turn develop their own interests and become a self-maintaining oligarchy.[11] With the above comment in mind, it is the intention of this paper to analyze the recent history of the Pan-African movement from the point of view of how the need to stabilize the movement by giving operational leadership to the Independent African States has "subverted" and traditionalized what otherwise was a radical movement.

There is still the tendency in some African quarters to think of African and Pan-Africanist Unity in very nebulous and emotional terms. This does not help either the understanding of our problems or the formulation of alternative policies. Robert Michaels wrote his *Political Parties* out of a commitment to democracy and was seeking to identify the variables that worked to thwart its realization. The present writer has such a concern for the unity of Africa implied in Pan-Africanism and wishes to identify those factors which have so far worked to change Pan-Africanist goals; what is the relationship between goals, methods of achieving the goals and the behavior of the relevant actors? To what extent has the environment of the 60's and 70's pressured the leaders to seek other more accommodative goals. If, as someone has remarked, politics is the art of making possible today what was impossible yesterday, we will ask—what is impossible today and what can be made possible tomorrow? In other words, does Pan-Africanism need a redefinition?

Pan-Africanism started as a political slogan, and like other such slogans it was a call to action. The action that it led to has been subject to change in content, scope and intensity according to the world view or historical consciousness of the users. Being primarily a political slogan devised by a group of people in a particular historical circumstance, and who saw Africa from a distance with its hills and valleys smoothed out, forest and desert as one continuous colorful picture, Pan-Africanism started with what might be regarded as "imminent myth" of African unity. The Afro-Americans and West Indians tended to impute a unity to Africa which in fact was not there. Neither pre-colonial Africa nor colonial Africa could be said to have a unity of its own. The black people in the New World, having been thrown together by accident of history into a "melting pot" of their own, were the first really de-tribalized Africans. It was to be expected, therefore, that they should look on Africa as one country which had only been divided by the evil machinations of European imperialism. At that stage, Pan-Africanism was a racial (not racist) idea. In their search for equality and dignity, the Afro-Americans thought that Pan-Africanism would be a way of raising not only the status of the "Negro" in Africa but that of the whole race everywhere. Commenting on the Pan-African Congress of 1919, the *Crisis* (organ of the NAACP) declared:

"The African movement means to us what the Zionist movement must mean to the Jews, the centralization of race effort and the recognition of a racial front . . . Any ebullition of action and feeling that results in an amelioration of the lot of Africa tends to ameliorate the condition of colored peoples throughout the world."[12]

In addition W. E. B. DuBois who is recognized as the father of Pan-Africanism has said that he envisaged a World organized of Black men which would "oppose a united front to European aggression."[13] There was also the sentimental longing to see a free and independent Africa which would possess for the Blacks of the New World "the same fascination as England does for Indian born Englishman."[14] The first goal therefore of the Pan-African movement was the independence of Africa. The earlier leaders of the movement could not fight on two fronts. The movement had to be "Africanized" if it was to achieve its goal. The slogan did not really become African until 1945 when a number of African students in Britain and delegated from the continent

attended the Sixth Pan-African Congress in Manchester. From
1945, Pan-Africanism went into action on the continent with the
following aims held by the nationalist leaders in a more or less
diffuse manner:

   a. That Africa was to fight colonialism and regain her independence.
      It was implied that this fight had to be territory by territory—
      each facing its colonial master.
   b. That Africa must unite, first as regional federalism and later
      linking these into a United States of Africa. (At this time, it does
      not appear as if the Arab countries in Africa were included.)
   c. That this United States of Africa will maintain a fraternal
      alliance with black people everywhere with a view to protecting
      themselves against white domination.[15]

Along with the Africanization came the nationalization—more
concisely "territorialization" of Pan Africanism. One did not hear
much about the movement until the era of Independence. Between 1945 and 1957, Libya (1951), Morocco (1956) and Sudan
(1956) became independent, but without as much fanfare as
was generated when Ghana became independent in 1956; Guinea
gained its independence (by default) in 1958. It was Ghana's
Nkrumah—one of the joint secretaries at the Sixth Congress—
who, as Prime Minister, called in 1958, first, the Conference of the
Independent African States and later, the All-African Peoples
Conference discussed earlier. It is instructive to note that of
the eight heads of state or government attending the CIAS only
Liberia and Ghana were from "Black Africa" whereas the others
—Egypt, Tunisia, Libya, Sudan and Morocco—considered themselves first as Arabs while Ethiopia was not quite sure whether
she was African. On the other hand, the All-African Peoples Conference was attended by nationalist political parties from many
territories in Africa; there were trade-union representatives, as
well as student organizations. The AAPC thus represented all
forces that were fighting colonialism and racialism in Africa—
including even white liberals from South Africa. It was in a sense
more truly African and its resolutions represented the mood of
Africa in 1958. This difference in composition accounts for the
difference in attitudes reflected in their resolutions. By 1961,
many African territories had tumbled over one another in the
scramble for independence and had successfully wrested the reins
of power (at least on paper) from their erstwhile colonial powers.
Many of those who attended the AAPC in 1958 as nationalist
parties or trade union leaders fighting for independence, were
then ministers in government, members of parliaments and
national assemblies while others became leaders of opposition

parties. As people in power, they were now faced with the recommendations which they had made to Independent States of Africa. It was for them to implement those recommendations. Let us note also that the third AAPC (Cairo 1961) introduced a new element in the Pan-African rhetoric. There was created the impression, that some Africans were not true nationalists, or were puppets. One of the clauses in the Resolution on the Liberation of Dependent Countries states:

> Aware of the fact that imperialists pour money into Africa in order to *promote puppets* as well as foster disunity *to thwart the struggle towards the true liberation of Africa* . . . . The AAPC condemns all those who, under *the guise of nationalism,* act as agents of colonialism and imperialism.[16]

Many of the delegates to this third AAPC were members of opposition parties or trade unionists in their states. So it was not unlikely that their respective governments would interpret the resolution as being directed against those of them governing the newly independent states. Who was a "true nationalist" and who was a stooge of colonialism? This was a matter which had to be dealt with at the territorial-state level. The effect was that those in power "killed" the AAPC as a potential threat to their position. The AAPC has yet to meet in its fourth Conference. The Conference of Independent African States had met a second time in 1960 and divided over the issue of the Congo and recognition of the Algerian Provisional Government. Coupled with other minor bilateral problems and quarrels—(Morocco and Mauritania, Senegal and Mali, alleged subversion by neighboring states, with the accusing fingers pointed toward Ghana, North Africa in search of her own unity with the Arab world)—all these were to lead to ideological splits that strained diplomatic relations among the states. As long as this situation lasted, efforts were spent in search of a rapprochement that would bring the states together. The issue of defining Pan-African unity further divided the states— soon one saw the emergence of what came to be regarded as Moderates and Radicals in the Monrovia-Brazzaville Group of States and the Casablanca Group respectively. After much diplomatic bluffing, bickering and blundering, the Organization of African Unity (OAU) was formed in 1963 to be the umbrella organization for the whole of Africa, to continue the ideals of the Pan-African movement.

A study of the Charter of the OAU indicates the conservative outlook of its authors. In terms of continental unity, it did four things. It ratified, as it were, the Berlin Conferences of 1885 in which expansionist imperialists demarcated what were to become boundaries of the new African states. It reduced inter-African cooperation to inter-state relations. By adopting a policy of non-interference in the internal affairs of member states, it limited itself from effectively handling intra-African problems and by resolving to respect the territorial integrity and sovereignty of each state, it voted for nationalism within the colonially created boundaries as opposed to the continental nationalism envisaged by Pan-Africanism.

To appreciate the retrogressive nature of this OAU charter, one can compare the structure it solidified with the situation in Africa around 1958. One can conveniently divide Africa into a number of more or less unified regions. There was the French West and Equatorial Africa (AOF & AEF) organized as federations with capitals in Dakar and Brazzaville, respectively. Since 1946 the administration of these political structures provided avenues for contact between the elite at both the Federal levels and in Paris. Even the first major political movement, the Rassemblement Democratique Africain (RDA) was inter-territorial. However, from 1956, the operation of the *Loi Cadre*, the growing attractiveness of each territory's independence (in terms of prestige for local leaders), the desire on the part of the French to forestall independence, and failing that, to control small weak states all led to the break-up. Were the leaders more forward looking and Pan-Africanist in ideals, then their first inclination would have been to resist the break-up of the federations.

The position in the British sector was not much better. The idiosyncracies of the scramblers for Africa had left Britain with the large chunk of Africa that was to be called Nigeria and three smaller ones—Gold Coast (later Ghana) Sierra Leone and Gambia. They were not blessed with the contiguity of the AOF or AEF. However, it was among these that Pan Africanist talk was loudest. Although there was a single currency system based on the sterling, a number of common research institutes, a tiny West African Airways and a legal system with a Court of Appeal for all four territories, British policy was directed toward separate development. Between 1945 and 1956, there was no counterpart of the RDA. But when Ghana became independent in 1957, she withdrew from the skeleton services that provided any kind of linkage between her and the other English speaking neighbors.

In East Africa (Kenya, Uganda and Tanganyika) Britain had an area in which she could experiment in Federation. By 1957, the ten-year old East African High Commission supervising some common services was the official structure that united these territories, but then, the African Nationalists fearing a concentration of power in the hands of white settlers were by 1957 opposing the Union and asking for independence for their separate territories.

In central Africa, then, there was still in being, a federation of the Rhodesias and Nyasaland which was imposed in 1953. By 1957 African Nationalist demands were in the direction of breaking it up for the same reason as in East Africa. Further north, the Belgians were still in control of Congo, Rwanda-Urundi, but there was no move to join these, largely because of the legal fiction that one territory was held in mandate (or trust) and the other was not. Elsewhere in North Africa, Algeria was still "French" and a Maghreb unity—Morocco, Algeria and Tunisia—was a possibility based on past association with France. Thus, by 1957, the colonial powers that arbitrarily divided Africa were creating building blocs for regional federations such as envisaged by Pan-Africanism as stated above, but territorial nationalism was undermining these building blocs. "Independence first, unity later" became the slogan and the strategy. After independence, the states were solidified by the OAU.

The OAU was seven years old in 1970. Its meetings, committees and commissions are all marked by a strict observance of diplomatic niceties. No one seriously believes that any other form of organization will emerge in the near future. On the contrary, as one student of African diplomacy puts it, "despite the contrary pressure of Pan-Africanism, the state as the African political unit seems here to stay."[17] Even with this sketchy history of the development since 1958, one can see that by any standards, the OAU is a very conservative organization.

The question then arises, why has the organization—OAU—abandoned most of the original radical ideas as embodied in the resolution of the Pan-African Congress of 1945 and the All-African Peoples Conferences? Here we shall identify four possible reasons for the change in character of the Pan-African movement.

1. *Environmental change and leadership.* The movement started among the New World Blacks as the response of a racially oppressed minority in a predominantly white world. This kind of historical consciousness was akin to the situation of colonial Africa hence there was an easy identification between colonial

students in London, Paris, or New York with the radical slogan
of Pan-Africanism. Many of the post-1958 leaders of Africa had
only the experience of colonialism in Africa; besides, they had to
deal with the problems of the emerging Africa which was by no
means an entity.

2. *Self-interest of the leaders.* It is one thing to be an agitator.
It is quite another to be a Head of State and/or Minister in the
government. In a situation of scarcity, those who have to make
authoritative decisions in allocating values acquire not only
prestige, but also a position of power, which, human nature being
what it is, they do not easily want to give up. In other words,
the leaders develop their own self-interest such as arises out of the
position of leadership. Were they to submerge the sovereignty
of their state in a larger continental state or even a regional one, they
would then lose the red carpet treatment they get as heads of state
in other countries. This is just one example. The rate at which
opposition parties disappeared, and the constant exposure of corrupt accumulation of wealth, support the view that there were
other interests clearer to the leaders than African unity.

We can couple with this, the lack of interest in the total
population for African unity. In his study of Europe, Ernst B.
Haas has pointed out that integration proceeds quicker if there
is a "discreet set of group motives, converging with motives of
cognate groups from across the border."[18] Further, if they are
modern "industrial-political" actors who fear that their interests
will not be safeguarded unless there is a structural change in the
form of integration, then these will demand integration and presumably will work to mobilize support around the demand. We
have already seen that in the case of Africa, the AAPC which
embodied people with cognate interests (nationalists fighting for
independence and trade unionists), died after 1961 when most of
the territories became independent. Thereafter, the all African
Trade Union Congress took over but was strangled by its own
ideological split. In this circumstance, there is no private political-
industrial group with Pan-African interest to push the States
towards further integration. Part of the reason for this may be the
extreme territorial nationalism that has been developed and
fostered by the respective leaders. There is the fear of subversion
from neighboring States (which, incidentally, was even written
into the Charter of the OAU); and also the genuine commitment
to do something first for those who elected them before thinking

of continental unity. In this regard even a confirmed Pan-Africanist, President Nyerere, was forced to admit that:

> "In order to fulfill its responsibilities to the people it has led to freedom, each nationalist government must develop its own economy, its own organizations and institutions, and its own dominant nationalism. This is true, however devoted to the cause of African unity the different national leaders may be . . . . But the people of this continent have been suffering the effects of poverty too long. They need to see some immediate attack being made on that poverty. They could not, and would not, agree to stagnation or regression while we pursue the goal of unity."[19]

3. *Responsibility of power*. This then leads to another factor: the responsibility that comes with power. As a critic, one can build grandiose schemes of what ought to be done, but once given the reins of power, a good leader strives to be more careful. Some leaders are genuinely afraid that a continental unity may topple the applecart. Others counsel gradualism to make sure that no precipitate action is taken, for fear of failure. In this situation of mixed motives, one cannot always tell when a leader is acting in good faith, for this can easily be a cloak for inaction.

4. *Factionalism among the leaders*. Perhaps we may add to the above, factionalism and lack of agreement among the elite. In the above sketch of the post-1958 history of the movement, it was pointed out that the leaders were divided into Radicals and Moderates. Even within each camp, more so among members of the latter, there were still gradations of moderation. While the radical definition of African unity was not acceptable to the moderates, they themselves ranged from those who would accept a loose confederation to those who desired no over-arching organization. Fraught with such division, leaders looked for a middle ground acceptable to most, if not to all the members. The result, as shown in the charter, was to adopt an ambiguous and at the same time conservative stand. In the search, the original goal was either abandoned, defined out of existence or camouflaged in legal and technical phraseology. All these influences, to some extent, contributed to the situation described. Everyone talked glibly about the desire for unity, meaning by it some form of political unification of Africa, but very few stopped to ask the awkward questions —who needed the unity and what were the conditions for this unity—and whether these conditions could be created and if so, how and by whom? Or would the peoples of Africa be better off with one continental government, three or four regional groupings or village democracy?

*Attempts at unity in Africa, 1958-1963*. Unity, union, unification, all belong to the class of words that are hazy as political concepts. The Random House Dictionary defines unity as: "The state of being one; oneness: one single thing; something complete in itself, or regarded as such. A whole or totality as combining all its parts into one. The state or fact of being united or combined as one, as of parts of a whole, unification. Absence of diversity . . . ." Using any of these definitions, Africa can be shown to have some kind of unity as well as disunity. However hazily expressed, African unity usually refers to some notion of coming together but as the above definitions show—this coming together could lead to "one single thing" or simply "absence of diversity" in certain respects without the uniting parts losing their identity. Here we will use unification to refer to the process of achieving unity. This process may be viewed at different points in time and at different levels. Thus studies of the political unification process usually attempt distinguishing between different kinds and levels of integration. Karl W. Deutsch, et al, for example, distinguished between "pluralistic security community and amalgamated security community." By pluralistic security community, they mean the kind of unification in which member units retain their legal independence of separate governments, whereas in the amalgamated type, there is a formal merger of the previously independent units into a single larger unit with some form of common government after amalgamation.[20]

Also Etzioni has differentiated between a political community and other kinds of political systems such as blocs, alliances and empires. The political community, one can say, is the highest form of integration or unification. In a way, it is what Deutsch would call an amalgamated security community provided that it has achieved three kinds of integration: "(a) it has an effective control over the use of the means of violence (though it may delegate some of this control to member-units); (b) it has a center of decision making that is able to affect significantly the allocation of resources and rewards throughout the community, and (c) it is the dominant focus of political identification for the large majority of politically aware citizens."[21]

Much discussion of African unity, like much political talk, tends to be imprecise. For example, in Nnamdi Azikiwe's much quoted speech he said, "As I see it, there is bound to arise an African Leviathan in the form of a political organization or association or union or concert of states."[22] Those who have read Hobbes will expect a Leviathan to subdue its composing members, but Zik was not quite expecting that for later he thought it had to be a "concert of African States." But what is meant by "concert" in this respect?

The difference between the so-called radical and moderate states could be put in terms of the level of integration which each bloc wished to see. The radicals want a political community (Etzioni ) or amalgamated security community (Deutsch) whereas the moderates want what Etzioni would call a bloc and Deutsch, "pluralistic security community."

There certainly have been several attempts at unity. None of these attempts qualifies for what Etzioni would call "political community." Since the formation of the OAU, they are now moving to the level of what Deutsch called "pluralistic security community" in the sense that all the members of the OAU accept, at least, peaceful means for settling their disputes. Probably this achievement is not unrelated to the fact that some form of permanent administrative organization is existing and functioning. Even so, many people in Africa still believe that the OAU is not doing much.

The continued debate over further unity has stemmed from some of the problems that the OAU has had to face but has been unable to solve: the continued oppression of Guinea, Angola and Mozambique by a weak country like Portugal; the inability of Africa to do what India did to the Portuguese in Goa; the effrontery of Ian Smith and his fellow 250,000 racists who want to control four million Africans; the apartheid policy in South Africa and the recalcitrance of its government over Namibia.[23] It is felt by many politically aware Africans that the continued inability of the OAU to deal with these problems is directly related to its structure and conservative outlook. This in turn is seen as an abandonment of the Pan-Africanist ideals. The question then arises, should we move to a different level of integration in order to correct some of the structural problems of the OAU, to give it more teeth? This will then involve moving to the stage of "amalgamated security community" or an increase in the degree of integration in respect of Etzioni's three criteria. It is easier to form a bloc or a pluralistic community than it is to form a political community that will give up monopoly of the use of means of violence, effective decision-making and the allocation of resources and develop a sense of community in the population. The question now arises, what sort of conditions are conducive to further integration. Do these conditions exist and to what extent were past attempts nullified by such situational factors?

1. *Values and expectations.*

Political unification proceeds quicker if the uniting states have the same values, expectations and similar institutions. In the case of Africa, we have already seen that the division between moderates and radicals stemmed from differences in ideologies of development and nation-building. Some have gone the way of African Socialism (variously defined). Others have adopted the one-party state structure; still others have multi-party systems. Sixteen of the states are now under military rule or a no-party political system. Some are monarchies, others have dictatorships. In such a situation, one is not likely to have unity of outlook on values or ends which the state ought to pursue. How will a union that includes Morocco, Ethiopia, Sudan, Ghana and Niageria (with a federal system) work? What will happen to Tanzania's African Socialism which perhaps is unacceptable to Ivory Coast? Besides, other intra-African quarrels, e.g., the Nigerian Civil War, the Sudan Civil War, the Somali-Ethiophia dispute—tend to exacerbate relations and factionalize views. In such a situation one finds very few compatible value premises held by all the members. There are a few countries in which the issue of African unity features in domestic politics. Since the military men started taking over and abolishing regular partisan political activities, it has become more difficult to determine the importance of any issues at all. Although most of the military rulers always take care to mention their adherence to the principles of the OAU, one should interpret this as a means of legitimizing themselves in the eyes of leaders of the other states rather than an expression of what they in fact believe. As regards expectations, it was also pointed out earlier that there are no groups within one state with interests spilling over territorial boundaries to create expectations of reward that may arise out of future unification. We must conclude therefore that this background condition does not really exist.

2. *Capabilities and Communication Processes.*

There certainly are official communications between the elite. Professional conferences and meetings like the Congress of African Writers and Artists help to get individuals and groups to maintain some kind of link across the borders of participating units. But Deutsch, et. al., talk of the necessity of main*aining "unbroken links of social communication both horizontally among the

main units and vertically linking different strata of the society."
Here again we find no such unbroken links of social communication. There is first the language barrier. Communication via
the radio is likely to be more intense within the English and
French-speaking sectors separately. It will be interesting to know
how many people tune in to the broadcasts from other African
countries.

### 3. *Mobility of Persons.*

The Deutsch study showed that "full-scale mobility of persons has
followed every successful amalgamated security community in modern times."[24] Anglo-Scottish, the American colonies and Italy are
cases in point. In the case of Africa, every State still maintains
passport controls against other African States. Sadly enough, it
was easier to travel to Ghana or Sierra Leone from Nigeria during
the period of British administration. (Ghana and Uganda recently expelled African foreigners.) Likewise it was easier travel-
ing in AOF than it is from Ivory Coast to Senegal today. The
position in East Africa is not much different. The existence of
common market ties did not deter Obote from repatriating Kenyans
who have been living and working in Uganda. It will be recalled
that, in respect of this mobility and the question of communication, the third all-African Peoples Conference as well as earlier
ones called for abolition of passport and travel certificates, and the
establishment of radio networks, etc. Nobody has seen it fit to do
this. Lack of inter-African travel is followed by lack of inter-
African mobility of capital and goods. The figures on inter-African
trade are simply appalling. A recent visitor to Nigeria and Ghana
was surprised to note that in neither Nigeria Airways planes nor
Ghana Airways planes would the air hostesses accept each other's
money in flights between Lagos and Accra! In fact, they do not
even accept anything but dollars or British pound notes!!

Two other conditions, "multiplicity and balance of transactions" and "mutual predictability of behavior" are closely linked
with the other three already discussed. If mobility of persons is
high, one should expect an increase in transactions between states.
At the present time the greatest amount of interchange is between
governments and this directly with the OAU Secretariat. One
would like to see in the areas of religion, education, sports and
trade greater interchange among the African states. In this respect
the East African Economic Community stands a better chance of
success than most other regions of Africa. Likewise, if there is
basic agreement on values and expectations, this will lead to

mutual predictability of behavior. But since we have found the
other criteria for greater interchange wanting one would not
therefore expect either a high level of transactions or predictability
of behavior. That these conditions do not now exist does not mean
that a greater degree of integration cannot be achieved, given the
will to do so. Here we begin to move into the realm of the possible,
into the areas in which something can be done or "engineered." The
goal of unity may seem utopian or a remote possibility, but if there
are conditions that will lead to the achievement of these goals, it
will help if the attention is directed to nurturing these conditions.
Action programs should be directed to the establishment of what
has been known in other circumstances, to be necessary if not
totally adequate conditions. It is just toward this re-definition of
goals and working out the proper action programs that future
efforts should be directed.

NOTES

1. See Colin Legum, *Pan-Africanism: A Short Political Guide*, Frederick
   A. Paraeger, New York, 1961, p. 230.

2. *Ibid.*, p. 232.

3. *Ibid.*, Appendix 4, p. 139.

4. *Ibid.*

5. *Ibid.*, pp. 239-40.

6. The Exchanges between Ghana-S. Nigeria were then widely discussed
   in the press of the two countries. See also Colin Legum, pp. 170-174.

7. See for example Rupert Emerson, "Pan-Africanism" in *International
   Organization*, Vol. XVI, No. 2 (Spring 1962), reprinted in *International
   Political Communities: An Anthology*, Doubleday and Co., Inc., New
   York, 1956. George Padmore, *Pan-Africanism or Communism*, London,
   1956. I. W. Zartman, "African as a Subordinate State System in International Relations", *International Organization*, Vol. XXI, No. 3 (Sum-
   mer 1967).

8. *International Encyclopedia of the Social Sciences*, Second Edition, Vol. II
   See article on Pan-movements.

9. Julius K. Nyerere, *Freedom and Socialism: Uhuru na Ujamaa*, A selection
   from Writings and Speeches 1965-1967. Oxford University Press, Dar-es-
   Salaam and New York, 1968, pp. 216-217.

10. Robert Michaels, *Political Parties*. Collier Books, New York, 1962.

11. Other examples of this kind of studies include: Paul M. Harrison, *Author-
    ity and Power in the Free Church Tradition*, Princeton, Princeton Uni-
    versity Press, 1959: P. Blau, *Bureaucracy in Modern Society*, New York,
    1956; Philip Selznick, "The Iron Law of Bureaucracy", Modern Review 3,
    (1950), pp. 162-63.

12. *Crisis* (Organ of NAACP), Vol. 17, Nov., 1919, p. 166.

13. W. E. B. DuBois, *Dusk of Dawn*, Stocken Books, New York, 1970, pp.
    274-75.

14. *Crisis*, op. cit.

15. Compare this with the summary given by Colin Legum, op. cit., and George Padmore, op. cit.

16. Colin Legum, pp. 247-48. Emphasis is mine.

17. Zartman, op. cit.

18. Ernst B. Haas, "International Integration: The European and the Universal Process", in *International Political Communities*, pp. 104-6.

19. Nyerere, op. cit., pp. 210-11.

20. Karl W. Deutsch, Sidney A. Burrell, Robert A. Kahn, et. al., *Political Community and the North Atlantic Area*. Reproduced in part in *International Political Communities*, pp. 1-92. See definition on p. 2.

21. Amitai Etzioni, *Political Unification: A Comparative Study of Leaders and Forces*. Holt, Rinehart & Winston, Inc., 1965, p. 4.

22. Nnamdi Azikiwe, "The Future of Pan Africanism", reproduced in part in Colin Legum, op. cit. Quotation is on p. 274.

23. Nor has the OAU been able to deal with such intra-African and intra-state problems as the Nigeria-Biafra war, the Sudan Civil War, Somali dispute with Kenya and Ethiophia. At best, it only provided opportunity for a friendly state to offer its good offices. On other occasions, it has depended on diplomacy-by-resolution approach.

24. Karl W. Deutsch, et. al., op. cit., p. 33.

# ABOUT THE CONTRIBUTORS

DR. MERVYN ALLEYNE
Professor of Linguistics at the University of the West Indies in Jamaica and visiting professor at Yale University 1970-71.

DR. UMA O. ELEAZU
Assistant Professor of Political Science at California State College, Dominguez Hills.

DR. ROSS A. EVANS
Assistant Professor, Department of Special Education and Assistant Director, Research and Demonstration Center for the Education of Handicapped Children, Teachers College Columbia University.

DR. DONALD HENDERSON
Formerly Director of Experimental Studies at Southern Illinois University is now Associate Provost at the University of Pittsburgh.

DR. S. OKECHUKWU MEZU
Associate Professor of French and Director of the African Studies and Research Program at the State University of New York at Buffalo. Also founder of The Black Academy Press, Inc.

WILSON J. MOSES
Lecturer in Afro-American History at Bryant College and teaching Associate and doctoral candidate in History at Brown University.

DR. G. C. M. MUTISO
Professor of African Political Thought in the Department of Government at University College in Nairobi, Kenya.

DR. FELIX OKOYE
Professor and Chairman of the Black Studies Department at the State University of New York, College at Brockport.

DR. HENRY J. RICHARDS
Associate Professor of Foreign Languages and Dean of Developmental Studies at the State University of New York, College at Buffalo.

DR. ARTHUR L. SMITH
Associate Professor of Speech and Director of Afro-American Studies at the University of California at Los Angeles.

JAMES TURNER
Director of the Africana Studies and Research Center at Cornell University.

RONALD WALTERS
Professor and Chairman of the Department of African and Afro-American Studies at Brandeis University.

This anthology is dedicated to the thirty-three students (at the State University of New York, College at Buffalo) who spent the academic year 1969-70 studying and developing with me a program in Afro-American Studies: Mary Barber, Orlando A. Boykin, Jerrell J. Braxton, Isadore J. Burriss, Dwight Clemons, Willie F. Cole, Nancy Conway, Dennis Dean, Robert Denson, Janice Earle, Danny Floyd, Emily Freeman, Christine Garmon, William Golden, Arthur Greene, Tyrone Gwinn, Charles Henry, Joseph Hicks, Ronald Hinkle, Carmenita Jones, Clifford Jones, Dennis Keeys, Mary Lewis, Harold Nolley, Prentis Parks, Derrick Pearson, Barbara Sampson, Eddie J. Swaggard, George Thomas, Philip Triggs, Delores Washington, Gloria J. White and L. Jean Young.

Henry J. Richards
Buffalo, New York (1970)